LINES OF FIRE

LINES OF FIRE

POETRY OF THE AFRO-ASIAN WRITERS MOVEMENT

EDITED BY TARIQ MEHMOOD

Published by
Daraja Press
https://darajapress.com
Wakefield, Quebec, Canada
and
American University of Beirut Press
Beirut, Lebanon

@ 2025 American University of Beirut

ISBN:978-1-997742-26-5

This publication may not be reproduced, stored in a retrieval system, or transmitted in any form by any means, be it electronically, mechanical, recording, photocopying, or otherwise, without the prior written permission of the American University of Beirut Press.

The opinions, findings, interpretations, and conclusions expressed in this book are entirely those of the authors and do not reflect those of the American University of Beirut or of Daraja Press, their affiliated organisations, or members of their respective boards.

For requests and permissions, contact aubpress@aub.edu.lb

Library and Archives Canada Cataloguing in Publication

Title: Lines of fire : poetry of the Afro-Asian Writers Movement / edited by Tariq Mehmood.
Other titles: Lines of fire (Compilation)
Names: Mehmood, Tariq, editor.
Description: 2nd edition. | Includes bibliographical references. | Introductory material in English. Poetry in English, translated from various languages.
Identifiers: Canadiana 20250330040 | ISBN 9781997742265 (hardcover)
Subjects: LCSH: Lotus (Magazine) | LCSH: Call (Journal) | LCSH: Afro-Asian Writers Association—History. | LCSH: African periodicals—History. | LCSH: Asian periodicals—History. | LCSH: African poetry. | LCSH: African poetry—Translations into English. | LCSH: Oriental poetry. | LCSH: Oriental poetry—Translations into English. | LCGFT: Poetry.
Classification: LCC PN6101 .L455 2026 | DDC 808.81/9895—dc23

Acknowledgements	9
Preface	xi
Foreword: Lotus and the Literary Torch	1
Introduction	17
Poems	
Exile	63
Independence and National Liberation	111
Place and Land	183
Hope and Endurance	263
Solidarity	413
Biographies	433
Lists of Poems and Images	451
Bibliography	459

Be angry, and you will find the earth a volcano,
And your bleeding voice becomes the anthem of the weary.
— *Farouq Jwaideh*

ACKNOWLEDGEMENTS

From Beirut, Lebanon, *Lines of Fire* comes to you after weathering an unrelenting series of existential crises: economic collapse, social upheavals, a devastating port explosion, the global pandemic, mass death, destruction, displacement, and never-ending wars. Despite these overwhelming challenges, many individuals played vital roles in collecting, curating, and commenting on the materials from the Afro-Asian Writers Movement that form the heart of this collection. To those whose names I may have forgotten, I ask your forgiveness—your contributions remain deeply valued.

My deepest gratitude goes to Virinder Kalra, Mjiba Frehiwot, and Firoze Manji for their generous feedback and detailed comments, which have profoundly shaped this book. Heartfelt appreciation to Elham Bakdash, who stepped in as the distribution editor of *Lotus* during its rebirth in Tunis. I am also thankful to the many graduate assistants at the American University of Beirut who supported me throughout my time working on the collection. Special thanks to Ali Faraj, Mohammad Fakhreddine, Tanite Chahwan, Brigitte Ghorayeb, Tamara Sleiman and Jana Khaled.

No words can express my gratitude to the AUB Press team for bringing this to life. The graduate editorial assistants of the AUB Press—Sarah Abu Zeid, Fadel Atwi, and Jude Abu Haidar—from their research and fact-checking, to manually typesetting the photos and scans of both *The Call* and *Lotus* journals, you were the base on which this was built.

To Mohammad Alameddine for designing the book and hand-drawing each of the artworks across the pages, thank you.

And to you, Danah El Kaouri—for your irritatingly precise eye for detail—and to Yasmine El Hajjar, for your re-reads of the ever-changing manuscript, your commitment to due diligence, and your unwavering faith in this book, I give my eternal appreciation.

PREFACE

As we were discussing the final touches of this book in 2023, the genocide in Gaza went into full swing. With so much pain and suffering, I was angry—glued to the television—feeling the growing shadow of an impending crisis in Lebanon. Soon enough, a full-scale war began.

On July 30, 2024, Israel assassinated Hezbollah's senior commander, Fouad Shukr, in Beirut. On September 17, Israel detonated hundreds of pagers simultaneously, targeting markets, nurseries, pharmacies, streets, homes—everywhere people lived. Nearly fifty were killed, hundreds lost their eyes, and 4,000 were injured. Dr. Ghassan Abu Sittah described this carnage as "the largest act of mutilation."[1] On September 23, expanded large-scale attacks on Lebanon displaced 1.5 million people. Just days later, on September 27, Hezbollah Secretary General Hassan Nasrallah was assassinated, alongside other top leaders. By November 27, with its objectives unmet, Israel agreed to a ceasefire—one it broke on a daily basis.

---

1 Ghassan Abu-Sittah, "Israel Bombs Lebanon After Blowing Up Pagers in 'Act of Mass Mutilation.' Is Ground Invasion Next?" interview by Sintia Issa, September 23, 2024, video, 35:43, https://www.democracynow.org/2024/9/23/israel_lebanon.

With the horrors of the genocide in Gaza, the mass destruction and displacement in Lebanon (and suffering in wars in the DRC, Sudan, and elsewhere across the world), it was difficult to return to poetry, especially poetry written in the 1960s and 1970s by the Afro-Asian Writers Movement, without raging at one atrocity after another.

One day as I was reading the Resistance News Network, I came across the following verses, in a statement attributed to Hamas. The anger in them echoed many poems in this collection:

> Be angry, for the earth bows its head to the angry.
> Be angry, for the wind slaughters the wheat spikes.
> It storms as it wishes through the branches of jasmine.
> Be angry, and you will find the earth a volcano,
> And your bleeding voice becomes the anthem of the weary.

I would later discover that these words were a translation of a poem of Farouk Goweda. Reading these words reminded me why poetry matters, especially in times like these. It reminded me that poetry is not just an outlet for anger, grief, or love. It is resistance. It is resilience. It is the refusal to be erased. That power pulses through the poetry of the Afro-Asian Writers Movement.

In the introduction to this collection, I narrate the history of the Afro-Asian Writers Movement—its conferences, internal conflicts, and most importantly the journals it produced, *The Call* and *Lotus*—all under the watchful eye of Anglo-American intelligence services. Most of the poems in this collection are from the *Lotus* journal's early years. I have included nearly all of them, leaving out only a few where I felt the poet had already been well represented. From *The Call*, I've included every poem I had access to.

The final section of this book contains biographies of selected writers whose work was published in the journals. While it would have been ideal to include every contributor, many are little known, and information on them proved difficult to find. Likewise, many of the poems were translated into English by translators whose names are listed after the poems, but little else is known about them—only their names are preserved in the pages of the journals.

Over the years, I have met some of the renowned poets and writers who shaped the history discussed in this book. One of them is Ziad Abdulfattah, who became the editor of *Lotus* in 1983 and who has written the foreword to this book. He shares his first-hand experiences of rebuilding the journal after the death of its only non-Arab editor, Faiz Ahmad Faiz of Pakistan, and reflects on how the journal continued to develop and resonate across the world.

This preface cannot end without honoring the Palestinian poet Refaʿat Alʿareer, who spoke to the world and predicted his own murder by Israel. In his words:

> If I must die,
> You must live
> To tell my story
> To sell my things
> To buy a piece of cloth
> And some strings,
> (make it white with a long tail)
> So that a child, somewhere in Gaza
> While looking heaven in the eye
> Awaiting his dad who left in a blaze—
> And bid no one farewell
> Not even to his flesh
> Not even to himself—
> Sees the kite, my kite you made, flying up
> Above
> And thinks for a moment an angel is there
> Bringing back love.
> If I must die,
> Let it bring hope.
> Let it be a tale.[2]

---

[2] Refaat Alareer, "If I Must Die," *In These Times*, translated by Sinan Antoon, December 27, 2023, https://inthesetimes.com/article/refaat-alareer-israeli-occupation-palestine

مقدمة:
لوتس والشعلة الأدبيّة

FOREWORD:
LOTUS AND THE LITERARY TORCH

In 1984, the idea of the *Lotus* journal came to me. This idea would be a cultural test, not just for me, but for the editorial board, translators, and artists. I had to make a choice of either pursuing this test or abandoning it completely. Ultimately, I chose to go through with my vision, which became a respectable publication.

Are we merely looking at a periodical issued by the Writers' Union of Asia and Africa, reflecting their concerns, dreams, and aspirations? Perhaps it would be an impactful venture aiming to elevate literature in all its forms, and art in its diverse expressions. From plastic and cubist to abstract, experimental, miniatures, and even calligraphy in all its splendor and creativity.

عندما مضيت قُدمًا في فكرة إنشاء مجلّة *لوتس* عام ١٩٨٤ احترت بين أمرين، أوّلهما إمّا أن أُضيف إلى الفكرة وأُغنيها وأنقلها بما يخدم غايتها النبيلة، إمّا أن أبتعد وأنأى بنفسي عن الدخول في هذه المغامرة التي هي بمثابة اختبار ثقافيّ ليس لي وحسب، إنما لكلّ هيئة التحرير والمترجمين والفنّيّين، ولهذه المجلّة التي بدأت فكرةً ثمّ أصبحت مقامًا عاليًا يليق بنا ونليق به.

هل نحن أمام مجرّد إصدار دوريٍّ يصدر عن اتّحاد كتّاب آسيا وإفريقيا فيعكس همومهم وأحلامهم وأمانيهم، ورهانهم على الأثر والتأثير، والدخول بعمق ليرفعوا الأدب بكلّ صنوفه، والفنّ بتنويعاته وتراوحه، بين التشكيليّ والتكعيبيّ والتجريديّ والتجريبيّ والمنمنمات وحتّى الخطوط بكامل ألقها وإبداعاتها؟

The poem, the short story, the novel, and all the arts that delve into the depths of human experience—whether through sculpture, charcoal, fire, oil, or water—are not enough to declare that we at *Lotus*, the voice of the Asian and African Writers' Union, have achieved, or are on our way to achieving, our goal.

The most important task was to explore the unanswered cultural questions. It was about discovering creators and human beings filled with promise, whose talents lift them from the abyss of the unknown. These discoveries are then brought to a public stage, where their value is recognised, capable of enriching and elevating human creativity.

In the beginning, with its rich and transformative editorial board made of elite group of poets, writers, and literary figures from Asia and Africa, *Lotus* was able to diversify its content and select from the creativity of young writers from every country and colour. However, the magazine faced obstacles driven by ideological and political motives that imposed conflicting visions. At times, compromises were made, and there was a tendency to accommodate personal affinities.

لا تكفي القصيدة والقصّة القصيرة جدًّا والقصيرة والطويلة والرواية، وكلّ الفنون التي تخوض في عمق التجربة البشريّة بما في ذلك النحت، والتشكيل بالفحم والنار والزيت والماء، لنعلن أنّا في مجلّة *لوتس* الناطقة باسم اتّحاد كتّاب آسيا وإفريقيا قد حقّقنا أو أنّا في طريقنا لتحقيق الهدف!

كان الأهمّ هو البحث في مجال الثقافة المجهولة، التي تضمّ مبدعين وأناسًا مفعمين بالوعد، وبمواهب ترفعهم من غيهب المجهول، إلى خشبة مسرح عامّ يعلن اكتشافهم الثرّ، القادر على إغناء الإبداع الإنسانيّ وإعلائه.

وفي البدايات كانت هيئة تحرير مجلّة *لوتس* مؤلّفة من نخبة الشعراء والكتّاب والأدباء من آسيا وإفريقيا، وهذا ما مكّنها من تنويع اختياراتها وانتقاء إبداعات الكتّاب الشباب من كلّ بلد وكلّ لون، لكنّها ولدوافع تتعلّق بالإيديولوجيا حينًا وبالسياسة أحيانًا، كانت تواجه عقبات تفرض رؤى لا تأتلف مع الأهداف العليا. كانت هناك أحيانًا مجاملات!

I met the renowned Pakistani poet Faiz Ahmad Faiz in 1984. At that time, I had become his deputy, heading the editorial board. He and I extensively discussed developing the journal with modern ideas to push it further. I remember that Faiz declared at that meeting without ambiguity, "Literature and the arts have no identity, even if they have noble goals. *Lotus* must capture creativity, especially the creativity of young people in all continents of the world, embrace it, spread it, and elevate it in every place."

Faiz added, "One red line that *Lotus* cannot tolerate is literature that serves colonialism, occupation, racial discrimination, or any other form of racial or religious discrimination." He continued, "Beyond that, our magazine remains open to all forms of creativity, regardless of their origin." Faiz further emphasised, "We may differ within the commission in evaluating the creativity of one writer or another, but on that red line, we are united." Faiz and I agreed completely, and this marked the beginning of our journey.

وفي أوّل اجتماع مع الشاعر الباكستانيّ المجيد فايز أحمد فايز عام ١٩٨٤ كنت أصبحت نائبه في رئاسة هيئة التحرير، تحدّثنا طويلًا عن تطوير اختياراتنا وتجديد أفكار مجلّة *لوتس* العتيدة، والقفز بها خطوات واسعة إلى الأمام. وإنّني لأذكر أنّ فايز أعلن في ذلك الاجتماع وبدون مواربة: "إنّ الآداب والفنون لا هويّة لها وعلى مجلّة *لوتس* أن تلتقط الإبداع بخاصة إبداع الشباب في جميع قارات العالم لتحتضنه وتنشره وتعلي من شأنه في كلّ مكان."

أضاف فايز قائلًا: "خطّ أحمر واحد لا تتحمّله *لوتس* هي ذلك الأدب المكرّس لخدمة الاستعمار والاحتلال، والتمييز العنصري، وكلّ تمييز آخر عرقيّ أو ديّيّ". و تابع: "ما عدا ذلك فإنّ مجلّتنا ستظلّ منفتحة على كلّ إبداع مهما كانت خلفيّته. يتابع فايز، "أنّنا قد نختلف داخل الهيئة في تقييم إبداع من هنا أو آخر من هناك، ولكنّنا عند الخطّ الأحمر لا نختلف." فاتّفقنا أنا وفايز أحمد فايز تماقًا، وبدأنا.

An introduction is essential as we review and evaluate the progress of the distinguished *Lotus*. From Faiz and other members of the editorial board who experienced the early days, I learned that for the initial issues, they selected renowned poets, writers, and storytellers to establish a strong foundation. The goal was for *Lotus* to emerge as a cultural beacon, attracting not only promising young writers but also those who had not yet received the opportunities they deserved.

It's rare to find an issue that doesn't feature or write about these distinguished figures: from Faiz Ahmad Faiz of Pakistan to Adonis from Syria, Pushkin from Russia, Mahmoud Darwish from Palestine, Badr Shaker al-Sayyab from Iraq, Salah Abdel Sabour from Egypt, to Ostliche Prudencio from Nigeria, Vernard Dadeh from Ivory Coast, Sissi Ousmane from Senegal, Oda Makoto from Japan, and Chingiz Aitmatov and Rasul Gamzatov from the Soviet Union.

كانت هذه مقدّمة لا بدّ منها ونحن نستعرض ونقيّم مسيرة هذه المجلّة العتيدة، مجلّة *لوتس*، ولقد فهمت من فايز ومن آخرين في هيئة التحرير الذين عاصروا البدايات أنّهم في الأعداد الأولى مضوا إلى اختيارات اعتمدت كبار الشعراء والكتّاب والقصّاصين ليتمثّلوا في الأعداد الأولى، ولتبدأ *لوتس* بقوّة ولتكون منارة ثقافيّة تجتذب الأقلام الواعدة والشابّة وكلّ أقلام أخرى لم تُتح لها الفرصة.

في هذا الإطار قلّما تجد عددًا لم يكتب فيه أحد هؤلاء الأفذاذ، من فايز أحمد فايز من الباكستان، إلى أدونيس من سوريا، إلى بوشكين من روسيا، إلى محمود درويش من فلسطين، إلى بدر شاكر السيّاب من العراق، إلى صلاح عبد الصبور من مصر، إلى أوستلش برودنسيو من نيجيريا، وڤيرنارد داديه من ساحل العاج، إلى سيسي عثمان من السنغال وأودا ماكوتو من اليابان، وجنكيز إيتماتوف، ورسول حمزاتوف من جمهوريّات الاتّحاد السوفياتي.
لقد ساهم هؤلاء الأفذاذ في جعل المجلّة مرجعًا قيّمًا وملتقى

These intellectuals helped establish the magazine's value, turning it into a significant forum. The publication maintained its momentum through the first twenty issues, but then setbacks began to occur, leading to multiple interruptions. Wars, coups, conspiracies, and sudden relocations from one capital or country to another all contributed to the journal's halts.

Lotus operated in Cairo from 1968 until 1976 and resumed its activities in Tunisia in 1983. The restart was challenging, particularly after the Palestine Liberation Organisation (PLO) left Lebanon in the fall of 1982. Despite their remarkable resilience, the invaders were ultimately unable to breach their defenses and force their departure. However, the prolonged siege eventually took its toll, weakening the resistance forces and diminishing their ability to hold out. The PLO exited Lebanon with only limited weaponry, emerging from a period of historic resistance but with a sense of defeat.

ممتنًعا، وهكذا مضت الأعداد الأولى حتّى العدد العشرين، حين بدأت العثرات تؤدّي إلى توقّف المجلّة مرّات عديدة بسبب الحروب والانقلابات والمؤامرات، ثمّ بسبب الانتقال المفاجئ من عاصمة إلى أخرى ومن بلد إلى بلد.

بدأت المجلّة نشاطها في القاهرة منذ عام ١٩٦٨ حتّى ١٩٧٦، وانتقلت بعدها إلى تونس عام ١٩٨٣، كانت البداية صعبة حيث كانت منظّمة التحرير الفلسطينيّة قد خرجت في خريف ١٩٨٢ من لبنان في صمود عالٍ لم يتمكّن خلاله الغزاة من اقتحامها، وإجبارها على الانسحاب. لكنّ الحصار، في النتيجة، فعل فعله حين أصبح يُطبق على القوى الوطنيّة واللبنانيّة والمقاومة، ليقلّص أمد صمودها، ولقد خرجت المنظمة مشرّعةَ الأسلحة الفرديّة، لكنّها في النهاية خرجت وسط صمود تاريخيّ، ولكنّه بطعم الهزيمة.

In Tunisia, the organisation started anew, and *Lotus* began to flourish, sharpening its cultural capabilities to their fullest potential. During this time, Muʿin Bseiso served as the deputy to Faiz Ahmad Faiz, the editor-in-chief, and, more precisely, could be considered the executive editor-in-chief.

After that, the magazine relaunched, but time was not on Muʿin's side, as he passed away soon after. Faiz also did not have much time and passed about a year later. I then found myself facing the vast cultural legacy left behind by two great knightly poets: Faiz Ahmad Faiz from Pakistan and Muʿin Bseiso from Palestine.

The editorial board met in Tunisia, then in Moscow, New Delhi, Senegal, Berlin, and other capitals in Asia and Africa, where it began planning for the future with steadfastness and in the spirit of modernity, which called for diversity and a range of creative types.

في تونس بدأت المنظّمة من جديد، وبدأت مجلّة *لوتس* تنهض، شاحذةً قدراتها الثقافيّة حتّى حدودها القصوى، كان معين بسيسو في ذلك الوقت نائبًا لفايز أحمد فايز رئيس التحرير، وللدقّة يمكن القول بأنّه كان رئيس التحرير التنفيذيّ.

بعد ذلك، بدأت المجلّة انطلاقتها مرّةً أخرى، لكنّ الوقت لم يكن لصالح معين إذ سرعان ما رحل، ولم يمهل فايز فرحل بعد معين بقرابة العام، لأجد نفسي أمام هذا الإرث الثقافيّ الضخم الذي خلّفه اثنان من الشعراء الفرسان الكبار، فايز أحمد فايز من الباكستان، ومعين بسيسو من فلسطين.

واجتمعت هيئة التحرير في تونس ثمّ في موسكو ونيودلهي والسنغال وبرلين وعواصم أخرى من عالم آسيا وإفريقيا حيث راحت تخطط للمستقبل بثبات وبروح الحداثة، التي استدعت التنوّع والتراوح بين صنوف الإبداع البشريّ.

كان لا بدّ أن نواكب العصر،

It was essential for us to adapt to the times. After more than a quarter of a century, we aimed to embrace a modern approach that would allow us to explore new horizons. Our focus was on African and Asian creators, as well as others who had not yet engaged with contemporary, literary, and artistic developments. We paved the way and navigated challenging paths, with the International Editorial Board dedicating itself to thoughtful, creative, and sometimes controversial choices. While the board worked from their respective countries, the executive editorial board in Tunisia managed translation, editing, and proofreading, preparing the journal for print and publication. This significant and meticulous effort propelled *Lotus* forward, enabling it to take bold and assured steps toward fulfilling its enduring promise.

As we embarked on our challenging yet fulfilling mission, we often asked ourselves: Have we arrived? Have we achieved our goals? One of our primary objectives was to reach those obscure writers or artists who, despite their dedication to creation, lacked the means to share their work with the world.

فنمضي بعد أكثر من ربع قرن الى مواءمة عصريّة تجعلنا في مركز القدرة على اجتراح آفاق جديدة. كان هقّنا أن نجمع بين المبدعين الأفارقة والآسيويّين وكلّ المبدعين الآخرين الذين لم تسنح لهم الفرصة، مع العصر الآليّ واللحاق بكلّ تطوّر أدبيّ وفتيّ. ممهّدنا الطريق، رصفنا الشوارع الوعرة، أكبّ أعضاء هيئة التحرير الدوليّة على اختيارات دقيقة إبداعيّة وخلّاقة، وفيما كان أعضاء هيئة التحرير الدوليّة يفعلون ذلك كلّ من وطنه ومكان إقامته، كانت هيئة التحرير التنفيذيّة في تونس، تكبّ على الترجمة والتحرير والتصحيح والتدقيق حتّى الأعداد للطباعة والنشر. لقد أدى ذلك الجهد العظيم والعميق إلى تقدّم مجلّة *لوتس*، بحيث راحت تخطو خطوات واسعة وواثقة نحو تحقيق الوعد الذي راودها.

وكنّا نسأل دائمًا ونحن منغمسون في مهمّتنا الشاقّة، والجميلة أيضًا: هل وصلنا؟! هل حقّقنا الأهداف؟! كان أحد أهمّ أهدافنا الوصول إلى كاتب مغمور أو إلى فنّان منذور للخلق والإبداع، ولكنّه لا يملك الأدوات التي تقدّمه للناس.

We committed to showcasing their talent as prominently as possible. At that time, computers, Facebook, the Internet, and email had yet to emerge, so we relied on traditional methods like air mail and land mail, which extended and complicated communication. Despite these challenges, we persevered, driven by our duty to address the difficult question:
Have we succeeded?

A critical question arose after the journal's publication: Was it distributed effectively? Did it reach our intended destinations—both large and small cities and the distant worlds we had long dreamed of reaching? The answer remained uncertain until we unexpectedly received two separate letters, one from Senegal, and the other from Morocco. These letters confirmed our efforts with undeniable clarity. While I will not delve into the details of the first letter, the second one, from Morocco, is particularly noteworthy. I find it valuable to include it in this introduction as it vividly illustrates the impact of our journal and reflects our journey. The message expressed what we could not articulate ourselves, capturing the essence and significance of our work.

فآلينا على أنفسنا أن نقدّمه نحن بأعلى ما يكون، إذ لم يكن الحاسوب قد ظهر بعد ولا الفيس بوك والإنترنت ولا البريد الإلكترونيّ الذي سيختزل ساعات السفر بالطائرات والبريد الجوّي والبرّي، وكلّ بريد آخر يهدر الوقت ويمدّد الزمن، وعلى الرغم من ذلك اجتهدنا في اجتياز كلّ العقبات، وأجبنا عن السؤال الصعب والشائك...هل وصلنا؟
كانت النقطة الحرجة تحيلنا إلى سؤال آخر حول المجلّة بعد صدورها، هل تمّ توزيعها جيّدًا؟ وهل وصلت إلى حيث استهدفنا أن تصل إلى المدن الكبيرة والصغيرة، وإلى عوالم لطالما حلمنا في أن نصل إليها؟ ظلّت الإجابة صعبة وغير حاسمة بالنسبة لنا، إلى أن تلقّينا فجأة رسالتين مختلفتين، إحداهما من السنغال والأخرى من المغرب. بعثت الرسالتان في قلوبنا يقينًا لا يتزعزع: لن أتحدّث عن الرسالة الأولى ولكنّي سأتحدث عن الثانية اختصارًا، فهي رسالة وردت إلى مجلّة لوتس من المغرب، أرى من المفيد نشرها في سياق هذه المقدّمة لكي نقدّر بامتياز آثار خطواتنا ومواقع أقدامنا. تلك الرسالة قالت ما لم نستطع قوله، كانت أصدق قول وتعبير وترجمة لموقع المجلّة ودورها.

Below is the text of the message:

Tonight, my solitude is eased only by the lotus flower my mother brought me along with some supplies and food. The flower still carries its intoxicating scent, leaving me unable to write my letters. Greetings to you, Ziad. We send you our heartfelt prayers and wish a long life to the budding project.

My mother, Ziad, like many mothers, is illiterate and cannot read letters, but something within her drew her to buy this issue of Lotus in the fall of 1986. She told me she didn't haggle over the price, even though it was higher than for other books, which were thicker and had more pages. When the guard handed me the book, she said, "Is it worth it?" but I didn't respond; my eyes spoke for me before I even touched the book. The guard was flipping through it.

Tonight, the flower was a luxurious treat that I enjoyed alone, setting aside my plans. Tomorrow, I'll return to my commitments, awaiting another flower that might bring a new surprise.

You have my sincere greetings, Ziad.
Al-Rahbani Saeed 59337
Civil Prison "Aghbla" Casablanca

وفيما يلي نصّ الرسالة:

"وحيد الليلة، لا تؤنس وحدتي سوى زهرة اللوتس، التي حملتها لي أمّي اليوم مع المؤونة وبعض الطعام، لا تزال الزهرة تحمل عبيرها الذي أسكرني، ففاجأت حروفي فأبت إلّا أن تحفر في الورق. تحيّة لك يا زياد ونشدّ على يديك بحرارة ونتمنّى للزهرة مزيدًا من العمر."

أمّي يا زياد، كأغلب الأمّهات، أمّيّة لا تفكّ الحرف، لكنّ شيئًا ما جذبها، شيء داخليّ ربّما، دفعها لاقتناء هذا العدد من اللوتس الذي يرجع إلى خريف ١٩٨٦. قالت لي إنّها لم تساوم عليه كثيرًا، ولو أنّ الثمن الذي طلبه صاحب الكتب يفوق ثمن كتاب آخر يحمل أكثر ممّا تحمله لوتس من ورق وعلى حدّ تعبيرها "غليظ" بعد أن أعطاني الحارس الكتاب قالت "واش مزيان" (هل يستحق هذه التكلفة؟) لم أجبها لأنّ عيني قد أجابتها قبل أن ألمس الكتاب بيديّ متى كان الحارس يتصفّحه.

الليلة شكّلت الزهرة وليمة لي فاخرة استأثرت بها وحدي دون باقي الرفاق، لذا اختليت هذه الليلة وتجاوزت البرنامج الذي وضعته. غدًا سأعود للالتزام في انتظار زهرة أخرى قد تحملها مفاجأة أخرى.

لك منّي يا زياد تحيّاتي الصادقة.
الرحباني سعيد ٥٩٣٣٧
السجن المدنيّ أغبلة" الدار البيضاء

In this brief review of *Lotus*' prospects, I want to highlight how the journal has evolved, changed, and broadened its scope. As it moved beyond the 1980s and into the era of computers and new communication networks, it enriched our dreams and goals. For instance, if we look at issues from 1986 onward, we see a notable shift from the early editions. The journal has become richer, more diverse, and more creative.

There is one final question: Can the journal return to achieve the same objectives? I would assert that these goals, rooted in humaneness and nobility, remain timeless. From the dawn of creation, humanity has been a reflection of divine creativity, bringing light and meaning to life. However, I cannot speculate on the possibility of reviving the journal without a thorough study and new considerations that require a different approach and context.

Ziad Abdulfattah

أردت من خلال هذه القراءة المستعجلة لآفاق مجلّة *لوتس* أن أؤكّد أنّ المجلّة قد تطوّرت وتغيّرت واتّسع مداها، بخاصّة أنّها وهي تقطع مسافة الثمانينات من القرن الماضي، كان الحاسوب وما ترتّب عليه من تنويعات في شبكات الاتّصال والتواصل قد بدأت تظهر فتثري ما ظلّ يراودنا من أحلام وأهداف. إنّنا لو تصفّحنا أحد أعداد المجلّة عام ١٩٨٦ وما بعده، فلسوف نجد اختلافًا عن الأعداد الأولى أو أعداد البدايات. لقد أصبحنا أكثر ثراءً، أشدّ تنوّعًا وأكثر إبداعًا.

ثمّة سؤال أخير، هل يمكن للمجلّة أن تعود من جديد؟! وإلى الأهداف والغايات نفسها؟ سوف أسارع إلى القول إنّ الأهداف والغايات التي نشأت من أجل تحقيقها هي غايات إنسانيّة ونبيلة ولا تتغيّر بتغيّر الأزمان، فالبشريّة منذ بداية الخليقة هي ظلّ الله على الأرض وهي خليفته في الإبداع والتكوين الأدبيّ والفنّي، الذي يجعل من الحياة نورًا ومنارة. غير أنّي لا أستطيع الإجابة ولو افتراضيًّا عن إمكانيّة صدور المجلّة من جديد، فذلك يحتاج إلى دراسة معمّقة وحسابات لها نسق آخر وسياق مختلف.

زياد عبد الفتاح

INTRODUCTION

The story of resistance to Zionism is deeply embedded within the Afro-Asian Writers Movement. The movement paid special attention to the ideological claims of Zionism, its origin, and role in relation to imperialism. The Afro-Asian Writers Movement held firmly to the Resolution on Palestine passed at the Third Afro-Asian Writers' Conference in 1966. Given that we were producing this book at the time of yet another genocide against the Palestinian people, this time live for the world to watch, it is instructive to revisit this resolution and see the resonance of the present in its opening words.

In the last six clauses of the resolution, it called on all writers to unite in solidarity with Palestine, saluted the resoluteness of the Palestinian writers living under occupation, and affirmed support to "liberate Palestine and to regain their usurped homeland by any means."

RESOLUTION ON PALESTINE

The Third Afro-Asian Writers' Conference :

1) Considers the Zionist movement as colonialist by nature, expansionist in its aims, racist in its structure, facist in the means it is using;

2) Considers Israel as an imperialist base and a docile tool used for aggressive purposes against Arab states in order to delay their progress towards unity and socialism, and as a bridge-head which neo-colonialism relies on in order to maintain its influence over African and Asian states;

3) Views the aggressive Israeli presence in Palestine as artificial, usurping and demographically imperialist, resorting to violent means and consequently considers the liquidation of this presence as a liberatory and urgent task;

4) Considers that a revolutionary solution to the problems of the Arab Nation, i.e., the liquidation of the reactionary and colonialist regimes, economic emancipation and progress, is primarily bound to the liquidation of Israel as a base intended to maintain backwardness in that region;

5) Views the Israeli presence as a fascist and racist system, in terms of a setback to civilization directed against human progress;

6) Appeals to Afro-Asion Writers, and to all progressive writers in the world, to stand in the face of the wide cultural conspiracy launched by the Zionist movement through writers who have betrayed the honour of the written word in order to serve interests that are contradictory to the rudiments of truth and History, and to take action, as strongly as possible, in order to stem that misleading cultural aggression through a quest for truth and an appeal to consolidate it.

7) Denounces the heavy cultural siege laid by Israel on one quarter of a million Arabs living in occupied territory under a hateful racial oppression in their own land.

8) Hails Palestinian Arab Writers living in occupied Palestine under terrorist rule, for their valiant stand in defence of the rights of the Palestinian people to liberate their country, and denounces the continuous oppression to which they are subjected at the hands of the occupational forces.

9) Hails progressive writers from Asia, Africa and the rest of the world who have, through their consciousness and courage, stood up to Zionist falsehoods and exposed them ; and those who have, through their honourable and responsible pens, considerably reinforced the cause of the Palestinian people in their struggle for self-determination.

10) Considers the support given by the writers of Africa and Asia to the people of Palestine in their struggle for the liberation of their territory as an integral part of the support given to liberation in the world.

11) Supports the Palestine Liberation Organisation which leads the struggle of the Palestinian Arab people to liberate Palestine and to regain their usurped homeland by any means.

Figure 1: Scan from Lotus. Issue 1 Vol 1. 1968, p.140.

I had originally opened this book with the words:

I wrote on the clouds, down with censorship – they confiscated the sky.

I was introduced to this verse by a friend in the 1980s, the late Javed Akhter Bedi, who mentioned it was by the Palestinian poet Mahmoud Darwish to whose work Bedi had also introduced me, along with the work of Pablo Neruda, Ahmad Faraz, Habib Jalib, and Faiz Ahmad Faiz. Working on this book I learned that the opening words were in fact those of Mu'in Bseiso and not Darwish.

Not unlike today, the 1980s were also a time of conflict and strife. Britain was at war with Argentina over the Malvinas Islands; Ireland was in the throes of "The Troubles"; bloody anti-colonial struggles were raging in Africa; the United States of America and its allies were involved with overthrowing regimes and imposing rulers with their backing; and Afghanistan was occupied by the Soviet Union, to give but a few examples. This was the time when the West, led by the USA and its acolytes, was pumping money and arms into the mujahidin in Afghanistan, through the Pakistani military dictatorship of General Muhammad Zia-ul-Haq.

I saw in the opening words echoes of the struggle for democracy in Pakistan. They carried a spirit of resistance amidst the oppressive days of censorship during the dictatorship of General Zia-ul-Haq. General Zia and Pakistan's military establishment, apart from facilitating support for the mujahidin, were pushing the "Islamization" of Pakistan.[1] Any challenge to the dictatorship was brutally suppressed; even poets were imprisoned and exiled. But poetry could not be locked up and continued to inspire hope, for in the words of Roque Dalton's "El Salvador," poetry is "not made of words alone."[2]

---

1 Haqqani, "From Islamic Republic to Islamic State," 131.
2 Harlow, Resistance Literature, 31.

During this time, I was active in black (Afro-Asian) youth organisations in Britain, primarily fighting against racism and fascism including murderous attacks. I was imprisoned briefly in the case of the Bradford 12. We had grown up in Britain and were determined not only to fight for the right to live but for a dignified life as well. We believed that this fight was not only a working-class struggle in Britain but concerned all those fighting for national liberation and for the creation of a fairer world. This was an era of victories in numerous national liberation struggles across the world.

Many of my youthful dreams have been crushed by retrogression of the very organisations that led national liberation struggles in the past into dictatorial regimes across Africa and Asia. The resources that they had promised to liberate for the peoples of their countries were plundered for their own cliques, often working hand in glove with the same imperial powers they had fought earlier.[3] Whilst new robber barons have emerged aplenty in many former colonies, they could not stop the robbed from struggling for a fairer world and the desire for economic, social, and political justice from being written, if at least in poetry. During the time of the Afro-Asian Writers Movement, "A light that glimmered in the dawn,"[4] would lead us to a place where "Not a finger shall be missing, from the hand of light, which shall hold the torch, of the universal."[5]

Learning about the movement

In 1984, the poet Bedi took me to a *mushiara*, a poetry recital in London where I met Faiz Ahmad Faiz briefly for the first time. This was shortly before his death. At the time, I was not aware that Faiz had been based in Beirut as the only non-Arab editor of *Lotus*, the journal of the Afro-Asian Writers Movement[6], nor did I know that I too would end up in Beirut working on an edited collection of poetry from *Lotus*. Faiz's poetry inspired generations of people resisting dictatorship, injustice, and obscurantism in Pakistan and the country's diaspora. One of his poems, "Hum Dekhengey" (We Shall See), has become a battle cry in the current struggle in India against the far-right Hindu nationalist movement of the Bharatiya Janata Party.

---

3   Mohan, "African Liberation Struggle," 4.
4   Abdel Halim, "All of Life," 168.
5   Prudencio, "We Shall Be There," 43.
6   Aydelott, "Memories of Faiz," 309-308.

In it he writes:

> And we oppressed
> Beneath our feet will have
> this earth shiver, shake and beat
> And heads of rulers will be struck
> With crackling lightning
> And thunder roars.[7]

Through working on this book, I became familiar with the works of many Afro-Asian writers. Amidst the work of the Afro-Asian Writers Movement, I discovered a treasure trove of poetry committed to a struggle for progressive change, a transformation as needed today as it was then. It is indeed as Mohammad Asim Siddiqui writes:

> A poem by its very nature is a kind of overcode, a discourse that exploits both emotive and metaphorical dimensions of language. Hence, poetry passes the test of time: it retains its relevance even in a different context [...]. This is what has happened to the progressive Urdu poet Faiz Ahmad Faiz of late. The widespread protests against the controversial Citizenship Amendment Ac, 2019, which began on 12 December 2019, has given his famous nazm, Hum Dekhengey [We Shall See], an entirely new context. Hum Dekhengey was written 40 years ago by an avowedly atheist poet in protest against the fundamentalist military dictator ruling over Pakistan at the time, Zia-ul-Haq. It has sparked a controversy in India now because the premier technology institute, IIT Kanpur, has set up a committee to decide whether the poem is "anti-Hindu."[8]

Why focus specifically on the poetry of the Afro-Asian Writers Movement when their journals were dedicated to a wide variety of writings such as political papers, folklore, and linguistic issues? Perhaps it is to negate something I often heard as a child, "What good is it to aim to be a poet?" To those who have asked me this question, I would like to retort and mention Mao Zedong and Ho Chi Minh, two published poets who laid the foundations that changed the lives of hundreds of millions of people and continue to do so today.

---

7 Faiz, "Hum Dekhengey (We Shall See).
8 Siddiqui. "How to Read Faiz"

These two writers led movements that defeated imperialism in their countries, inspiring hundreds of millions around the world to also resist and fight for a better future; some may dismiss this poetry as political sloganeering, but for people like Marwan Makhoul whose words embody the spirit of this book and were being circulated against the backdrop of the war on Gaza:

> In order for me to write poetry that is not political,
> I must listen to the birds
> And in order to hear the birds
> The warplanes must be silent.[9]

Indeed, Afro-Asian poetry changed the world, for "[p]oetry is capable not only of serving as a means for the expression of personal identity or even nationalist sentiment,"[10] as Barbara Harlow writes in *Resistance Literature*. She also writes, "poetry, as a part of the cultural institutions and historical existence of a people, is itself an arena of struggle." Quoting Amilcar Cabral in the same book, "[t]he national liberation of a people is the regaining of the historical personality of that people, it is their return to history through the destruction of the imperialist domination to which they have been subjected."

After all, if we had nothing else linking us directly to each other's struggles, we had each other's poetry. At times this was reflected in the rhyming slogans we shouted in the streets, and at other times in echoes of rebellious poems, penned by poets who would write on the clouds if need be. In our public meetings, speeches were often punctuated by defiant poems, which we saw as an integral part of our culture of resistance.

---

9 Makhoul, Untitled.
10 Harlow, *Resistance Literature*, 33.

Whilst the protest poetry of the streets is often expressed in the chants during demonstrations, the slogans themselves are embedded in the narratives and demands of specific struggles. These slogan-poems are not the work of the pen of an individual poet but often the direct product of shared experiences, which burst into life, sometimes spontaneously, and sometimes old slogans reemerge to regain new meanings.

The colonial project not only deprived the colonised of their human and material resources but also often created mass poverty and illiteracy.[11] Given the widespread illiteracy during the height of the colonial era, many poets often wrote for their class in a language not meant for the masses but for the class of readers who enjoyed the finer things in life yet empathised with the downtrodden. An anecdote from Pakistan has it that when Faiz Ahmad Faiz was questioned about this, he replied that he does not write for the masses but about them. The fact that his words live on today is testimony to the power of the written word. By writing on paper, the resistance poets of the Afro-Asian Writers Movement were among those who helped to negate the oppressive power of the written word as used by the colonial and imperial edifice. As Hugo Blanco said:

> [...] for centuries the oppressors of the peasants made them regard paper as a god. Paper became a fetish: Arrest orders are paper. By means of papers they crush the Indian in the courts. The peasant sees papers in the offices of the governor, the parish priest, the judge, the notary - wherever there is power; the landowner, too, keeps accounts on paper. All the reckonings you have made, all your logical arguments, they refute by showing you a paper; the paper supersedes logic, it defeats it.[12]

---

11 Banya, "Illiteracy, Colonial Legacy and Education," 164.
12 Cited in: Harlow, *Resistance Literature*, 12.

The Call and *Lotus*

When I started working on this book, I thought there had been only one Afro-Asian Writers Movement, with *Lotus* as its journal. While working to collect and archive *Lotus*, I learned that there were in fact two wings within the movement; one produced *Lotus*, and the other *The Call*, which preceded *Lotus* by almost a decade. Both journals were concerned with the cultural arena of resistance. *The Call*'s position on culture followed Mao Tse-Tung's thought, "[i]n the world today all culture, all literature and art belong to definite classes and are geared to definite political lines. There is in fact no such thing as art for art's sake, art that stands above classes, art that is detached from or independent of politics."[13] *Lotus* was produced by a split in the organisation, fermented and orchestrated by writers funded by the Soviet Union, including one of its editors, Faiz Ahmad Faiz. On behalf of the General Secretary of the Soviet Writers' Union in 1964, Faiz wrote to the Central Committee of the Soviet Union requesting funding for a new journal:

> In light of the anti-communist and anti-Soviet campaigns conducted by imperialist circles through different cultural and press organisations (such as *Encounter* in England, as well as *Thought and Current* in India), the question of the founding of a progressive, multilingual literary and political magazine somewhere in Asia or Africa has become particularly pressing. The importance of such a journal has also been reinforced by the activities of the Chinese schismatics, who have financed different foreign journals, such as *Eastern Horizon* in Hong Kong and *Revolution* in Africa, Asia, and Latin America to utilise them in their interests. These magazines systematically publish writers and journalists from various countries who criticise the policies of the Communist Party of the Soviet Union and other fraternal parties.[14]

It is clear that there are two central concerns in this letter. Firstly, "the anti-communist and anti-Soviet campaigns conducted by imperialist circles" and secondly, "the activities of the Chinese

---

13 Afro-Asian Writers' Bureau, "The Struggle Between the Two Lines," 2.
14 Ernst and Djagalov, "The Road to Lotus," 701.

schismatics" for which funding is sought for a new journal. Faiz was aware that his move would divide the Afro-Asian Writers Movement, as he firmly made his position clear in Cairo:

> I tried to explain to the writers of UAR [United Arab Republic] the situation in the Permanent Bureau and the Executive Committee of the Afro-Asian Writers' Association, talked about the schismatic actions of the Chinese and the damage they have done, and insisted on the necessity of cleansing our movement, ideally at its next conference in Jakarta.[15]

Faiz makes no mention of *The Call* despite being a part of the movement. At the time, *The Call* was already publishing various literary works, including poetry and short stories by writers from across former colonised nations. Faiz's efforts to split the movement resulted in the inception of a journal called *Afro-Asian Writings*, which later evolved into *Lotus*. Despite major differences between the two wings of the movement, both were clear on one central point: that the cultural arena of struggle against colonialism and imperialism was no less important than any other arena of battle. In this they represented the spirit of Bandung.

In the first edition of *Afro-Asian Writings*, Youssef el-Sebaʿi, who was appointed as the first editor, declared, "What is more serious, however, is the danger that threatens national culture and literature in the form of an avalanche of imperialist 'quasi-cultural' products [...]. This destructive phenomenon which threatens the whole of the world in the form of a diffusion of cheap publications abounds with a shameful insinuating call to boost up violence and racial discrimination, racial supremacy, the support of war and imperialism, the cheapening of ethical and moral values[...]."[16]

---

15   Ernst and Djagalov, "The Road to Lotus," 709.
16   El-Sebaʿi, "The Role of Afro-Asian Literature and the National Liberation Movements," 10.

Bandung Spirit

Anti-colonial struggles not only laid bare the utter brutality of the coloniser, especially in their dying days, but also showed that the colonised had no choice but to unite with their respective countries as well as across continents against their common enemies. This desire, as Vijay Prashad notes in *The Darker Nations*, would force them to come together in Bandung in 1955, "[a] vast section of the world that had once bowed down before the might of Europe now stood at the threshold of another destiny."[17]

The dreamers of this new destiny were clear that not only was it necessary to take back control of human and material resources from the colonial powers, but also vital to reclaim history and culture as well. Prashad observes in the same book:

> Empires generally attempt to direct the cultural history of a people —to set one community against another (divide and rule), adopt one group as the leader above the rest, or else disdain the cultural traditions of a region and propose its subjugation by the empire's own cultural traditions at least for the select few.[18]

While fighting with guns, pens, or songs, anti-colonial struggles were also in search of ways in which they could communicate among themselves—a bridge that they could cross to find each other. Although there was a desire to forge unity between formerly colonised peoples, there were serious contradictions among those who had gathered at Bandung. The leadership that emerged at the end of colonial rule in many countries often reflected the interests of the newly developing indigenous ruling classes.

Whilst direct colonialism might have been taking its last breath, imperialism certainly was not; it wasted no time in consolidating its hold over former colonies. This battle was not just for material control but also for cultural and ideological domination. Prashad argues

---

17   Prashad, *The Darker Nation*, 33.
18   Ibid., 45.

that the most powerful agreements were made at Bandung in the field of cultural cooperation:

> The lack of agreement on the nature of the global political economy, resulted in a weak combined position. Progressive nationalisms drew from the class interests of those who predominated in their various societies. What united these various classes however, was a forthright condemnation of the indignity of imperialism's chauvinism.[19]

It was this agreement that would provide the impetus for Afro-Asian writers to unite in the cultural arena of words.

Afro-Asian Writers and Tashkent, 1958

Following Bandung, this determination would continue to resonate through the desire for South-South unity. It would lead to the largest-ever gathering of Afro-Asian Writers in Tashkent in 1958. The movement for the unification of Afro-Asian Writers was itself part of a broader Afro-Asian movement, incorporating Afro-Asian People's Solidarity Organisation (AAPSO), the Afro-Asian Women's Association, and the Afro-Asian Journalists Association.

To fully grasp the historical significance of the Tashkent meeting and its influence through the following decades, perhaps it is time to reflect on what was missing in the lives of writers, particularly progressive writers of the time. Whilst organisations such as the Progressive Writers' Association in India and writers' associations in the Arab world existed well before the conference, there was no common platform for writers from Africa and Asia. Furthermore, there was no internet, nor the plethora of publications that exist today, and many of these writers had lived under the shadow of colonial and imperialist repression. Thus, this meeting was significant as it was the first time that many writers speaking different languages united across two continents with the common objective of sharing similar

---

19   Prashad, *The Darker Nation*, 45.

experiences of oppression, exploitation, and resistance through an organised structure without any reliance on colonial masters, past or present. Shirley Graham Du Bois, who attended the conference of 1958 with W. E Du Bois, recalled:

> In ancient times along a road not far from the present city[20] travelled caravans of merchants bearing silk from China and ivory from the Congo. Over this road ancient cultures contacted and influenced each other, languages mingled, and scholars from Timbuctoo met scholars from Peking. So now, in our own day, scholars of Africa and Asia travelled the road to Tashkent. Only now, they had come as strangers, having lost the ties of the past. And though they came in jet planes, Ghana's poetess Efua Theodora Sutherland correctly describes the conference as "a step towards unification of the disrupted soul of mankind."[21]

In black-and-white silent footage of this meeting,[22] hundreds of delegates are welcomed by horns, drums, and applauding crowds. Even without sound, you can almost hear the music, the clapping, and the cheering. The expressions on the faces of both well-wishers and delegates undeniably reflected the joy of participating in this occasion. Shirley Du Bois wrote a minute of the event:

> With a far larger representation from Africa than was present at the Bandung Conference in '55, writers from all over Asia and Africa gathered Oct. 7-13 here in Tashkent, the ancient capital of Uzbekistan, in one of the most important international conferences ever held. Never before have so many Africans and Asians from so many different countries met together. From 48 countries abroad came 168 writer-delegates; delegates from Soviet Asian republics brought the total delegates to over 200. Additional writers from Western Europe, guests and visitors filled to overflowing the magnificent Alisher Navoi Theatre where the Conference took place.[23]

Shirley Du Bois noted that an "appeal" unanimously adopted by the conference called on writers of the world to "Raise your voices against

---

20 Tashkent, Uzbekistan.
21 Du Bois, "I am an American, I am an African," 2-3.
22 British Pathe, Uzbekistan: The Tashkent Conference.
23 Du Bois, "I am an American, I am an African," 2-3.

all the evils which are being committed both against individuals and against whole nations, against injustice, colonialism, exploitation." The conference reminded the world, "We express the regenerating spirit of one and a half thousand million people. It was on the banks of the Hwang Ho and the Yangtze, the Indus, the Ganges, the Euphrates, the Nile and the Niger that man emerged for the first time from the darkness of prehistoric existence and created the means for fashioning intellectual and material culture."[24]

Figure 2: W. E. B. Du Bois delivering an address at the
Afro-Asian Writers Conference in Tashkent in October 1958

It was at this conference that W. E Du Bois, who was ninety at the time, gave his famous speech, "I am an American—I am an African." He received the only standing ovation for an individual at the conference. When speaking as an "American African" he warned Africa against "economic imperialism" and called for "patriotic sacrifice" for the good of all of its peoples. In an informal discussion on African unification with writers from Angola, Dahomey, Ghana, Madagascar, Nigeria, Somaliland, Guinea, and Senegal, Du Bois recalled the superior mores of Africa's original community of life before it was corrupted by white invaders.

---

24 Du Bois, "I am an American, I am an African," 2-3.

He was fervently applauded when he urged his listeners to draw their strength and sustenance from within Africa rather than from without, to give cooperation rather than accept "gifts."[25]

Figure 3: Scan from The Call. Special Supplement of The Call on the Occasion of Palestine Day (May 15), 1968.

The Tashkent conference established the Afro-Asian Writers Bureau (AAWB) in Sri Lanka (then Ceylon). It was tasked with producing translations of Afro-Asian writings, publishing books, and a journal. Subtitled "The Bulletin of the Afro-Asian Writers Bureau," the first journal to be launched by the AAWB was *The Call*. The first edition was published in the early 1960s and was produced in English, Arabic, and French from Beijing and Colombo.[26] Initially, *The Call* mainly published reports on the activities of the movement, but it would go on to produce a variety of articles on culture and resistance, including poetry and short stories.

---

25 Du Bois, "I am an American, I am an African," 2-3.
26 Incidentally around this time a journal of Afro-Asian Journalist was also produced.

The Afro-Asian Writers Movement itself consisted of an amalgam of writers' organisations from different countries, such as Vietnam and Syria, along with the individual writers. This movement was born under the intensifying conflicts between the Soviet Union and China over the question of whether it was possible to peacefully coexist with capitalism.

Intelligence Services

The activities of these cultural organisations were closely followed by British and American intelligence forces, whose documents offer detailed insight into the 1958 conference and some of the discussions that took place at the time, albeit from an imperialist perspective. The American CIA noted that the executive committee:

> [...] despite some opposition, passed 35 resolutions, all violently anti-imperialist, anti-American, and anti-colonialist. Heavy stress was laid on the theme of imperialist economic penetration "since imperialism depends upon them for raw materials for the sale of its industrial products and for the investment of its capital."[27]

The CIA report comprehensively lists core disputes that existed between pro-Soviet and pro-Chinese wings of the movement, which would have a direct impact on the Afro-Asian Writers Movement about five years later. Interestingly, the CIA notes:

> Although there were reports of ideological differences between the Soviet delegation, which allegedly wanted the theme of the conference to be "peaceful co-existence" and ending the Cold War and the Chinese, who preferred "liquidation of imperialism," a Sino-Soviet compromise was apparently reached and both slogans were incorporated, side by side, in the final resolution.[28]

---

27 Central Intelligence Agency, The Afro-Asian Peoples Solidarity Organization from April 1960 – April 1961, June 15, 1961, 9.
28 Ibid., 11.

The proceedings of the Tashkent conference were also monitored by British Intelligence. In a confidential NATO report, the British embassy in Moscow dismissed the significance of the gathering:

> From the point of view of serious literature the Writers' Conference had been practically worthless. Its only achievements had been to bring about some stimulating and interesting meetings between Asians and Africans and to enable the Communist elements to put out propaganda on the usual lines.[29]

Such dismissal of African and Asian literature recalls the racist attitudes expressed in Macaulay's infamous minute from 1835: "A single shelf of a good European library was worth the whole native literature of India and Arabia."[30] The report also consolidated anti-African stereotypes and racism:

> In this propaganda the emphasis had been mainly on the need to write on the current themes (i.e primarily anti-colonialism). This had more effect on Africans, who for the most part have no literary traditions, than on the Asians who have. Indeed, it was the Africans who, throughout the proceedings, played to the Soviet point of view, and spoke more violently.[31]

The British assessment also predictably dismissed the idea of Afro-Asian unity, noting:

> The whole "Afro-Asian" idea to some extent is vitiated by the profound mistake of ignoring that many - perhaps most - Asians, especially the Indians (to say nothing of Mr. Sei Ito) have much more in common with the West than Africa. On one level, this appears to have emerged fairly clearly at the conference on the question of "imperialism".[32]

---

29 North Atlantic Treaty Organization, Committee on Information and Cultural Relations Afro-Asian Writers' Conference, 1.
30 H. Sharp, "Minute by the Hon'ble T. B. Macaulay," Selections from Educational Records, Part I (1781-1839).
31 North Atlantic Council, Committee on Information and Cultural Relations, Afro-Asians Writers Conference, Tashkent, October 1959, Note by the United Kingdom Delegation, 1.
32 Ibid., 3.

Under the Shadow of the Sino-Soviet Split

The shadow of the conflict between the Soviet Union and China would affect the Afro-Asian Writers Movement even before the movement formally split into two different wings, according to the AAWB's reflection. Divisions in the movement existed even during the preparations for the conference of 1958, stoked by the pro-Soviet camp, which the AAWB labeled "Soviet revisionists."

> When the conference finally opened in October 1958 they (Soviet revisionists) expressed in clear terms of the opening session their wish that the conference would be a tool to serve their policy of "peaceful coexistence" and "peaceful cooperation." They prattled on about "peace" and cooperation" and "exchanges" between the East and the West, brushing aside the Afro-Asian people's anti-imperialist and anti-colonialist struggle which was flaring like fire set to dry timber.[33]

Whatever the conflicts between the Soviet and Chinese groups, the CIA had already reached its conclusion on the Soviet concept of peaceful co-existence and its implications for the West's relationship with the communist bloc. In an internal document by the CIA from 1959, they concluded:

> The desire for peaceful coexistence is, itself, genuine. This does not mean, however, that peaceful coexistence is to be equated with peace as we understand it. It is, in a sense a prolonged armistice while the political and ideological struggle as well as the economic competition, goes on. It also implies that since "hot" war is no longer regarded as an instrument of foreign policy in the traditional sense, the "cold" war can be conducted more boldly, though far more subtly. It also means that peaceful coexistence may endure for a long time if the capitalist "system" remains militarily, technologically, economically and politically strong. If we were to become weaker, the concept of peaceful coexistence would lose its meaning in proportion to the degree of our weakness and vulnerability.[34]

---

33 Afro-Asian Writers' Bureau, *The Struggle Between the Two Lines*, 6.
34 Central Intelligence Agency, Peaceful Coexistence, 4.

Under this climate, the 1958 conference of Tashkent approved the setting up of the Afro-Asian Writers' Bureau to be based in Colombo, Sri Lanka. In 1961, with the election of R.M. Senanayake as the Secretary-General of the AAWB, the pro-Chinese faction effectively took control, and launched *The Call*. It was a grand visionary endeavor that sought to counter what they saw as an imperialist attack using culture as a weapon:

> Imperialist cultural aggression, especially waged by the US, is launched particularly by means of flood-like mass media such as immoral, sex, and terror literature, decade films, and music. This kind of cultural expression is being used by the imperialists as a weapon to paralyse and disarm the ideology of the peoples' struggle to destroy the self-respect, patriotism, and moral solidarity of the Afro-Asian peoples. They use many ways to divide our people on the basis of religion, caste, tribe, etc. "Art for art's sake" is one of their pet slogans. It is an attempt to isolate the writer from his people and their struggle for political, social, and ideological emancipation in order to open the gate for the propagation of harmful, dangerous, and reactionary imperialist ideologies. The purpose of imperialists' ideological propaganda is to create confusion among all the progressive, anti-imperialist cultural movements. All types of methods, such as bribery, slander, and blackmail, are used to achieve this objective through organisations like "The Cultural Freedom Congress," "Moral Rearmament," "Peace Corps," and others.[35]

The Call envisioned a major international plan for the exchange of knowledge through book production.[36]

Given that the Soviet Union was placing great importance on the cultural arena to expand its global sphere of influence, as noted by Zaid Abdulfattah,[37] who became the editor of *Lotus* after the death of Faiz Ahmad Faiz, it could not let the Afro-Asian Writers Movement slip out of its hands. Writers who supported the Soviet Union's line, with Afro-Asian Writers' assemblies and meetings would continue to try to push different aspects of the peaceful coexistence line, especially to its opposition to all wars. This argument was passionately rejected

---

35   The Call. "A Review of the Past and a Call for the Future," 6.
36   I managed to locate most of the missing copies of *The Call* only at the end of 2021, well into the writing of this book.
37   Ziad Abdulfattah, interview by Tariq Mehmood, 2019.

by the pro-China AAWB, who rebutted that this was "making no distinction between the just wars and unjust wars."[38]

A CIA internal report with the sub-heading: "Sino Soviet Struggle for Writers' Allegiance: Who Smashes Whom?" noted:

> Nowhere is the struggle for the leadership of the Afro-Asian movement more pronounced than in the Writers' Movement. The Afro-Asian Writers' Bureau (AAWB) split last summer and set up two separate secretariats, one in Peking and (Soviet-controlled) in Cairo, each claiming to carry on the functions of the former Ceylon secretariat [...]. In recent weeks representatives of the Peking based Bureau have toured Asian and African countries trying to enlist support for a Peking-oriented writers conference which is to rival a Soviet sponsored writers' meeting to be held in Beirut...The Chinese have bitterly and repeatedly denounced the Soviet "Spiritist" activities... [and] strongly condemned the Soviet revisionist clique for having engineered the Cairo preparatory meeting for the "bogus" Third Conference of Afro-Asian Writers.[39]

The pro-Soviet writers' conference was declared "illegal" by the AAWB as it had bypassed internal protocols of the Afro-Asian Writers' Movement, which at that time was based in Colombo. The conference would indeed be convened in Beirut from 25 to 30 March 1967. Claiming the entirety of the Afro-Asian Writers Movement, Youssef el Seba'i, Nasser's culture minister and the first editor of *Lotus*, who was present at the Tashkent conference, remembered Japanese writer Yoshi Hotta:

> Our only means of getting in touch with Afro-Asian literature in the past was through American and imperialist books and publications which, of course distorted, perhaps perverted and falsified everything in the service of imperialism and imperial interests, but now we have a wide-open window overlooking the panorama of Afro-Asian literature. That window is *Lotus* magazine.[40]

---

38   Afro-Asian Writers' Bureau, The Struggle Between the Two Lines, 12.
39   Central Intelligence Agency, Sino-Soviet Struggle for Writers' Allegiance, 5.
40   Interview with Ziad Abdulfattah, Cairo 2019.

The writers who would assemble in Beirut were well aware that the American CIA was heavily engaged in promoting cultural activities through organisations like the Congress for Cultural Freedom. At the Beirut conference of 1967 these writers resolved to counter "the various forms of imperialist cultural activities such as aids granted to universities and educational institutes and other organisations and bodies responsible for issuing magazines, books, films recordings, and other communication media, as well as organs with guised imperialist activities such as the 'Congress for Cultural Freedom.'"[41]

The scale of the work undertaken by the Congress for Cultural Freedom was noted by Frances Stonor Saunders in the introduction of *Who Paid the Piper: The CIA and the Cultural Cold War:*

> At its peak, the Congress for Cultural Freedom had offices in thirty-five countries, employed dozens of personnel, published over twenty prestige magazines, held art exhibitions, owned a news and features service, organised high-profile international conferences, and rewarded musicians and artists with prized and public performances.[42]

It is important to remember that this was the era of the Cold War where the West, led by the United States and the Soviet Union, fought for influence over countries that had newly gained independence and those that were in the throes of the struggle for independence under the threat of a nuclear Armageddon which hung over the world. Apart from battles on the ground in some areas around the world, such as Southern Africa, this Cold War was also fiercely fought in the realm of culture, and particularly among writers through US-backed organisations. In order to fight back against those programs, the pro-Soviet conference set about the task of creating a publishing house, awards (Lotus Award), a magazine, and acquainting writers from different countries with each other.

---

41 Afro Asian Writings, V1. N1, P142.
42 Saunders, *Who Paid the Piper,* 1.

In this great battlefield of culture, it would be an oversimplification to look at the whole movement for progressive literature through either the mechanisms of US-funded bodies or through the prism of Sino-Soviet lenses, for the interests of the newly independent countries and their political leaderships. As Ziad Abdulfattah, the third editor of *Lotus,* commented, "This was the time when Nasser (President of Egypt) was dreaming of a united Africa and *Lotus* provided him with the sort of projection he needed, and he in turn provided full support for *Lotus*, including money."

He continued, "The Soviet Union wanted to promote itself through culture as well, especially among the Non-Alignment movement, and this played a major role in the conception of the *Lotus* idea. Cairo was very important for the Soviets because it is the capital of a huge influential African country."[43]

The Two Wings of the Afro-Asian Writers Movement

Both wings of the Afro-Asian Writers Movement upheld their opposition to racism, colonialism, and imperialism, and both resolutely opposed the US war on Vietnam and supported the struggle of the Palestinian people and Southern Africa against apartheid. *The Call* was overtly the journal of a Marxist-Leninist organisation supporting armed resistance against colonialism and imperialism in Southeast Asia and Africa. It based its ideological positions, as stated earlier, on the teachings of Mao Tse-Tung, who clearly saw literature and art as a tool to complement armed struggle. *Lotus* was much more concerned with literature and art both as a means to an end and as a form in itself.

The ideological differences between the two wings lay in what the CIA had correctly identified: the pro-Chinese position was one of the liquidation of imperialism and the pro-Soviet position promoted "peaceful co-existence." These conflicts came to a head with the formal splitting of the organisation following the Soviet invasion

---

43   Abdul Fattah, interview.

of Czechoslovakia in 1968. *The Call* condemned the Soviet Union's actions declaring:

> The armed invasion and military occupation of Czechoslovakia by the Soviet Revisionist ruling clique with their flunkeys in Poland, GDR, Bulgaria, and Hungry on the 20th August, 1968, is a brazen act of brutal aggression committed in a fascist manner against the Czechoslovak people by these renegades following the footsteps of U.S. imperialism and its gangster logic. This is the outcome of the Soviet revisionist collaboration with U.S. imperialism in a vain attempt to divide the world into two spheres of domination and establish supremacy over the respective sphere, making other countries their puppets.[44]

Lotus, on the other hand, did not refer to either the invasion of Czechoslovakia or the existence of a journal before it, nor did it mention any split in the organisation. The AAWB published a pamphlet detailing the split in the movement in which it pointed to the fact that the differences between them went back to the Tashkent conference of 1958. Radshidov, who presided over the opening session, said, "The strength of the conference lies in its expression of the desire of Afro-Asian people for peace. . . road of peaceful co-operation . . . cultural relations and exchanges between East and the West."[45] The AAWB noted in this pamphlet that differences had been simmering since the very inception of the movement and quoted Mao Tse-tung's famous position, "[either] the East wind prevails over the West wind, or the West wind prevails over the East wind; there is no room to compromise in the struggle between the two lines."[46]

* * *

Both *The Call* and *Lotus* were produced in English, French, and Arabic. However, how much was produced trilingually is difficult to establish. Unlike *Lotus*, *The Call* did not publish the names of its editorial board nor did it publicise all the authors, which is hardly surprising since the writers hailed from countries where armed struggles against colonialism and imperialism were raging and the AAWB was supporting the resistance. Some of the writers' names which were

---

44 Afro-Asian Writer's Bureau, *The Struggle Between the Two Lines*.
45 Ibid., 6.
46 Mao Zedong, "Speech at a Meeting."

published in *The Call* included R. D. Senanayake (Sri Lanka), Chanid Sairpradit (Thailand), Tabaka (Madagascar), Hamid Mohammad Wafi and Ahmed M Kheir (Sudan), Jamaluddin Aali and Ahmad Faraz (Pakistan), H R Lwekamwa (Tanzania), Awar Hakim (Jordan), Tokumatsu Sakamoto (Japan), Rew Alley (New Zealand), Mazisi Kunene (South Africa), Wadya Kamal (Palestine) and Khaddour M'Hamsadji (Algeria).

"Is there a free pen that can remain silent?"[47]

Unlike *The Call*, *Lotus* was a much larger publication in terms of pages, and consequently published a vast collection of poetry, short stories, folklore, studies, and positional papers that explored issues relating to the development of arts and culture in the former colonised nations of Africa and Asia. It also addressed burning issues of the time, such as the Vietnam War, the struggle against colonialism in Africa and Asia, the struggle against the apartheid regimes of South Africa and Zimbabwe, and the struggle against Zionism. *Lotus*'s published writers included Mahmoud Darwish and Ghassan Kanafani (Palestine), Adonis (Syria), Soheil Idriss (Lebanon), Youssef el-Sebai, Abdel Aziz Sadek, and Edward el-Kharrat (Egypt), Faiz Ahmad Faiz (Pakistan), Mulk Raj Anand (India), Mouloud Mammeri (Algeria), Mohamed Soleinian (Sudan), Ousmane Sembène (Senegal), Alex La Guma (South Africa), Mário de Andrade (Portuguese Colonies), Hiroshi Noma (Japan), Sonomyn Udval (Mongolia), Anatoli Sofronov (USSR) and many more. Notably, at least three writers featured in *The Call* and *Lotus* (Ahmed Sékou Touré, Léopold Sédar Senghor, and António Agostinho Neto) were instrumental in anti-colonial movements in Africa and served as the first presidents of their independent countries. *Lotus* published several literary giants; it would be impossible to discuss them all in detail here. In the first editorial of *Afro-Asian Writings* (predecessor of *Lotus*), Youssef el-Seba'i, its editor, wrote stingingly:

> Today there are clear indications that the imperialist system with its allies and agents is desperately clinging to whatever strongholds still remain and is vainly attempting to recuperate whatever it has already lost. These attempts have taken the form of either flagrant

---

47   Afro-Asian Writings, "General Declaration," Vol 1, Issue 187 ,(1968) 1.

neo-colonialist infiltration, through sowing division...reinforcement of their footholds in the few territories still under the yoke of direct colonisation...insurance of the continuity of the inhuman and repulsive system of racial discrimination.[48]

It was also under the editorship of Youssef el-Seba'i that the journal would print a statement from the 8th Arab Writers Conference, Damascus, 11-15 December 1971, "the Arab writers realise that the battle of destiny lies in resisting the forces of imperialism, Zionism, colonialism and racism; for establishing the basis of freedom, progress, socialist reconstruction, peace and social justice and for the spiritual and cultural prosperity of man."[49] Contradictorily, el-Seba'i would go on to idolise Anwar Sadat and the Camp David agreement which recognised Israel, which resulted in his assassination in Cyprus in 1978.

Rise and Fall of the Writers' Movement

Following el-Seba'i's death, Faiz would eventually be appointed the editor. Faiz was close to the leadership of the Palestine Liberation Organisation (PLO), which had begun to provide financial and logistical support to the journal. However, after the Israeli invasion of Lebanon in 1982, the PLO was expelled from Beirut and Faiz Ahmad Faiz was lucky enough to escape with his life. *Lotus* had to be re-established in Tunis, where Ziad Abdulfattah became the deputy editor under Faiz following the death of Mu'in Bseiso in 1984.

Ziad Abdulfattah recalls his first meeting with Faiz who asserted, "One red line that *Lotus* cannot afford is literature becoming dedicated to the service of colonialism, occupation, racial discrimination, and any other ethnic or religious discrimination. Otherwise, our journal will remain open to all creativity, no matter what its identity. We may differ within the body in evaluating creativity from here or there, but at the red line we do not disagree."[50]

---

48 Editorial, Vol 1 Number One, Afro Asian Writings, 1967.
49 From the 8th Arab Writers Conference," 205.
50 Abdulfattah, interview.

According to Ziad, *Lotus* would come to an end following the 1989 conference in Tunisia of the Afro-Asian Peoples Solidarity Organisation and the Afro-Asian Writers' Association, "This took place against a backdrop of a struggle between Egypt and Syria over influence. Egypt wanted to restore the Arab League to Cairo. The Syrians who were close to the Soviet Union also had the same ambition. However, Gorbachev's Soviet Union was not interested in supporting *Lotus* anymore, and obviously neither was Mubarak's Egypt."[51]

Over the years, there have been a number of attempts at reviving *Lotus*, the latest in 2016, when it was published with the title "Afrisan." Like its predecessors, it produced in English, Arabic, and French, albeit by the African-Asian Writers' Union. A year later it was published by the Writers of Africa and Latin America. Although still publishing literature from across Asia, Africa, and Latin America, the journal does not possess the former zeal born out of an anti-imperialist struggle. I am still searching for how *The Call* came to an end.

Language and Translation

The poets of the Afro-Asian Writers Movement, irrespective of wing, were living, loving human beings who were both trapped in the social and political trauma of the times and in the conflicts and contradictions of their own existence. The work, especially by *Lotus* writers, covered everything from the philosophy of poetry, questioning existence itself, resistance, religion, love, anger, self-denial, and self-searching. Much of it was translated from an array of indigenous languages, and at times poems can read as if they were translated from other translations. It is important to remember that this was the first time writers from the furthest corners of Africa and Asia shared their poetry, not only across continental barriers but linguistic and imperialist barriers as well.

---

51 Ibid.

Notwithstanding the fact that this first edition of *Lines Of Fire* is being published in English, I have not privileged the poems that were originally written in that language, but I have included a cross-section of the poetry to give a taste of the excitement of freedom from centuries of colonial censorship.

That *Lotus* was heavily funded by the Soviet Union was not a secret at the time among the writers it published or in the general body of the Writers' Movement. Criticism echoed in the words of the poet Adonis, who was published in the very first edition of *Afro-Asian Writing*, "The bringing together of African and Asian writings was a great idea, and the notion of unifying all these works in *Lotus* magazine, along with the Afro-Asian Writers' Association itself, was a wonderful endeavour. However, when it came to execution, I believe that it became overly political in the sense that it gave literary importance to writers who did not deserve these merits simply because of their political standing. Mostly everyone who worked with *Lotus* recognised this, but we never brought it up. The blending of politics and literature sometimes gave literary distinction to a few writers and poems that didn't necessarily deserve it."[52]

Poetry of Resistance and Categorization of the Poems

The poetry from *Lotus* published in this anthology dates from 1967 to 1973. I decided to focus on the early years for manageability, given that the journal published hundreds of poems over the decades of its existence. The *Lotus* and *The Call* poems have been divided into the following categories: Exile, Independence and National Liberation, Place and Land, Hope and Endurance, and Solidarity.

---

52   Interview to my student, Mohamad Fakhredine, 2019.

1. Exile

Many of the poets and writers in this collection were exiled at one time or another, including the editors of *Lotus*, such as Faiz Ahmad Faiz, Mahmoud Darwish, Muʿin Besesio, Dennis Brutus, Keorapetse Kgositsile, Mazisi Kunen, as were many others from across Africa and Asia. Abdel Wahab El-Bayyati tells us that this place of exile could be in:

> Cities in whose eves the people sleep
> unburied
> Like birds upon a wall of light.[53]

In Muʿin Bseiso's "The Island of Ancient Mottoes,"[54] the island is a place where there "are the nests of exiled birds." A tragic stanza in the poem reads, "O Seas of sand, O bread of homeless storms."

J.J Rabearivelo personifies exile:

> Exile — and you, its ineluctable shadow, forgetfulness,
> You will cover me under your obscure remains,
> Like Autumn with his proud forehead defeated.

And here is Mahmoud Darwish's exile, in "A Lover from Palestine":

> One stormy night:
> I opened my door and windows
> And watched a petrified moon
> No matter how much the pain of exile and suffering,
> there was always
> the hope of a better future.[55]

---

53 Haddad, "Listen and I am Calling You," 34.
54 Bessisso, "The Island of Ancient Mottoes," 37.
55 Darwish, "A Lover from Palestine," 81.

Tawfik Ziad says in "Bury your Dead and Rise":

> Bury then your dead and rise
> If tomorrow flies away, we will not let it flee
> We are not gone and lost ... But
> Once more ...
> We have been molded
> Anew...[56]

The pain of exile is at once a place of death and sorrow; it is a place where the injured want to speak out, but for the writers of resistance, it is never one of defeat. In the words of Khaled Aly Mustapha, from the poem "The Voice of the Wounded":

> O wind make of my ribs a quill
> Ink of my blood, a page of my brow, and write:
> In my bones are still
> The wounded moans, a deep black well bitter to my taste.
> O wind make a black veil of my walls in which any years for a moment did fade
> I saw the sun die beneath my lids in pain
> And beneath them I saw it rise again.[57]

Precisely because the poems could all sit here, perhaps they can speak for themselves in this collection.

2. Independence and National Liberation

The second category, Independence and National Liberation, perhaps runs through the heart of ideas about a new world, as such the poems in this category could be in any other category. However, they are here because the objective of independence and national liberation struggles has always been to expel the coloniser from the land of the colonised. Nevertheless, the road to this future is not set in stone.

---

56   Ziyad, "Bury Your Dead and Rise," 178.
57   Mustapha, "The Voice of the Wounded," 149.

As Ho Chi Minh writes in "A Milestone":

> You are only a little milestone,
> Which stands at the edge of the highway.
> To people passing by
> You point the right direction.[58]

But the direction at once is raging and angry, where "you will find the earth a volcano," or as Mazisi Kunene puts it in "Poisoned Mind":

> Was I wrong to erect monuments of blood
> Was I wrong to avenge the pillage of Caesar.[59]

The road to independence and national liberation was not only marked by milestones of struggle but, as Agostinho Neto, in his "Fire and Rhythm," writes:

> Sounds of shackles on the roads
> songs of birds.[60]

The anger of the dispossessed was shared in poems from South Africa to Palestine, as in Fadwa Toukan's "The People's Liberty":

> With an angry spurt of words
> Beneath the bullets and in the flames.
> I shall ever seek my liberty.[61]

Fadwa's struggle for her liberty is tied to the liberation of the land from the usurpers, and there is no night long enough to stop this fight until the emancipation of the common people. Fadwa's anger runs in the words of Afro-Asian poets published in *The Call* and *Lotus* for whom independence meant resistance not only against colonisers and imperialists but also their comprador accomplices. These include those who would build their castles, whether on historical myth, as Zionists in Palestine, or in fields tilled by the toiling labor of peasants.

---

58 Minh, "A Milestone," 192.
59 Kunene, "Poisoned Mind," 89.
60 Neto, "Fire and Rhythm," 25.
61 Touqan, "The People's Liberty," 62.

As Antonio Jacinto writes in "Monangamba," "On that big estate there is no rain, it's the sweat of my brow that waters the crops."[62]

This poetry published by the Afro-Asian Writers Movement was clearly a poetry of resistance. In Ghassan Kanafani's "Resistance Literature in Occupied Palestine," published in 1968's *Afro-Asian Writings,* we read: "poetry of resistance sprang up from the land of commitment and commitment to the land, revealing through practice and confrontation, its depths and dimensions."[63]

Keorapetse Kgositsile's "My People No Longer Sing" delves into the depths, suggesting the suppression of the joys of the people. The poet says in the opening:

> Remember
> When my echo upsets
> The plastic windows of your mind
> ...
> To remind the living
> That the dead cannot remember.[64]

But simply because the dead cannot remember doesn't mean the poets who dream of changing the world are despondent, as the poem concludes with the words "to carry the banner of humanism across the face of the Earth, Our voice in unison with our poets proudly says 'Change is gonna come!"

This change is one which Marcelino dos Santos writes about in "The Earth Trembles":

> We're are, all of us, just like you
> exiled
> shackled
> rent up
> muzzled
> on the earth that belongs to us.[65]

---

62 Jacinto, "Monangamba," 172.
63 Kanafani, "Resistance Literature in Occupied Palestine," 65.
64 Kgositsile, "My People no Longer Sing," 177.
65 Dos Santos, "The Earth Trembles," 167.

3. Place and Land

Despite the pageantry in which colonialism draped itself, the central issue was not a mystery for the colonised: their lands had been occupied, and brutal military force was applied to control both human and natural resources. It was this occupation that triggered resistance, be it political or military, in the form of rising struggles at the time across nations including Vietnam, Africa, and Palestine. Whilst the forms of occupations differed between colonialism and settler colonialism—the latter in the case of Palestine —Zimbabwe or South Africa would see bitter armed conflicts. The resistance to the reclamation of land was also tied to the reclamation of culture from the occupiers. In this, the common theme was one of finding a place in the coming world that would be built following the defeat of the occupier.

In this second category, Place and Land are both real and metaphoric, where days can be measured in the suffering of people and where the poems themselves protested their categorization in this collection. South Africa's Mazisi Kunene writes in "The Night":

> Darkness descends from the path of the skies.
> The black tails of cows shake against the wind
> Beating the sea with the fence of dusk.[66]

As Mazisi Kunene's "fence of dusk" echoes in Hussein Marawan's Palestine, where

> "[the] light shall not die at the top of the lighthouse."[67]

The poems in this category cover the length and breadth of Africa and Asia. They are simultaneously about nature and the human appreciation of its richness, with anti-colonial sentiments.

---

66   Kunene, "The Night," 67.
67   Marwan, "Palestine," 80.

Some of the poems highlight the genuine humanity between the people of Africa and Asia, such as "The Dove":

> I climbed to the roof of the house
> To look upon my dove.
> I found my dove drinking
> From the canal of another.
> I cried from the depth of my passion:
> "O my dove!"
> She said "Your time is past — look for another!"[68]

Some poets of the Afro-Asian Writers Movement, such as Adonis, rejected their identification with a physical place, such as being described as a Syrian poet. Adonis rebuts this association by saying, "I don't belong to any nation or ethnicity. I belong to the Arabic language, and when I say the Arabic language, I don't mean or intend to involve an Arab nation or Arab ethnicity, as I don't give them any significance."[69] In his words which were published in the very first issue of *Afro-Asian Writings*:

> And in what language
> Shall I greet the Euphrates
> The cradle which lulled me to sleep
> And quenched my thirst with its kind waters?[70]

Similar to the first category, the main focus of the poetry in this section is not to pose philosophical questions on the art form but to bear witness to the struggle that aims to free all that has been occupied. Salah Abdel Sabour's "The Hanging of Zahran" talks about British executions following the incident in the Egyptian village of Denshawai, where a British soldier died of sunstroke and for which local villagers were hanged:

> That those misfortunes should have happened
> in so short a time,
> Since Zahran's kindly head drooped from the rope.[71]

---

68   Vyas, "The Dove," 137.
69   Interview with my student, Mohamad Fakhredine, 2016.
70   Adonis, "Chapter of an Old Image," 66.
71   Abdel Sabour, "The Hanging of Zahran," 44.

An example of an existential struggle that both *Lotus* and *The Call*'s poets placed at the forefront of their literary works was the theft and colonization of Palestine and the Palestinian people's Nakba. This poetic spirit resonates well in Fadel el-Azzawi's Songs for Jerusalem, "War and Revolution":

> Jerusalem is a book read in the house of dreams
> Jerusalem is the garden of my house in Baghdad.[72]

4. Hope and Endurance

The Afro-Asian Writers Movement strongly held the belief that resistance was the only solution to the ravages of imperialism. Hope and endurance were essential in this struggle. The determination to live for a better world is echoed in poem after poem in this collection. Those who are adamant about struggling against the forces of their own oppression, be it individual or collective, need hope to carry them through the journey, even if this hope lies in the distant future. To put it in the words of Tawfik Ziyad:

> We shall weigh like stone on your chests –
> Go hungry, go naked, defiant,
> Singing in our poems.[73]

Despite feelings of pessimism and hopelessness among writers, many of them were still engaged in armed struggles as defeat was not an option, regardless of the oppressor. Those engaged in this struggle believed they would endure and that victory was certain. Of course, these poems, perhaps like poetry itself, do not wish to be categorised according to my subjective feelings; they could just as easily spill over into many of the other categories. For example, Eustache Prudencio's "We Shall Be There" is not only full of hope and endurance but is clearly embedded in the historical injustice of colonization and slavery, whose vestiges will one day be conquered:

> They had
> the guns
> They had
> the alcohol
> And most of all
> the lies and hate.[74]

---

72 El-Azzawi, "Songs for Jerusalem, War and Revolution," 82.
73 Resistance Themes in Palestinian Literature, V1 Issue 2-3, 76.
74 Prudencio, "We Shall be There," 42.

Though the poem is a little romantic, it still brims with the desire to bring humanity together. This poem, just like Malek Haddad's "Listen and I am Calling You," is a testimony of the desire to speak to future generations, where even the dead will not be silenced. Malek Haddad writes:

> Listen to me, I speak
> With the mouth of the dead.[75]

Both Eustache Prudencio and Malek Haddad, like the rest of the poets in this collection, shared a belief that while they may live across oceans and are scattered across seas of languages, they can still be united as those who endured the brutalities of colonialism and were adamant to not only document history but speak out no matter the consequences or conditions. This is not to say that these poets did not suffer from the insecurities of life, as beautifully summed up by Frank Parkes's "Blind Steersmen":

> How can I, who cannot control
> My own waking and dreaming, ever hope to make my voice heard in the wrangling for mankind's soul?[76]

Poets like Buland al-Haidari not only broke the conventions of Arabic poetry but have left us with an enduring vision:

> Bring back to us
> O age of ours
> . . .
> Bring back to us
> Our ancient eyes.[77]

5. Solidarity

The core concept of the organisation of Afro-Asian writers was to create a literary mechanism whereby they couldexpress solidarity with each other, as clearly shown in the Tashkent conference of 1958. This solidarity would rise from collective common experiences of

---

75 Haddad, "Listen and I am Calling You," 34.
76 Parkes, "Blind Stersmen," 73.
77 Buland Al-Haidari, "The Age of Rubber Stamps," 108.

historical oppression and resistance, and help forge connections across their struggles. Ousmane Sembène shows this most clearly in his poem "Fingers":

> Across the rivers and languages
> . . .
> Let us join our fingers to take away
> All power of this finger
> Which keeps humanity in mourning.[78]

Solidarity was a cornerstone of the movement that sought cross-continental unity. Vincent Tsoungu-Ngono, like Ousmane Sembène, sought integration of the Afro-Asian continents. His poem "Afrasia sees":

> a spirit new   piercing at last   the sleep of centuries.[79]

For the Writers' Movement, solidarity was not simply about consolidating ancient continent links that had been disrupted by colonialism and imperialists but also in recalling the memories of leaders killed by these forces. *Lotus,* for example, included a set of poems that were published in memory of Patrice Émery Lumumba, the first prime minister of the now Democratic Republic of the Congo, who was assassinated with British involvement in 1961.

> But when the martyr's blood is shed
> It freezes into a drop of immortality shining ruby-red![80]

Lotus published a few verses from the Russian writer Alexander Pushkin (1799-1837), extolling poetic solidarity,

> Poets from ancient days are used
> wwwIn sweet alliance to unite;
> True votaries of a single muse,
> A single flame their souls ignite.[81]

---

78 Sembène, "Fingers," 101.
79 Tsoungu-Ngono, "Afrasia," 165.
80 Ludhianvi, "Martyr's Blood," 132.
81 Pushkin, "Preface," 60.

Poetry of *The Call*

The Call, like *Lotus*, publised short stories, poems, plays, and memoirs. However, similar to the articles, the poems were first and foremost ideologically driven, in either supporting Marxist-Leninism or else eulogising particular struggles. As the poem "Lead We Follow O Great Helmsman!" by Challezh Khaphezh Mourax-qui Mahida from Kenya shows:

> In the word the red sun of immortal thoughts
> Of Marxism-Leninism shines bright!
> O helmsman of the destiny of the world lead we follow.[82]

The content of *The Call* was fiercely internationalist and uncompromising with what it saw as its mortal enemy and all those who tried to appease it. Its internationalism ranged from showing solidarity with workers in the West, such as France, the Black people of America, and the peoples of the colonies and former colonies across the world.

> In Vietnam where ride rough-shod the US imperialists,
> The heroic people refuse their rule and shackle
> And united they wage a valiant struggle.
> And on the land where Lincoln
> Freed the slaves
> There millions of Negroes
> Are debased and enslaved
> Now the Black Power avows:
> Violence for violence.

Poem after poem called out for solidarity with those struggling against racism and imperialism, with a special focus on Vietnam. In this context, China's support was seen as central to the inevitable defeat of the US. Rewi Alley from New Zealand wrote, "Victory in Red River Bridge, at our rear lies China; at your rear a pack of jackals."[83]

The Call's poetry aimed at building an internationalist unity to pave the way for a socialist revolution and liberation. The journal carried

---

82 The Call, "Lead We Follow O Great Helmsman?" 7.
83 Alley, "Red River Bridge," 12.

reports of progress on various anti-colonial battles, but also carried reports from liberated areas of some countries such as Mozambique.

Jose Maria Sison wrote "From the Philippines to Vietnam" in solidarity with Vietnam:

> Curse the birds of prey
> That drop their iron eggs.[84]

Sison concludes this poem with an inference to Mao's East wind prevailing over the West wind,

> Let the eastern wind
> Strike at the western terror in flight.[85]

In the poet's mind, the victory lies in defeating American imperialism in Vietnam. Not only did *The Call* publish poetry in solidarity with Vietnam, but also poetry by Vietnamese poets, showing their determination to continue struggling against the US. Hanh Can in "A Hundred Mountain Ranges" writes:

> On the vermilion dirt tracks
> I've been battling the US foe three full years.[86]

"A Hundred Mountain Ranges" was one of three poems published over images of Vietnamese resistance marching through the mountains where poetry was being recited.

Poetry published in *The Call* was not only concerned with the major global issues of the time, such as apartheid in South Africa and Palestine, the Vietnam War, and the general contradictions between imperialism and China's vision of a socialist world order. It also raised everyday issues about the working masses. In "Letter to My Brother," Indonesia's Sutojo writes:

> Class-hatred is burning on,
> And blazes everywhere —
> In the huts of the peasants,
> And also in the prisons.[87]

---

84   Sison, "From the Philippines to Vietnam," 13.
85   Ibid.
86   Can, "A Hundred Mountain Ranges," 10.
87   Sutojo, "Letter to My Brother," 21.

This class struggle was seen as a global revolutionary fight, and poetry could be an "Oath of the Revolutionaries" under the byline, a popular Arab revolutionary song, which clearly referred to the central line of division of the Afro-Asian Writers Movement:

> Every bleeding wound the oath cries,
> The shouts of the oath pierce the skies.
> No "peaceful solution", no surrender, a million no's.[88]

Mexico's Roberto Crespo y Payno's "3,000 Million and One Thought" situates the class struggle as an integral part of national liberation that involves all of humanity:

> March forward thundering steps
> On the long, long road
> Coloured like fire
> By the sun.
> Take this road we must
> From the five continents
> To the horizon of aurora
> That illuminates the whole world.[89]

National Liberation was not seen as a gift the colonial masters could give to their colonised peoples; it had to be snatched by force of arms. This is made clear in the poem "Fire! Fire!" by Guinea-Bissau's Gracade, who wrote:

> Granted independence,
> We do not want it;
> Bestowed independence,
> Keep it for yourselves!
> Independence can't be begged,
> Nor purchased.
> To gain independence,
> We must take up arms.[90]

---

[88] The Call, "Oath of the Revolutionaries," 16.
[89] Crespo y Payno, "3,000 Million and One Thought," 16.
[90] Gracade, "Fire Fire!," 16.

Although the editorial focus of *The Call* was firmly on the anti-imperialist struggles raging at the time, particularly in Korea, Vietnam, Portuguese colonies, South Africa, and Palestine, what was happening in the heart of the imperial country was not ignored. The struggles taking place in the colonies were linked to those in the heart of the empire.

In the poem "In Memory of G. Jackson," M Tolliver wrote:

> Who will make America a people's democracy?
> that's genuine.
> Attica has fought well, so did Ashkalon.[91]

The poem is set below an illustration of Jackson, armed, fist clenched, surrounded by flames, and looking leftward. In an asteriated note, Tolliver explains, "George Jackson, a young American progressive, was imprisoned in 1960 and killed at the age of 29 by the American reactionaries in the summer of 1971." Another note was on Ashkalon, "Prison in occupied Palestine, where prisoners revolted after Attica and other U.S. prison uprisings."

Given the endless massacres in Gaza and the resilience of the Palestinian people in their steadfastness to fight for their land and dignity, I begin concluding this section with words about Palestine's S.A. Hussain. In His "Ode to Fighting Gaza," he points out that there is no peace under occupation:

> At every place where the enemy camp,
> Laid in store
> Are fear, death and destruction.[92]

---

91 Tolliver, "In Memory of Jackson," 19.
92 Hussein, "Ode to the Fighting Gaza," 5.

Figure 4: Scan from The Call. Issue 3. 1972, p. 19.

As I reach the end of this introduction, I ask myself, why do hundreds of millions of people across the world identify with the pain of Palestine when many have to endure pains and challenges of their own? Is it simply because many of us share a history marked by systems of oppression by our former imperial masters who are now engaged in genocide in Palestine? In Kashmir, for example, slogans such as "Free Kashmir" are followed by "Free Palestine." In Indian-occupied Kashmir the former slogan was deemed offensive and often erased. As a result, people only wrote "Free Palestine" and that slogan alone was understood as "Free Kashmir."

Afro-Asian Unity

The poems in this collection are awash with aching angry words, protesting at the long injustices inflicted on Africa, of the legacies of racism, of its slicing into different colonial parts, of the plunder of its human and natural resources, and of the dehumanization of peoples of the continent. Just as in Palestine, "bleeding voices become the anthem of the weary."[93] And this anthem is not going to be a song that is soft and gentle, recited in the halls of the mighty, but according to Femi Fatoba in his "Home 1968", it will be a place of:

> Tongues Blazing
> . . .
> Vultures pecking
> Mad elephants among vegetation.[94]

For many African poets in the collection, this maddening rage demanded an undoing of the past injustices, where Africa would be given the dignity it deserved. This was, for many, seen as in the ideology of Pan-Africanism, which demanded not just the end to colonial ravages but a unified Africa, a pan-African state. Both wings of the Afro-Asian Writers Movement unequivocally supported a unified stand against colonial and imperialist injustices, such as in Palestine and Vietnam.

Many a poem in this collection captured metaphors that spoke of Africa as a whole and not just of individual countries. Anoma Kanie of the Ivory Coast writes to Africa, in "All That You Gave Me":

> Makes me walk just so
> with a step unlike any other,
> My hip broken beneath the weight of time,
> My feet wide with all the walking.[95]

---

93 Fatoba, "Home 1968," 24.
94 Ibid., 24.
95 Kanie, "All That You Gave Me," 35.

Africa is at once fatherland and motherland, and for Mirzo Tursun-Zade, it is "Africa My Sister":

> Who does not know about Africa, continent black and remote,
> Off the main sea-ways, burning in fires that few cared to note?[96]

Poets such as Agostinho Neto, who was the leader of the Mozambique People's Liberation Army (MPLA), and who would go on to become the first leader of an independent Angola, sought to unite people within Africa as well as those of African descent living in the West. Black was at once a color of oppression, but it was also one of resistance and unity. Agostinho Neto, wrote in "The Voice of Blood":

> Blacks from all the world,
> I join my poor voice
> And simple beat
> to yours.[97]

Like Agostinho Neto, Marcelino Dos Santos too sees Africa beyond the divisive scars of the demarcation of borders defined by colonial states. In his "To a Child of My Native Land," the poet narrates the murder of fourteen-year-old Emmett Till, who was lynched in 1955 because a white woman was offended by his presence in the grocery store. The poem embraces Till as a child of Africa:

> It was there, far away,
> O child of my native land...
> It was there, far away
> on the American land
> built with the hand
> of black slaves
> from Africa.
> That Emmett Till
> . . .
> with his tortured face,
> and his blood
> cemented
> the blood-tinted lake of the race.[98]

---

96   Tursun-Zade, "Africa my Sister," 66.
97   Neto, "The Voice of Blood," 24.
98   Dos Santos, "To a Child of my Native Land," 170.

In Saido Tidany's "Martyrs" and Neto's "Fire and Rhythm" the fire and pain of the voice of Africa is marked in every line:

> Rhythm in the bleeding shackles of naked feet
> Rhythm in the pulled out nails.[99]

Tidany's "Martyrs" are transformed by Bernard Dadie who writes:

> I will twine for you a crown
> ...
> In letters of fire
> Of fire
> Your
> Name
> O, Africa!

When I began this introduction, I was certain that I wanted to end it with an imaginary vision of a crown made from soft beams of light in letters of fire. But for me, these burning words would today spell Gaza, as well as Africa. Whilst the words would still demand the crown of justice for Africa, if this crown had a voice, it would remind the world of the words of Nelson Mandela, who said, "We know too well that our freedom is incomplete without the freedom of the Palestinians,"[100] and it would scream out in the words of Refa'at Al 'areer:

> If I must die Let it bring hope Let it be a tale.

---

99 Neto, "Fire and Rhythm," 25.
100 bush, "Related Somehow to Africa," 73.

EXILE

Exile

J.J. Rabearivelo, Madagascar

Exile—and you, its ineluctable shadow, forgetfulness,
You will cover me under your obscure remains,
Like Autumn with his proud forehead defeated
By the arrows of a dark blue sky—
I'll cry of fear, so that they rescue me
As a bull caught in a hedge of thorns
In vain, I will be but drunk with my pains:
My ruin will be your answer—
Everything speaks of wreckage, everything speaks of death.

The red signal marks and covers the horizon . . .
Where are you taking me, you brutal hands of Destiny?
On what peaceful turf
Or on what bitter grass with venomous flower
Will you put me down one day, at the end of the voyage?
To what purpose will come my adventurous life
To the bottom of seas or to the shore?
It doesn't matter—embark me since I have to be embarked
Let's have a single glance at the fires of the morning
Of whom the glory might have come to encourage me
In the hardship of my destiny.

Tomorrow, it's thick darkness and mystery;
Tomorrow, on departure, it is the painful poem
That could speak of a soul attached to earth;
Tomorrow . . . It's life itself.

From *Lotus*

In Alien Land

Joke Moeljono, Indonesia

The heart is almost lost in anguish and despair;
If I could hold it in my hands,
I'd fasten it in bonds
Or squeeze it flat: a bloody catch.

What lasts the longest says the Book of Books?
But now I'd rather have the courage to endure
The plaguing of the blood
Until it danced itself to death.

One day I shall abandon Europe—
Her anxieties aren't mine;
But I shall never hate her,

For I've been liberated through her sorrows,
And found again lost homesickness
Out of her wounds.

Translated by James S. Holmes.

From *Lotus*

The Angel with Broken Wings

J. F. William, Somalia

I dreamt
that in the antique legend
of my native country there was an angel
Banished for ever
from the vibrant nothingness
with wings broken
by the fire of Evil

Since that faraway day
that moment
fixed
in heavenly infinity
the angel wanders about
in the Universe
of stars and concrete matter
taking sometimes
the form of man
and walking in his steps,
sometimes
the form of a fluid thought.
His path is recognized
by this fluid
which he leaves on the steps
of men . . .

His thought is life
unknown
to men
leaving traces
of good and evil
in his spirit
tell me

have you received
the grace of this
angel with broken wings
or do you embody him
in the moment of his thought . . .

It is still said
that this angel weeps
in the night of time.
His tears are
a harmonious song
for those who wander about
in the immense span
of heavenly thought.
Since time
Has become a moment
and the moment
the eternal thought
this song
guides their steps
in the eternal
labyrinth
of nothingness

It is still said
that this angel with broken wings
creates fluid thoughts
some beneficent
others malefic . . .
Tell me
from which thoughts
you hold your grace.

From *Lotus*

A Lover from Palestine

Mahmoud Darwish, Palestine

Your eyes are thorns that pierce the heart
They hurt and yet I worship them,
I shield them from the wind
And shelter them behind the night,
Behind the pains
I shelter them
Their wound kindle the light of lamps
Making my present their morrow, dearer to my heart
Than my soul,
Until I forget, when our eyes meet,
That once behind a door, we were two!

One stormy night
I opened my door and windows
And watched a petrified moon
And said to my night: Go seek
Beyond night and fence . . .
The promised words and light
You, my virgin friend . . .
So long as our songs am swords when drawn
And you're as faithful as the grain of corn . . .
So long as our songs
Nourish the earth when we plant them.
And you're like a palm-tree in my mind

That has never been broken by storm or man
Nor were her locks ever raped
By beasts of wilderness of forest
But it is I who am banished beyond fence and door.

Hold me beneath your eyes,
Take me wherever you are
Take me however you are,
Restore to me the tan of body and face . . .
And the light of heart and eyes . . .
Restore the salt of bread, and the melody
Restore the taste of soil, restore the country.

I have seen you at the cave's mouth,
Hanging upon a line the clothes of your orphans,
I have seen you in fireplaces, along the streets,
In sheds ... and in the sun's blood,
Seen you in laments of death and misery,
Seen you in the salt and sand of the sea,
And you were as pretty as Earth . . . as children,
As the jasmine.

. . . And I swear:
To weave a kerchief of my lashes,
And scribe on it poems for your eyes
And a name I shall water with a heart melted in songs ...
Until [it] stretches into shady trees;
I shall write a phrase more sweet than martyrs, than kisses:
"Palestinian she was, and still is!"

Glory to you . . .
Your echo—in my imagination—
Endowed jail and chain with wings;
I see you, a young mare, galloping,
If I rest against a pillow,
I feel you on cold nights
A sun
That chants in my blood.

I call you childhood
And there it stands before me,
I call you Spring
And soon roses and herbs bloom proudly,
I call you the Sky
And the rain laughs and the thunder bellows . . .
Glory to you!

From *Lotus*

Listen and I am calling you

Malek Haddad, Algeria

Over and above the songs of the shattered bush
Listen to me, I speak
With the mouth of the dead
Listen to me, I write
With my hand broken on its guitar.

I am your mirror
The assassin is handsome-looking
I have the exact ugliness
Of this truth which it hurts to say.

"Catch thief!" is the cry that rings out
Every time a poet is drowned
In the heart of his music and in the heart of words,
As for me, the words I write arc mathematics
So many Algerians have been murdered!

"Catch thief!" is the cry that rings out
Every time the dressed-up rhyme, in its finery,
Awaits the neat, too neat Alexandrine.
To know love, I know the telephone
And the bathtub.

"Catch thief!" is the cry that rings out
When, to write a poem,
One makes of History an affected gallantry
One courts the words and woos their favour
One looks at himself in the mirror.

The hut and the heart?
On the heights of Algeria
The Sesini Villa
Is the castle of my loves.

All my truths are one innumerable dream
I was told that tenderness lies on the side of childhood
But I
Have counted
the living
the dead
the survivors
We should need a thousand years to be able to forget.
My music has come
Avoiding
to disturb
those who sleep everywhere
On the Algerian soil.

LISTEN AND I AM CALLING YOU

Remember this
When I dragged on my corps in exile,
When my eyes looked at you without meeting your eyes
And if I open my newspaper before I read my mail
If I no more appreciate how tender the roses
If I take up again at a distance the refrain that they hear
If my heart is no more
Wherever yours is, humming a tune for me,

LISTEN AND I AM CALLING YOU
Remember this: TOGETHER WITH THEM, I AM DEAD.

From *Lotus*

The Visitor Who Did Not Come

Nazek Al-Maleika, Iraq

The evening passed and the moon's brow was on the wane,
We were about to say farewell to another evening
And witness how happiness was moving towards the abyss
You did not come and were lost with the other hopes,
You left your vacant seat
To hold our fading gathering in [anxious] expectation
Clamouring about a visitor who did not come.

I did not know that in your absence beyond the years
You leave your shadow behind in every word and every meaning
In every angle of my vision and every curve.
I did not know that even in your absence,
You overshadow those present.
That hundreds of visitors
Are lost in a moment of yearning
Which ebbs and flows, longing for a visitor who did not come.

Had you come and had we sat with the others
Had the talk gone round in circles, from friend to another
Wouldn't you have become like the others,
The evening would have passed while we with wondering eyes,
Questioned even the empty seats
About [those] absent behind the eves
And cry that we have, among them, a visitor who did not come?

For should you come one day—and still I would rather you came not,
The fragrance of the colourful emptiness in my memory would dry
The palm-tree wing would have been shorn and desolate would be my songs
I would hold in my hands the wreckage of my innocent hope
And realized that I love you as a dream.

Since you have come in flesh and bone
I shall dream of the impossible visitor who did not come.

From *Lotus*

Evening

U Win Pe, Burma

Where in the emerald evening the hills change color
From murky sea green to estuarine blue,
The thickets breathe scents of childhood, trees burst aflame
And buds are liquid spurts of soft fresh light.

The rutted road is old and ivy-wise with mysteries,
The patient boulder ponders on another day's close,
There is a sudden scamper of bats in the gables
And a shudder of wings in the mazy tamarind.

Across the stubble fields, bubbled through the palms,
The crow-pheasant's low call beats against the evening's throb;
I hear it in the tombs and sepulchers of my breast
Like moon-echoes through ancient temples at Pagan.

The lazy cattle come home beside the rising river,
On the tangled earth-banks the swelling pools gurgle,
[The] boatman stirs the swirling muddy water
While the [sun tide] ebbs and the [sea tide] flows.

On the lead pipe in the garden the drop has poised too long,
Too long has the equivocal haze lain on the hills.
Why are you like the haze and the droplet?
Our days leak through these emerald sieves too soon.

From *Lotus*

The Island of Ancient Mottoes

Muʻin Bseiso, Palestine

This is you, and your bells
Are the nests of exiled birds.
From what island, friend,
Have you come back, carrying
No crosses of "ancient mottoes"
To fences you have left the fences 'bites
And to thorns of the painful wounds
"The narrators" told me, and in the strings
Is the tragic stanza of this poem:
O Seas of sand,
O bread of homeless storms,
My poet had been in that island
In the field of "ancient mottoes"
He was cast among "flags" and broken bells
His heart a honeycomb.
To him there came a ship [. . .]
Oh, he did not set his flags on fire for it
Nor did he burn a "poem,"
And he cried, begging the "narrator" to repeat
The wounds of the tragic stanza of this poem:
The cargo burdened the ship
O friend, the "ancient mottoes" burdened it
Cast the "ancient mottoes" away to the fish, friend,
Cast them away, the fish do not read,
And the depths are dumb, and deep the secret [. . .]
The biting of earthquake, "and the awakening, friend,
And the breeze of new storms [. . .]
Remove them, remove the "ugly parrots"
From the road of the return poet
From this island.

From *Lotus*

Self and Sin

Mahmud Hassan Ismail, U.A.R.

I carried my yesterday, and my morrow
And made for the appointment.
Then I reached a shore of whispered prayers
Whose horizons were ablaze with light and worship.
"Fly, O Self, and ascend," I said. "There lies your origin."
But weeping, it tremblingly repeated:
"Thy sins fill my hand, O God postpone my judgement.
Repentance is not yet born within me."

Still, I pray God to grant my body another life
To house my new life, the life of the spirit,
Purified of all that troubles my sleep,
And grant me faith, now an exile, within my soul.
Living like light imprisoned in the silence of the temple
Tormented like the thoughts of the persecuted
Or a bird that loses its way in the rigours of autumn
Whose call is like a black dream of sorrow.

O God [. . .] grant me light! For darkness has surrounded me
I have murmured faithfully, in an eternal wasteland
For your light my heart feels the ecstasy of eternal love,
Ascending into a heaven whose door is never closed,
But my body is weighted with every mortal sin.

Still I knocked at the door [. . .]
The fire of sin was near to consuming me.
O God, accept my prayers, and forgive me!
I snatched at my soul [. . .] and [forever] have I lost my identity!
I prayed God to give my body another life!

From *Lotus*

The Voice of the Wounded

Khaled Aly Mustapha, Palestine

- 1 -

My wound astride the wind is bound with string
Pulling ribs to the mountain's wing
Stretched is the nightmare with its fettered voice
Throbbing with the pain of exodus
Its bandage is the dust.
In my palm I plant a flag O wound, made of waves of blood
My finger points to a well in whose eyes the light turns dark

Of my ribs do make a mast,
Of my shirt a flying banner.

To call upon the wind for rain which the mountains hold
That their thunder may arise in prayer.
My bow upon my breast is made of wounded moans
A song of sands
Where are the arrows to be feathered
They died on the mountain the flock of arrows
And my hands fell upon the earth wiping
It with blood and writing
A melody of hearts.

What if the earth opened to me the gates of time
In their depths my heart I'd see, treading the dark tomorrow
Unseeing without light
(Tear from your eyes the veil of illusion and carry in them flames of dust)
I bear the burden of the orbiting question in search of an answer.

O wind make of my ribs a quill
Ink of my blood, a page of my brow, and write:
In my bones are still
The wounded moans, a deep black well bitter to my taste.
O wind make a black veil of my walls in which my years for a moment did fade
I saw the sun die beneath my lids in pain
And beneath them I saw it rise again.

The wind, why hast the wind stretched its hand into a darkened well
From which the brook emerges not knowing where to turn
Come hither for mine is a loving heart, I'll twist its veins
Into a path for you to pass
Pass O winds of flame and set to flame all man's illusions.

- 2 -

I open my window to the wind and its caravan of spears
Like poles sailing across my ribs
Their masts red with blood across the desert of my pain
Like fingers bearing the gorged wound, the bleeding wound
Come, open my breast
Its roots are sands which dried my years and nailed my hands
To a thread wandering in vain, without pain.
Stretch your arms into a sacred well of burning coal
And wash away the tragedies, cleanse the depths of my heart.

I stand by my window
Leaving my masts across the sea seeking a hand to anchor them
    in the dawn
I am weary of the fields of waves in which my sails are planted.
I stand by my window
For the wind is my caravan
In it I have dipped my veins
So that each dream in its naked breast may come true
I stretch to it my hand each vein a fierce pain

Take my hand O wind and in it read each line of hidden fate
And all my secrets do reveal.
Take my breast O wind, let each of your spears embrace
    one of my ribs unveiled.

- 3 -

Make my hand heavy O wind with the spears of your caravan
Stretch the masts across my breast and I will make my breast
   a sea for them.
And of my wound I'll make a shimmering wave.
The open wound will sail, tomorrow on my breast, quenching
The thirsty olives on my way.
Sing of exile O wind, the open wound is yours
Sing of exile
The sea in my breast is turbulent
For in its arms your eyes have shed their tears of blood.
Heal my wound O wind
With nectar drops which are the longing of the dead for resurrection
A nectar drink in which the well of your tolling bell is melted
Ringing, not only in the eyes of God.

Translated by Nihad A. Salem.

From *Lotus*

We Have Come Home

Lenrie Peters, Gambia

We have come home
From the bloodless war
With sunken hearts
Our boots full of pride—
From the true massacre of the soul
When we have asked
What does it cost
To be loved and left alone?

We have come home,
Bringing the pledge
Which is written in rainbow colours
Across the sky—for burial
But it is not the time
To lay wreaths
For yesterday's crimes.
Night threatens,
Time dissolves,
And there is no acquaintance
With tomorrow.
The gurgling drums
Echo the star
The forest howls—
And between the trees
The dark sun appears.

We have come home
When the dawn falters
Singing songs of other lands;

The death [march]
Violating our ears
Knowing all our lore and tears
Determined by the spinning coin.

We have come home
To the green foothills
To drink from the cry
Of warm and mellow birdsong

To the hot beaches
Where boats go out to sea
Threshing the ocean's harvest
And the harassing, plunging
Gliding gulls shower kisses on the waves.

We have come home
Where through the lightning flash
And thundering rain
The [pestilence], the drought
The sodden spirit
Lingers on the sandy road
Supporting the tortured remnants
Of the flesh
That spirit which asks no favour
Of the world
But to have dignity.

From *Lotus*

Fateh on the Day of Karameh[1]

May El-Sayeg, Palestine

In Bethlehem the neighbours told
Of a new star
Which over Karameh glowed.
They spoke of Gabriel's Annunciation
To the banks of the Jordan,
Of a sign he had bestowed:
An olive branch
A gun
A lance

The name of Fateh.
The edge of the dawn
The night sets down
A new history.

The joyful heartbeats flutter
In the depths of the river.
Blessed are these shores
For they shall inherit the earth,
They shall remove the agony and the fears
From the source of tears
A thousand paths into the sky they will open
Paths as yet untrodden save by saints,
Hallowed are their steps upon the water
Spelling a pledge.

Rejoice O mother
For the sword of terror
Cannot reach heads
Beyond reach.

---

1 Town in which Fateh scored a victory over Israeli forces.

If Herodotus had but known
The truth
He would not have dared to do what he did.

From the blood of babies the dawn gives birth
To infants
Whose hearts are made of steel
Whose eyes are glass
Who, in their hands bear the dead yesteryear
With its hands seared.

Twenty years
And in my exile,
And in the dark,
I carried the cross of wood decayed.

Twenty years
Cursed years
Bitter laughter in the hollow vales
And on the roofs of a thousand tents.

In every vale a song
And laughter in the night
In the bright month of March
Fearing the breath of day
How can we promise Fateh[2]
When Fateh is born today.

---

2   Fateh also means victory in Arabic.

I have removed the thorn from my eyes
And from my heart
The face of humiliation now
Is turned to anger on my brow
To angry mountains at my door.

When the weary quails
Fly ashore in the month of August
I'll spread the earth beneath their beaks
With a rug of fertile green,
For in my exile

The shores of longing are now covered with leaves
Tomorrow they will blossom into fruit
And plenty will be our harvest.

Go free O mother
From the gates of pain
For the path home shall be vast

And the shore of dreams extensive,
For arms are building in the heat of day
And your promised son
From his executioner does not turn away.

For around his neck
Are garlands of tears and moans
And pain
And years of exile and despair
Of prison
Some have been left in the square
Trodden by injustice.

Over our graves, Barabbas
Drinks a toast to his chosen hour.
A toast to the slaughter of babes,
There by the church of the Child Jesus
A toast of my blood [. . .]
So, mother, if tomorrow
You see the fortune-teller

To him, do say:
"In my son's eyes, the flowers have blossomed
On his path, the flowers bloomed
The soul of Jerusalem guards him on his way
And guards his horizon grey."
Weep not,
mother heed not,
mother
His croaking voice: he lies
And if in his anger he doth say
Your son's cross is up today

Answer:
"Glory to the olive branch
To the gun
To the lance
And to Fateh".

Translated by Nihad A. Salem.

From *Lotus*

The Song of Songs

Sulafa El-Hegawy, Palestine

Lost is my love, Bisan,* upon whose eyelids cast its shadows
And Haifa* I in whose pomegranate cheeks spread its meadows
His hair like waves of the sea, full of Acre's* fragrance
And Jaffa* does at His lips the song and cup enhance.
Lost is my love, bearing the memories of
Our scythes
Our flowers
The olives of our orchards
The limes of Hakoura[1]
And the songs of the birds.

Ours is the solemn oath
O maids of Jerusalem, of Aghwar and Ramleh both
Ours is the solemn oath to bring Him back
A palm tree to our barren sands
For Him our arms we'll stretch
Up to the stars, a stairway.
And in the dark of night we'll wipe away
The darkness from His eyes.

On the path of His return we'll sow the seeds of our deed
And we'll water His eternal path
With the heart blood of our betrayers.
And from the stars of night we'll make
A home for Him
We'll light the oil jars
As flames for its terraces
And all the bodies of our imprisoned virgins will be His fence.
Flower baskets we shall fill to scatter at His feet
And the flowers will be our hearts.

Translated by Nihad A. Salem.

From *Lotus*

---

*Cities and towns of Palestine.

Self-Exile

Tsegaye Gabre Medbin, Ethiopia

- I -

Seeking asylum
In the bosom of an ailing world,
Ever remaining
Preys of our own shortcomings,
[Focused] by the narrow chapters
Of private ends,
Prostituting greater causes
For which the past heirs died to keep aflame,
Cashing principles
In favour of tin-gods
At the cost of blighted hopes,
Scared of total death
Unlike the hard old days
When many had faith,
Now, one prefers to move half-dead
In the shades of a doomed era.

- II -

They say:
Where the growth of weeds
Is cultivated
To undermine the plants
(Lest it may yield a surplus)
One must learn
To befriend not for friendliness
But to uproot
While the friend is unaware.

They say:
Where the choking smokes are let out
To eclipse heaven's sunshine
(Lest the earthlings are over-brightened)
One must learn
To love to walk the earth
Not to enjoy it
But to exist in spite.

They say:
Where the breed of rats
Are raised
To nibble at healthy bodies
(So as to keep them [dependently] docile)
One must learn
To develop hard skin covers
Not to be secured
But to protect oneself from life.

They say:
Where the shadow of fear
Is spread
To over-cloud spring flowers
(Lest they escape weather disillusionment)
One must learn to look contented
With the naked layers
Of these white shining teeth
Without the heart's consent.

- III -

Then, alas, it is fear
With its shame-sprinkling nozzle,
It is like you are suddenly [unborn]
Undelivered
   Unconceived.
It ravages the brain
Gnaws the spirit
Saps the hope.

It leaps up
From the dark corners of ill-fate
Dimming your light of day
Lurking in your innermost
Clinching your raison d'être,
It catches to consume
Like a strange disease in the wilderness

It runs deep
Like the cult of inherited sin.
There is no shame like despair
No sin like fear
No death like self-exile.

From *Lotus*

At the Peak of a Passion

Tchicaya U'Tam'si, Congo

- 1 -

I hand a deck of cards into the hands of the passer-by
More fertile in dialogues than the silent fate
Of my perishable heart
Which resists no more the road to Damascus, embraced
By the naked belly of a hill of shades
At the peak of my passion to undress
O my improbable genealogy
From which tree to descend? What flowers toll the death-bell
A bell like an [orphan's] tear in the night!
A tree at the top of a hill
Raises a branch of blood like a candle;
The branch, in its first, bears a green leaf
Image of a flame, soft and in silhouette
Hooted by jinnis!

- 2 -

Amidst this pus of well-made things
To see my better world,
I carve orange-blossoms upon my retinas
May they turn not into flames
May they be white to cool
The dead belonging to my slow conscience
Reeking of this slowness, I win by sleight of hand
May a better cheat than I
Follow me to this paradise where men
With naked daggers
Live in their own gangrene
Will he, then,
Revive the fire which they put out, by robbing
The heart
Whose barely uncovered mystery
Uncovers me, flays me, crucifies me
At the peak of my passion.

- 3 -

Your eyes predict a pain
Like three heaps of debris, like three hills of ashes!
But do tell, whose ashes are they?
The sea, already then, heeded the slave ships alone,
And the negroes were taken in
Despite the magic of their smiles
The bell would then toll
With a kick in the belly
Of the pregnant passersby:
A curfew reigns
To spice their agony.

- 4 -

The jungle fires mostly give bad dreams
As for me
What crime will I commit?
If I were to rape the moon
Would I bring them back to life?
What pain do your eyes predict?
If they were to return as seeds
Of the bread- tree for a black life
Amid black clouds
Will I be then set free?

- 5 -

This knot on my nightmare,
Could it be the blue river,
The key to the fields, opening
A certain door to all, to the wind of fire?
I came,
Of a certain wood they carved a certain door
And I knew no more the essence of my soul
To open this very door
As would have done the ancestors of my shades.

- 6 -

Take then my conger-eels, my sea urchins
Caught in Landana,
Take this soft-fleshed Guembo here
And I,
I've come to the end of my tether made of turbulent seas.
Among you, I could be the sole of a foot
If the well in my Katanga villages
Could shorten by capturing it
The royal path of the Milky Way
The Congo, the Congo
For sure, for sure, for sure,
Strap then not your feet
For I live off the sight of colours
That certain paths take on
On certain evenings of the dance
Tied by the storm of my ardent fire.

- 7 -

This eve
What crime will I commit,
If I were to rape the moon
In the water-well which I have been offered,
They will say it is a poet's madness
With three horns and a hundred thousand bells
Play me a [lullaby]
On certain eves there still persists in me
The russet of certain household fires
When return the moths,
And for the djinns who clamour,
Sleep with a thousand layers of mire
Where night sucks the earth and the Congo clay
Come take my head
In return for the remnants of night upon my soul.

- 8 -

These lines in my palm are forerunner signs
Place a knife before my sleep
Upon which the course of ancient destiny may break its thread
I want to be free of my destiny
I give back its dew to the grass
May the lines of my palm
Open all paths to me.

Translated by Nihad A. Salem.

From *Lotus*

Bury your Dead and Rise

Tawfik Ziyad, Palestine

. . . Bury your dead and rise
. . .
For we had to drink all . . .
Down to the glass itself,
This our red and bitter drink

And we had to be slaughtered
. . . To be slaughtered like an ewe
When history went mad

And we also had to flee
. . . like a flock of geese, to flee
And feel shame down to our marrow

Never mind! Our flesh is now a bridge . . .
. . . On the high and angry sea
To shores that betrayed us not and which never we betrayed

O you earth of shining gold
Of red rubies and ivory
Our love is stronger than love, and richer too

Bury then your dead and rise
If tomorrow flies away, we will not let it flee

We are not gone and lost . . . But
Once more . . .
We have been moulded
Anew. . .

Translated by Nihad A. Salem.

From *Lotus*

The Descent of Orpheus to the Underground

Abdel Wahab El Bayyati, Iraq

The prayers of the wind in Assyria and the knight in armour clad
Undefeated in war he dies
And is scattered dust and ashes in the night

'Neath the wall of night, and the bull
of myth who flies
Striking with his horn the sun hung
by the priest in the ceiling of life

While the singers stand and see
Bowing low to the fire in the distance
by the shepherds lit
Cities born in exile and other 'neath
the ocean's depth and 'neath their
night do sink
Cities in whose eves the people sleep
unburied
Like birds upon a wall of light

—And I upon my brow bear them all
from age to age
Clad in their rags, playing 'pon the
lyre of life.
All your wounds did bleed to death
In the dawn of mankind and in the age
of ice
Why then stand you alone within the cave?

Tracing the mythical light upon the
walls with fire
Clad in the rags of exile
Crying o'er a lock of the sun's fair
locks, crying for what cannot be
Dreaming across the nights of leaving
Dreaming of shores of times when
man is born anew
—Why art thou in exile with death and
the leaves of fall?

You were their rags and are reborn in
every age
Seeking the needle in the hay, feverish,
exiled
Of thorn your crown, your feet in ice
encased
You cry in vain for long is the night
Its hours tread in flames the cities of
the night
Each time Astarte from her grave does
call to you and tend her hand

The ice does thaw
And in one instant all the ages go
And down falls night and crumble do the walls
And the corpse in its shroud cries as
the new-born babe
When the priest with bread and holy
water him does bless

—Oh how lonely my nights on Assyria's walls
with death and the leaves of fall
As I rise from the netherworld
towards light and the distant dawn
Dead, yet in armour again reborn

—O bull of myth who o'er vast cities
smoke
Do fly
O martyr light
In vain your cries for in things and
stones and flesh the world now dies
Maidens and spider-webs and butterflies
And ages of culture - everything dies

—In vain you hold the thread of light
in every age
Seeking the needle in the hay, feverish, exiled.

From *Lotus*

Diaspora

Akbar S. Ahmad, Pakistan

of the noon-pierced dust
settling in
to choke the vision with
mirages of things to be.
All fragmented
omnivorous
dreams hunger
starve and settle about me
like the daughter of kneme.

Bulbous domes in mist
shrouded confuse me as I
hear refuge in the gliding
itinerancy of the muezzins
echolalia. Through the
noon-heat edacity
of the seraglio lifts
the veil and I see the
squalor of pavement domesticity
the diaspora sticks in
a gullet of despair into
the heart of my alien stomach.

A sloe bat draws its fangs
and a thoughtful spider
spins its plampede web
across the Eastern horizon.
Lal Killa and
Hyderabad, Deccan
crumble into
those mosaic
tiles of my floral
incubus. The
awakening in the
actuality of parched Sindh.

Karachi: the harlot
of ethnic hungers
sucks me in; the
strange, lacerated hospitality of
a new skin excruciatingly growing
excruciatingly pealing
haunting lacuna
the worn pain of a
suspended past.

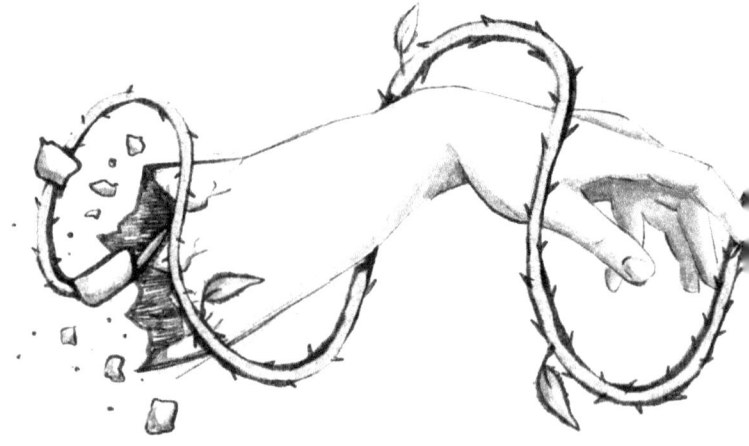

From *Lotus*

Love Exile Land

Cosmo Pieterse, South Africa

I shall not be sad
Though away from you
Who have harboured the love
Moving me—stage for my passion, my sleepless bed.

It is particularly and first of all you I
nestle in
Though till the wings of my dream
Seem to have strength to carry me over all oceans, and, safe,
Love, arriving with you, at last, to settle down.

In that thought is a moment: we shall come together,
Driven in the going of an instant
time as the social world gathers feathers
And contracts to its free common, that
we may flower and fly further
And become one, and grow on forever.

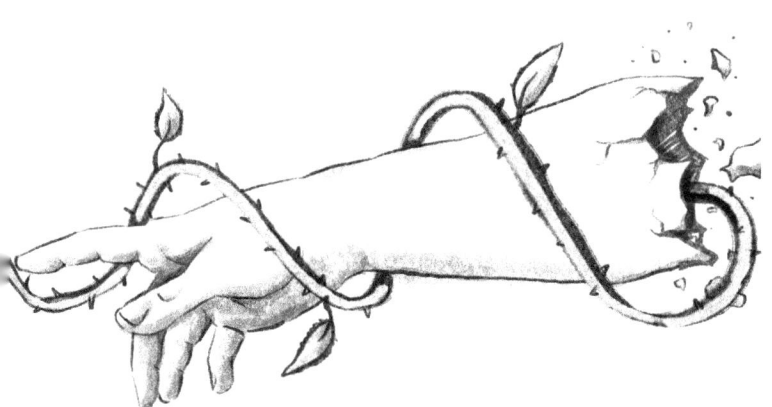

From *Lotus*

Old Form: New Life

Cosmo Pieterse, South Africa

Sahara; Gobi:
Snow-eagles nest in fire:
Hungry love tongues fruit.

From *Lotus*

Laila in Acca My Homeland

Abdel Rahman El Sharkawi, Egypt

Laila: All laurels set upon our brows were crowns of thorn
Were we then born to live in misery, pursued, exiled?
Strangers in the land of stars?
Guests at the feast of avarice?
We dreamed of coming back one day, of living like all others
No more than live just as other live . . .
I never dreamed of luxury . . .

Unlike the others, I had no right to dream of joy and luxury
I dreamed instead of living on my land in dignity
Of seeing father rest in his old age
did not want to exile those who banished me . . .
I did not hope to die, like Samson, in the temple's ruins!
I hoped to live my simple life with pride

No more than just to see my trials end
No more than just to live as [others] do!
No more than just to own the dust we tread!

I never used to dream of clouds
I dreamed of nothing save to have a homeland!
My homeland is the place of tears where all kinds of tears have flown!
Its builders lie beneath the ruined wall stretching their hands to all
My homeland gave civilization its most treasured gifts
My homeland gave to man the light of truth
My homeland whence the light of faiths did come
Has now become a beggar while you wait!
While others boast of counties only waved

Nothing will free our land save our young arms
Hope not for any force to set us free
However friendly it may be
Be then the first to strike the blow and you will get help that is not begged for
The cause is ours
It is our shame or else our pride
Shall I stand here and cry while [others] give?
Shame be upon us if martyrdom we should beg!

Laila: They are in all the grains of sand
They are in the glitter of stars
They are in all the strength of storms,
In strokes of lightning ... they fill all space
Search then in space!
And if you find them not, search then in rocks
They are in all the veins of rocks

They live in [every] heart, search then each heart
They are above the clouds
They are above the graves
They raised the dead from 'neath the graves
You'll see them in green pastures or within the heart of mills
You'll see them in victorious laughter or wherever tears do flow
You'll see them in the dew-drop glow
In echoes ...
In the storm ...
In sweeping floods ...

They are in every man who now lives free to think and feel
Search then in every mind that thinks ... in every conscience now alive ...
They are in every loving mother's love
They are in night's deep darkness

In heaven's tears, unshed since they are hardened in the light of stars!
They are in every sigh heaved by a broken heart
They are in dawning light
They are in all the sparks of sharpened scythes
They are the force of tide in the great march . . .

Ask for them Christ's crown of thorns
If you cannot go then to martyred John
And delve into Mohammed's heritage!
Search for them in David's wisdom and truth
If not then ask wise Moses.
Do you now see tomorrow coming forth? They are tomorrow's footsteps.

They are all that words can say
They are in every shot
They are the pulse of hope in the inner depth of hearts
They are in the dew of every dawn of hope, in every fragrance
They are in every axe that tills the soil to bring forth life and add
They are in every typhoon that brings fear
They are in every honest man . . . among our people or your own!

Jacob: I see . . . what be your name young girl? Come answer me!

Laila: I am the echo of all tears
I am the sun just risen from the heart of dark
You do not know my name, my name is Arab girl
Red freedom in my name . . . My name? My name is Hope
Bright future in my name, my name's a curse to fall upon your head in flames.

Translated by Nihad A. Salem.

From *Lotus*

INDEPENDENCE AND NATIONAL LIBERATION

Fire and Rhythm

Agostinho Neto, Angola

Sounds of shackles on the roads
songs of birds
under the humid green of the forests
freshness in the sweetened symphony
of the coconut trees
fire
   fire in the grass
      fire on the warm metal sheets of Cayatte

Wide pathways
full of people, full of people
full of people
in exodus from everywhere
wide pathways to the closed horizons
but pathways
pathways opened
over the Impossibility of the arms
   Fogueiras
      dance
         tomtom
            rhythm
Rhythm in the light
rhythm in the colour
rhythm in the sound
rhythm in the movement
rhythm in the bleeding shackles of naked feet
rhythm in the pulled out nails
But rhythm
      rhythm

Oh dolorous voices of Africa

From *Lotus*

The Martyr of a Song

Mahmoud Darwish, Palestine

They raised the cross upon the wall
And from my wrists removed the chains,
Fan is the whip; and the beat of the boot
Is a tune that whistles:
"My Lord!"
And bids the dead: "Beware!"

"You there!"
Howled the barking of a beast,
"I give you back your alley
If twice you kneel before my throne!
If twice you bashfully kiss my hand
Or else . . .
You mount the cross."
The martyr of a song . . . and a sun.

I am not the first to wear a crown of thorns
So I'll not bid the dark beloved: Cry!
You, whom I love as I love my faith,
And to whose name in my mouth, dipped in dusty thirst,
The taste of old wine kept in jars.

I am not the first to wear a crown of thorns
So I'll never say: Cry!

For my [cross] may be a courser's back,
And the thorns on my brow adorned
With blood and dew,
Maybe a crown of laurel!
And may I be the last to cry:
"I've longed for death!"

From *Lotus*

Poisoned Mind

Mazisi Kunene, South Africa

Was I wrong when I thought
All shall be avenged?
Was I wrong when I thought
The rope of iron holding the neck of young bulls
Shall be avenged?

Was I wrong to think that the orphans of sulphur
Shall rise from the ocean?
Was I depraved to think there needn't be love,
There needn't be forgiveness, there needn't be progress,
There needn't be goodness on earth,
There needn't be towns of skeletons,
Sending messages of elephants to the moon?

Was I wrong to laugh asphyxiated ecstasy
When the sea rose like quicklime,
When the ashes on ashes were blown to the winds,
When the infant sword was left alone on the hilltops?

Was I wrong to erect monuments of blood
Was I wrong to avenge the pillage of Caesar
Was I wrong? Was I wrong?
Was I wrong to ignite the earth
To dance above the stars
Watching Europe burn and its civilization of fire,
Watching America disintegrate with its gods of steel,
Watching all persecutors of mankind turn into dust.

Was I wrong? Was I wrong?

From *Lotus*

Song of a Revolutionary Without Identity
Rady Saddouk, Jordan

Cursed be fog, mirages and boredom,
The snow in the blood,
The clouds in the sky.
Grudging are the clouds.
No thunder, no rain.
While we wander in the lanes, killing time.
Losing our way.
No glimmer in the eyes, no colours.
The wind has blown out our candles, while we raise
Them, lighting them with our blood to give light.
[In spite] of the accumulated night, [in spite] of the wind
    and the smoke
We continue to light the road,
To pave it towards a colourful morrow.

We are on the way,
Our tents are [somber], with gaping eyes and bellies
Deep in their veins, misery and disease.
Their shades have a pale [luster],
Its frost is panting in our veins
Like the pipe of a low degenerate,
Spat out by London, Paris or Chicago into our roads
Licking up our blood,
Living on our flesh.
And we are hungry, grinding the rocks,
    kneading the sands, doing the impossible.

We move, adamant in spite of death, in the procession of life,
Caravans of flames in corpses of bones and veins
We are on the road, moving,
Eyeless caravans;
But we shall make the sun rise;
With eyes whose [luster] is dimmed,

We shall awaken life from the depths of nothingness,
We shake the graves, dig up the unknown, light the darkness, kill fate.
We, the hungry, there is food for life in our bones,
We who wake the spring and the stars.
For us, the hungry, the rains shall fall.
We are the gardens and the vineyards,
While others eat the fruits
And in existence, we are its soul, the flame of conscience,

We hunger, today, in spite of ourselves,
We die in life, unwillingly,
We, the foreheads, lower our eyes
And tomorrow, it is we who will make destiny.
Spark of life, run, shine on the roads,
Cursed be fog, mirages and boredom.
Our eyes are restored, and the blossom is blooming,
The seasons of abundance in our veins are laden with branches
And fate trembles in our mighty arms,
And our spears are brandished proudly,
Over the clouds of humiliation, over the haters.

We shall reap fangs and accursed claws,
We shall reap slim scythes in our fields,
We shall sweep up the dirt off our streets.

The meek shall kindle the flame of light
And dig, in the dimness of darkness, our road to morning.
Pour down, pour down,
You flame of resistance and struggle.
However long our roads may be
Planted with night, mines and arms,
However lean our bodies may be,

It is we who shall triumph
We shall plant the moon and olive trees in our humiliated gardens.
We shall wipe away the tears,
We shall awaken the dreams, love, and the spring.
Hunger shall triumph
The young and the women will be
fed and the suckling will have, enough.
And the gluttons will be in the depths of hell!

Translated by Mursi Saad Eddin.

From *Lotus*

The Song and the Sultan

Mahmoud Darwish, Palestine

It was no more than a description of the birth of rain
And the [sheets] of lightning that light up the mysteries of the trees,

    So why did they oppose it?
When it said that something other than this water
Flows in the river
That the pebbles of the valley statues and other things?
    Why did they torture it?
When it said that there are mysteries in the forest,
And a knife at the moon's throat,
And the nightingale's blood forsaken on that stone?
    Why did they oppose it?
    Why did they torture it?
When it said that my country is a rope of sweat
And in the square a man dying
    A darkness that burns?

The Sultan was angry—and the Sultan is an imaginary being,
And said: the defect is in the mirror,
So let your singer stop his singing, and my throne
Will extend from the Nile to the Euphrates!
Then he screamed: Throw this poem into jail!
The cell of detention is better, for the sake of security and quiet,
Much better than an anthem or a newspaper.

Tell the Sultan that the wind
Is not wounded by a sword blow
And that a million trees
Turn green leaves on the palm of a single letter
And all the clouds of summer would not
Shed enough rain to water the summer grass on its edges!

The Sultan was angered, and the Sultan in every photograph
And on the back of every [postcard]
Is as pure as the psalms—on his forehead the brand of slaves—
Then he called out commanding:
Execute this poem!
But the execution yard is the place
Where the obstinate songs refuse to die!

Tell the Sultan that the lightning cannot be imprisoned in a stalk of maize.
Songs have the logic of the sun and the history of streams
And the temperament of the earthquakes
And songs are like the trunks of trees
If they die in a land
They flower in every land.

The blue song . . . an idea
That the Sultan tried to obliterate
And thus it became the birth of an ember
The red song was an ember
That the Sultan tried to jail
And lo! [The] fire rayed into a revolution!

The voice of blood was immersed in the colour of the storm
And the pebbles of the square were the mouths of screaming wounds
And I stood laughing infatuated with the birth of the wind
When the Sultan resisted me I took hold of the keys of morn
And groped my way with the lanterns of wounds
Oh, how right I was when I consecrated
My heart to the call of the storm
So let the storm blow! Let the storm blow!

Translated by Shafik Magar.

From *Lotus*

A Negro Labourer in Liverpool
David Rubadiri, Malawi

I have passed him
Slouching on dark backstreet pavements
Head bowed
Taut, haggard and worn.
A dark shadow amidst dark shadows.

I have lifted my face to his,
Our eyes met
But on his dark negro face
No sunny smile,
No hope or longing for a hope promised;
Only the quick cowed dart of eyes

Piercing through impassive crowds
Searching longingly for a face
Feeling painfully for a heart
That might flicker understanding.

This is him—
The negro labourer in Liverpool
That from his motherland,
A heart heavy
With the load of a century's oppression,
Gloriously sought for an identity
Grappled to clutch the fire of manhood

In the land of the free.
But here are only the free dead—
For they too are groping for a light.

Will that sun
That greeted him from his mother's womb
Ever shine again?
Not here—
Here his hope is the shovel,
And his fulfilment resignation.

From *Lotus*

The People's Liberty

Fadwa Toukan, Jordan

My liberty!
My liberty!
My liberty!

A phrase which I repeat
With an angry spurt of words
Beneath the bullets and in the flames.
I shall ever seek my liberty
I shall, despite the night, pursue it.
Carried away by a tide of anger
Whilst struggling for my liberty

My liberty!
My liberty!
The sacred river, the very bridges
Will always echo:
My liberty!
The two banks will repeat:
My liberty!
The paths of the angry wind,
The thunder, the storm, and the rain

In my country
With me repeat:
My liberty! my liberty! my liberty!
I shall carve its name, whilst fighting,
On the ground, on the walls,
On the doors ... where the sun rises,
On the Virgin's temple, on the altar,
and
On pathways through the field.
On every mound, on every slope,

At every turn, on every street,
In jail, in the torture cell, and
On the gallows.
Despite chains, demolitions
And conflagrations
I shall go on carving its name
Until I see it
Stretching forth in my country and
expanding

Expanding
Expanding
To cover every inch of its soil
Until I see red liberty open each door,
Night escape, and its light destroy
The pillars of fog.

My liberty!
My liberty!
The sacred river and the bridges echo:
My liberty!
The two banks echo:
My liberty!
The voice of the angry wind
The thunder, hurricane and the rain
Of my country
Repeat with me:
My liberty! my liberty! My liberty!

Translated by Dr. Shafik Megally.

From *Lotus*

The Hum of the Spinning Wheel
Giang Nam, Vietnam

You held your breath skulking behind a hillock,
Your eyes opened wide. in the dancing darkness.
Which village is it? O! Also haystacks,
Canals and [coconut trees] . . .
And shaking [bamboo bridge]!

You heard children play in front of houses,
The thumping of pestles, even humming of spinning wheels . . .
You bit your lip . . . Heavens! The humming sounds of spinning wheels!
Why were they as eager as beloved voices!
You knew that in your village at this time your wife had not yet gone to bed,
Still spinning threads by the lamp,
Her eyes with rings from sleeplessness and worry.

You knew that your son still "stormed strongholds" and "blew up bridges"
Eager in his play late at night;
Your gun was pointed there   .
In the direction of your son, your wife!
The humming of spinning wheels always sweetly gentle!
"Don't tremble!" You were told,
"This is the Viet Communists' area!"

Where was the enemy? Where should be pointed
The steel barrel of your gun? You let down your gun, shaking
Behind your back was darkness.
The murderous pincer was driving you to crime!
the humming of spinning wheels always insistent, gentle . . .
Your head fell on the gun-butt wet with dew.

The dark sky cleared! Cock crowed in hamlets,
The clouds reddened, the birds sang melodiously,
The green silhouettes of coconut tress raised
Their tops over the thatch roofs.
The [thumping] of pestles again resounded by the [kitchen fire]!
And the humming of spinning wheels, insistent, gentle . . .
Order to go forward! Bewildered, you trembled;
Guns had fired! No going back!
Your gun was pointed before you,
It was cocked! Heavens! Whom to shoot at?
You glanced round: other guns fell down,
Other hands also shook like yours!
A baby cry behind a threshold
A familiar silhouette dashed across the road

"Shoot?"—"Compatriots, no! Don't shoot, brothers!"
The levelled guns suddenly lowered their heads!
Our mothers! Our wives! Damn the villains!
You bit your lip, blood ran out:
"Shoot?"—"Never! No shooting!"
A deafening explosion, you sprang up,
"The enemy is behind!" you shouted for the last time.
Before your eyes, the sky collapsed!
You heard the soft vibrating hum of a spinning wheel
Like a mother's voice rocking her baby by the river side
    in your native village.

Now at night people in my village do not go to bed
When hearing the intimate, soft humming sound of spinning-wheels.
U.S.-Diem raids cannot break the people's will.
The spinning wheels hum steadily by the [kitchen fire]!

From *Lotus*

A Milestone

Hochi Minh, Vietnam

Neither high, nor very far,
Neither emperor, nor king,
You are only a little milestone,
Which stands at the edge of the highway.

To people passing by
You point the right direction,
And stop them from getting lost.

You tell them of the distance
For which they still must journey.
Your service is not a small one.
And people will always remember you.

From *Lotus*

Crossing the Demarcation Line

Thanh Hai, Vietnam

Last night I crossed the demarcation line,
Coming to the North to see you.
So many days of longing,
I walked quickly, very quickly

I walked through ricefields
Fields of green rice plants,
I went through streets.
Who was that in the distance looking like you?

—It's you! You, you, you!
It's you! I started running,
—Darling, stop!
It's me, [don't] go!

—No. I don't go,
I've recognised you in the distance
Among hundreds, thousands of women,
I've seen only you.

Burying my face on your breast I wept.
It's already five years past!
You hugged me tightly
So much you wanted to tell me.

You asked me about our [rice fields]
You inquired of our village.
How could I tell you all
About these past bitter years.

From *Lotus*

You touched my arm
On which you had rested your head in days gone by
Suddenly you became agitated
"Your arm has a long scar!

Who has mutilated your arm?
I have waited for you these five years,
I have not let you down
And married again."

"I have not forsaken you, the enemy hunted me,
I have not abandoned you, I was arrested,
The enemy cut off my arm
On which you formerly rested your head."

I could not utter a word,
I cried to lighten my heart
Your breast was afire with hatred,
You hugged me and caressed me . . .

A cockcrow resounded,
I woke up, startled,
O! It was a dream!
My heart bled with suffering and longing.

Are you aware, darling,
That from this South of extreme misery
Night after night my heart
Crosses the demarcation line to see you?

From *Lotus*

Permitted to Take a Walk in the Prison Yard

Hochi Minh, Vietnam

After this long inactivity, my legs are like cotton.
While trying my first steps, I totter and stagger.
Immediately the chief warder calls out after me:
"Attention—about turn! That's enough of dawdling around!"

From *Lotus*

The Flute of the Fellow-Prisoner

Hochi Minh, Vietnam

Suddenly a flute sounds a nostalgic note:
Sadly the music rises, its tune is close to sobbing:
Over a thousand miles, across mountains and rivers,
Journeys an aching grief. We seem to see a woman
Climbing a far-off tower, to watch for someone's return.

From *Lotus*

To the Soldier in the South
Thanh Hai, Vietnam

Southern soldier! To what does your mind turn in the evening
When shadows again come to put out the sun.
Every day you go out with them,
And blood is shed and tears flow!

On their orders you burn down thatch huts,
That child who writhed in the flames, do you remember him?
When your son calls you and runs to you in the evening.
Taking him in your arms, are you not sick at heart?

You mount guard while the monsters
Slash women's breasts and cut men's throats.
For three years our sister Ly has seen her wounds bleed.
Is your wife proud when looking at you?

Keeping in your mind's eyes the sight of a target
They urge you to shoot wherever you go.
They want to turn your heart into lead.
It is your gun or your heart that spits out cartridges?

O Southern soldier! To what does your mind turn,
You with a gun in hand and always on the way?
In the [daytime] you are a shooting machine, a guillotine,
But at night, your sleep is troubled by bloody nightmares.

You are a worker, or a peasant
Who, enslaved for a hundred years, still drags along in misery.
You are said to kill in workers' quarters,
To terrorize villages. Do you do so?

Your parents gave you life
Only for you to defend your country and bring happiness.
The bandits coming from the other side of the Pacific
Want to turn you into a heap of shame.

Southern soldier! To what does your mind turn every evening
When shadows again come to put out the sun?
At night the sun sets but not your conscience!
Be strong tomorrow, don't let them send you out.

From Lotus

The Earth Trembles
Marcelino Dos Santos, Mozambique

- I -

The stifled long drawn-out voice
in the night
covered the man
killed in the mine
Your son,
Your father,
Your brother,
was quiet still,
Broken in the gases
and the carbon stones of the mine
tied up forever to the mine.
Death came along, stalking,
a creeping hyena,
To inscribe once more on the veins of your body
the lines of the grim destiny
that is meted out to the people of our country.
to mark you
with the will of the strangers.
There was no liberation,
a young shoot of maize
was plucked up from the dry earth.
Deep down in the mine
Death did not find you calm and steady.

It was a spasm of pain
as it has been all your life.
A leaf burnt out
in the continuous rebellion
on the earth
occupied by the whites.

- II -

It was hard, your life
on the earth to which you were born.
You have planted the cotton,
the [coconut] tree and the sisal,
your labour
built up
the riches of the "company"
you built up the city,
the road
and the port

You had wished to mould
human traits on the countenance of the earth
but all your efforts had scarcely gone
to provide you with a pass

[We] are, all of us, just like you
exiled
shackled
rent up
muzzled
on the earth that belongs to us.
The body walking
under a sky without stars
covered with sweat
all along the days that have no morrow,
It was hard, your life
on the earth to which you were born.
You have gone
to the Rand.

Your will under duress, constrained
by the will of the strangers.
News came
by the old-trodden road
to the mine.

- III -

The whole earth trembles
in the first crash
Men
Feel the world hemming them in
They run
in quest of the sun
They only find in front of them
the men of the company
a huge raven, throwing its shadow
to cover the sun under its wings
and the shrill voice:

"Go ahead
You must go ahead
You must
return deep into the mine!"
Then another crash
Men run
the earth trembles
Men fall down
in the ruins of the mine-drives that give way
dead bodies are warped up and writhe
in the gases and the carbon stones.

The hopes
in a world in which a man will live his life
are frittered away in the dust of the mine.
Dying men,
black men.

- IV -

From now on
faces will remain still and frozen
up in the gases and the carbon
stones of the mine
tied up forever to the mine.

Where
is the hope of joy
in a smile of love
in the offerings of wedlock?
Where is the longing
to see your black child grow up?
From now on
nothing but the ringing cry
amidst the gases and the carbon
stones
in the mine.
Putting the seal of its rhythm on another
sadness.

Tell me, Grandmother Ximane:
Where is your son?
And you, young girl:
What has become girl:
What has become of the man
who has stolen away your heart?

Slowly
the voice rings out in the mine
and breaks through:
"The contract is sealed!"

- V -

From now on
a yearning shoots forth,
in the mine,
for liberty.

From *Lotus*

My Father

Mahmoud Darwish, Palestine

He turned his eyes away from the moon
And bent to hug the earth
and prayed...
To a rainless sky
And told me not to leave!
The lighting hit the vales
Where my father used
To raise the stones
Of old... and grow the trees
His skin dark in the dew
His hand made the stone grow green
... And from afar a ballad wailed
—Odysseus was a knight...

There were loaves in the house
And wine, and covers warm
And horses, and shoes
And once my father said
When he had prayed upon a stone:
Turn your eyes away from the moon
Beware the sea... and travels far!
The day the hord beat the slave with a rod
I said: O people—let us turn away from God
And my father said ... as he bent his brow:

In a dialogue with pain
Job always thanked
The Maker of the worm ... and clouds
He made the wound [form]
Not for a corpse... or stone
Leave then the wound and pain
And help me to repent!

A star passed in the sky
Descending low . . . Descending low
And my shirt now stood
Between fire and wind
And my eyes now thought
Of tracings in the dust
And my father once said:
For him who has no homeland
There is no grave in earth's dust
. . . He also told me not to leave.

Translated by Nihad A. Salem.

From *Lotus*

Illusion

Nazih Kheir, Palestine

The fields of fog are in their hearts
And in their eyes the savagery of fire
They stretched the hand of destiny
To a world without destiny
The journey of the stream, a tale
Which passes in their hearts
Returning with the steps of misery
Pulled out . . .
From all which morn contains of hope
Pulled out from its true dawn
And illusion is still their eternity . . .
and still
The fields of fog are in their hearts
And in their eyes the savagery of fire . . .

Translated by Nihad A. Salem.

From *Lotus*

Apartheid

Arthur Nortje, South Africa

Winter parades as a mannequin.
The early scene looks virgin.
We sway past in a Volkswagen.

Nothing outwardly grieves,
so luxuriant are the trees.
Leaf-rich boughs ride past with spring's ease.

Yes, there is beauty: you make
the understandable mistake.
But the sun doesn't shine for the sun's sake.

Flame-sharp, it beats casual
sweat from my aching skull
and the May winds are mechanical.

A bird's clean flight
exhibits the virtues of light.
I skulk in a backseat, darker than white.
How should I envy the luminous
sky if the cold and anonymous
men of the world strengthen my enemies?

It matters little that
this lane, this door is separate.
In the rare air have we met.

From *Lotus*

A Wrong Headed Bunch

Dennis Brutus, South Africa

A wrong-headed bunch we may be
but the bodies of poets will always be
the anvils on which will be beaten out
a-new, or afresh, a people's destiny.
*
We must die;
We must buy
A new honest destiny:
*
not only tearing our flesh
to tear the shackles of alien oppression
*
but groping with lacerated fingers
to light, to our sense of right.
*
O may I be strong
and brave
and courageous to follow truth.
*
—Spirits of the brave
who have died for knowledge, truth and freedom
spirits of slave-ancestors knowing the bitter
price to be free make me strong and brave
make me too the brused and ready-ripened fruit.

From *Lotus*

To the Dark Singing

C. J. Driver, South Africa

This man's no hero; mad, perhaps,
Killed an old woman and burned
A child's face to a white skull
So he might make a god out of pain
To free his country from the praise
Of a golden beast. But we are fools
Who dose our disease with hate,
THOUGH WE SING WHEN WE DIE.

No praise then; and no prayer either—
For we are past the praying stage.
All prayers shout out too loudly
When one man goes alone to die
In a short falling, a short way
Through his little dark to the dark.
THOUGH HE SINGS WHEN HE DIES.

Each of us makes a separate peace
With the dark; he made his cruelty
Both ways, that his beast of fire
Might gobble the other golden beast
And that the sweet smell of flesh
Burning, burning, might crowd the gate
Where his country waits, unspeaking,
THOUGH IT SANG WHEN HE DIED.

I can see no beauty in this
Except that a man should sing
To his dark
Till the rope breaks his voice—
The flames burn white in his skull
And no one death repeats another,
THOUGH HE SANG WHEN HE DIED.

From *Lotus*

Freely

Cosmo Pieterse, South Africa

The exciting light of the stars
That steer our endeavour, is in
Us, as always, and still stirs us,
Explodes and attracts—so!—
Every tomorrow is here and so nearly distant.

From *Lotus*

My People no Longer Sing

Keorapetse Kgositsile, South Africa

Remember
When my echo upsets
The plastic windows of your mind
And darkness invades its artificial light
The pieces of your regrets hard to find Remember
I shall only be a sighing memory then
Until you look in the fiery womb of sunrise
Retrieving songs almost aborted
On once battered black lips
Remember
When you get sick and tired
Of being sick and tired
To remind the living
That the dead cannot remember.

Yes, Mandela, we shall be moved
We are Men enough to have a conscience
We are Men enough to immortalize your song
We are Men enough to look Truth straight in the face
To defy the devils who traded in the human Spirit

For Black cargoes and material [superprofits]
We emerge to sing a Song of Fire with Roland

We emerge to prove Truth cannot be enslaved
In chains or imprisoned in an island inferno
We emerge to stand Truth on her two feet We emerge

To carry the banner of humanism across the face of the Earth

Our voice in unison with our poet's proudly says
`Change is gonna come!'

From *Lotus*

For a Childless Woman
Popular folklore from Egypt

What is amiss with this woman?—her coffin as awry:
She has no son among the bearers.
What is amiss with the woman?—her coffin is tilted:
She has no son among those bearing her.
The consoler came to console, and withdrew—
She has no son: we are come to console woman.
The consoler came to console and withdrew, looking askance—
She has no son, we are come to console womenfolk.
Be careful with her, you who lay her down—
She has no son; take heed that you do not uncover her.
Be careful, you who set her down—
She has no son; take heed that you do not disorder her.

From *Lotus*

As Long as I Live

Mazisi Kunene, South Africa

I still can remember
When I still have eyes to see
When I still have hands to hold
When I still have feet to drag
So long shall I bear your name with all the days
So long shall I stare at you with all the stars of heaven
Though you lead me to their sadistic beasts
I shall find a way to give my burden-love
Blaming your careless truths on yesterdays,
Because I swear by life herself
When you still live, so shall I live
Turning the night into day, forcing her
To make you lie pompous on its pathways.
So shall I wander around the rim of the sun
Till her being attains your fullness
As long as I live . . .

From *Lotus*

The Echoes

Mazisi Kunene, South Africa

Our the vast summer hills
I shall commission the maternal sun
To fetch you with her long tilted rays,

The slow heave of the valleys
Will once again roll the hymns of accompaniment
Scattering the glitter of the Milky Way over the bare fields.

You will meet me
Underneath the shadow of the timeless earth
Where I lie weaving the seasons.

You will indulge in the sway dances of your kin
To the time of symphonic flutes
Ravishing the identity of water lilies.

I have opened the mountain gates
So that the imposing rim
Of the Ruwenzori shall steal your image.

Even the bubbling lips of continents
(To the shy palms of Libya)
Shall awake the long-forgotten age.

The quivering waters of the Zambezi river
Will bear on a silvery blanket your name
Leading it to the echoing of the sea.

Let me not love you alone
Let the essence of your being
Lie heavy on my tongue
When you count so many to praise.

From *Lotus*

Monangamba

Antonio Jacinto, Angola

On that big estate there is no rain
it's the sweat of my brow that waters the crops;

On that big estate there is coffee ripe
and that [cherry redness]
is drops of my blood turned sap.
The coffee will be roasted,
ground, and crushed,
will turn black, black with the colour of the contratado.
Black with the colour of the contratado!
Ask the birds that sing,
the streams in carefree wandering
and the high wind from inland:

Who gets up early? Who goes to toil?
Who is it that carries on the long road
the hammock or bunch of kernels?
Who reaps and for pay gets scorn
rotten maize, rotten fish,
ragged clothes, fifty angolares
beating for biting back?
Who?
Who makes the millet grow
 and the orange groves to flower?
—Who?
Who gives the money for the boss to buy
cars, machinery, women
and Negro heads for the motors?

Who makes the white man prosper,
grow big-bellied get much money?
—Who?

And the birds that sing,
the streams in carefree wandering
and the high wind from inland
will answer:

—Monangambeeee...
Ah! Let me at least climb the palm trees
Let me drink wine, palm wine
and fuddles by my drunkness forget
—Monangambeeee...

From *Lotus*

The Fourth Poem of a Song of Accusation

Fernando Costa Andrade, Angola

On earth
there are 50,000 dead whom nobody mourned
unshriven

on earth
50,000 dead
nobody mourned them.

A thousand Guernicas and the words of Orozeo's paints and
those of Siqueiros
A silence with the dimensions of the sea.
as if rains of blood fell down
as if strong wiry hair stood on end
tall grasses
as if mouths condemned
at the very moment of their 50,000 deaths
all the living on earth.

On earth
there are 50,000 dead whom nobody mourned
nobody . . .
The mothers of Angola
fell when their children fell.

Translated by Nihad A. Salem.

From *Lotus*

The Little Boy Enters Not in the Circle
Geraldo Bessa Victor, Angola

The little black boy enters not in the circle
of little white children, of little white children
dancing together in a lively circle
of joyful songs and open peels of laughter.

The little black boy enters not in the circle.
And then comes the wind all against the children
and dances with them and sings with them
songs and dances of breezes suave
songs and dances of violent tempests,
and the little black boy enters not in the circle.

The birds, in a flock, fly and twitter
o'er the tiny sweet heads of the children there
and set down in a circle. Finally
they dance their flight and sing their song.
and the little black boy enters not in the circle.
"Come here little black boy, come here and dance"
says one of the children with a happy air
the vigilant mother has seen all in a trice
and already the white child wants him not, wants him not . . .

And the little black boy enters not in the circle.
The little black boy enters not in the circle.
of little white children, dreamy and sad
he remains alone, his eyes fled like a blind man's
he remains alone, his voice mortally quiet.

Translated by Nihad A. Salem.

From *Lotus*

Ode to The Revolutionary Heroes: A Revolutionary Song of Thailand

Jitra Pumisakdi (a martyr of Thailand), Thailand

Sons and daughters of Thailand
Are fearless in struggle against tyranny,
Even under dictator's rule,
We are firm and steadfast forever till death!
Blood of our heroes
Reddens soil of our motherland,
Flames of anger
Burn and burn a blaze in our hearts!

Rise up, Thai's heroic sons and daughters,
Fight against imperialism and its lackeys,
Avenge on enemies our blood and lives!
Thailand belongs to her people, who want freedom!
Blood of heroes arouses our revenge,
We remain persistent, wipe out oppressors lock, stock and barrel.
Let's defy hardship and sacrifice.
Fight, fail, fight again till victory.
Comrades-in-arms' sacrifice stirs us up,
They die a heroic death, people will win freedom.
Their lives laid down for the country's dignity,
Like radiant sun, shine upon our motherland!

Sons and daughters of Thailand
Are fearless in struggle against tyranny,
Even under dictator's rule,
We are firm and steadfast forever till death!
Blood of our heroes
Reddens soil of our motherland,
Flames of anger
Burn and burn a blaze in our hearts!
Rise up Thai's heroic sons and daughters,
We can't bear comrades' blood shed for nothing.

Men and women, old and young, united as one man,
Ready for combat.
Thai's heroic sons and daughters,
We are powerful beyond compare,
We'll overthrow traitors, drive out U.S. imperialism.
Let's defy hardship and sacrifice.
Fight, fail, fight again till victory.
Comrades-in-arms' sacrifice stirs us up,
They die a heroic death, people will win freedom.
Their lives laid down for the country's dignity,
Like radiant sun, shine upon our motherland!

From *The Call*

Albanian Revolutionary Songs: Revolutionary is Marching Forward

F. Laro

Today the songs are echoing everywhere
Workers and peasants are united as one
We are happily celebrating our victories
And our country is shining under the sun of November*

Refrain:
The workers are marching on the forefront
The revolution requires us
To work with revolutionary impetus
So we can build socialism

Picks and spades in hand
We are building our country
We go to the difficult fronts of work
And we are soldiers as well

We are working full of vigour
In the plants, factories and everywhere
We are following our heroes' path
For we have the Party at the head

From *The Call*

---

*On November 29, 1944, the Albanian people, under the leadership of the Communist Party of Albania, which was renamed the Albanian Party of Labour in November 1948, won the final victory in their anti-fascist war and achieved nationwide liberation.

Oath of the Revolutionaries

A popular Arab revolutionary song

No "peaceful solution", no surrender, a million no's!
In the name of all-conquering "Assifa", we loudly swear the oath.
Every bleeding wound the oath cries,
The shouts of the oath pierce the skies.
No "peaceful solution", no surrender, a million no's!
Marching along the road to victory with big strides,
Holding their heads high.

They shout: No "peaceful solution", no surrender, a million no's!
Our people bearing arms will never stop their march
Till the dawn of liberation glows.
Together with our martyrs, bullets and arms, we shout:
No "peaceful solution", no surrender, a million no's!
Over Chungshan swept a storm, headlong,

From *The Call*

Poems of Chairman Mao Tsetung: Capture of Nanking by the People's Liberation Army

A Lu Shih

Our mighty army, a million strong, has crossed the Great River.
The City, a tiger crouching, a dragon curling, outshines its ancient glories;
In heroic triumph heaven and earth have been overturned.
With power and to spare we must pursue the tottering foe
And not ape Hsiang Yu the conqueror seeking idle fame.
Were Nature sentient, she too would pass from youth to age,
But in man's world seas change into mulberry fields.

April 1949
Granted independence.

From *The Call*

The title: On April 1949, 21, according to Chairman Mao Tsetung's order "Advance bravely and annihilate resolutely, thoroughly, wholly and completely all the Kuomintang reactionaries within China's borders who dare to resist. Liberate the people of the whole country. Safeguard the independence and integrity of China's territory and sovereignty", the Chinese People's Liberation Army forced the Yangtse River. On April 23, it liberated Nanking, the centre of the counter-revolutionary rule of the Kuomintang and proclaimed the downfall of the reactionary Kuomintang regime.

Line 3 & 1: Mount Chungshan, the other name is Purple Gold Mountain which stands to the east of Nanking. Chinese classical writers compared the city of Nanking to a "crouching tiger" and Chungshan a "curling dragon". Later, the two comparisons put together, specially refer to Nanking.

Line 6: In the third century B.C., Hsiang Yu and Liu Pang respectively led peasant forces against the Chin dynasty and Hsiang Yu self-bestowed the title of "the conqueror". Wishing to appear generous after Chin's main force was put out of action, he did not kill his rival Liu Pang when the opportunity offered. In the end, he was defeated by Liu Pang and committed suicide.

Line 8: According to an ancient Chinese tale, a certain woman was so long-lived that she several times witnessed the seas dry up and become fields covered with mulberry trees.

Fire! Fire!

Gracade, Guinea: Bissau

We do not want it;
Bestowed independence,
Keep it for yourselves!
Independence can't be begged,
Nor purchased.
To gain independence,
We must take up arms,
And fight, defying sacrifices,
Till final victory's won,
As has done Mao Tsetung's China,
And as Enver Hoxha's Albania.

Aim at imperialism, fire!
 Aim at revisionism, fire!
Aim at colonialism, fire! fire!

Granted independence,
We do not want it;
Bestowed independence,
Keep it for yourselves!
It is you who crave for war,
Making the world a chaos;
It is you eager to amass fortunes
Upon heaps of people's skeletons!
You can't live without war,
You, more brutal than beasts!

Aim at U.S. imperialism, fire!
   Aim at Soviet revisionism, fire!
Aim at new colonialism, fire! fire!

Granted independence,
We do not want it;
Bestowed independence,
Keep it for yourselves!
You open your beastly bloody mouths,
With an appetite to gulp all;
There's no satisfying your voracity,
Unless we bury you all.

We've known you scoundrels
Not for five days,
But five hundred years!
The bit of vitality left by our ancestors,
You want to suck it to the last drop;
Our gold, diamonds and riches,
You try to loot them all away.
Now that your day of misery's come,
You speed up your plunder;
The bell of freedom is ringing,
The sight of people's liberation
Makes your hearts ache and bleed.
Viet Nam! Thailand! Palestine!
Angola! Kinshasa! Colombia! Czechoslovakia!

Aim at U.S. imperialism, fire!
   Aim at Soviet revisionist social-imperialism, fire!
Aim at all reactionaries, fire! fire!

We do not want it;
Bestowed independence,
Only enjoyed by your running dogs,
Keep it, keep it for yourselves!

Our war is a just war,
    Our war is a people's war,
Our war is sure to triumph!

But my brothers,
We must carry on our battle,
For the freedom of Cape Verde,
For the freedom of the whole Africa,
And for liberation of Asia and Latin America!
Wherever there's exploitation,
The only way to liberation
Is to take up arms,
And fire! fire!

From *The Call*

United in Blood

Azanian Poems

United in blood,
Oh Karameh,[1]
United in blood!
Unity, Oh Karameh, unity!
On burning hills,
In rocky caves, Fedayeen[2]
Upon the forefront of the Arab land, we are united by our blood!

In our people's liberation war, we are united by our blood!
Invincible, Oh our revolutionary Fateh!
Invincible, the hand that explodes a tank!
Unity of the revolutionaries,
Oh Karameh,
Upon the land on fire!

Hand in hand,
Oh Karameh,
Under the torch of determination,
The revolutionaries are united,
Fedayeen!
Under the torch of determination,
Fedayeen, upon the forefront of the Arab land,
We are united by our blood!
In our people's liberation war, we are united by our blood!
Invincible, Oh our revolutionary Fateh!
Invincible, the hand that explodes a tank!

---

1   Karameh, a city where the Palestinian guerrillas fought a big battle_ in 1968 and won a great victory.
2   Fedayeen, plural of Fedayee.

From *The Call*

Militant Songs of Palestine

A Martyr's Last Word

Into my blood dip your reed-pen,
And put down my behest.
Look at my lips, firm and forceful,
I sing a few lines.

A wounded man expresses his wish with his lips,
This is the highest prayer,
As a hero's legend,
Written in the annals of life.
People believe in the bayonet
And in Fateh who has taken up the bayonet.
Land has turned red with blood.

Into my blood dip your reed-pen,
And put down my last word.
To my brothers, kinsfolk and all,
Leave the behest of mine:
You're the symbol of daybreak
And the end of dark night.
Carry on my cause after my departure,
On, on and still hold on!
This is the mission of our generation.

Debt In Blood

Brothers,
I have great faith in my lost and fettered people!
So I took my gun in hand,
For the generations after us
To be free to wield the sickle!
And I made my blood from my wounds a stream,
To flow through the fields
And valleys of our land!
Our blood is a debt that must be repaid!
A debt that cannot be delayed!

Beladi .... *

Beladi, Beladi,
Fateh revolution on the enemy!
Palestine, our fatherland,
Back to you I'll return.
Fateh revolution will see victory;
Al Assifa** is my country's hope.
Beladi!

Palestine, my great love,
You're my aim and destiny.
Back to you I'll march and fight,
Meeting oppression with determination.
Beladi!

Palestine, the cradle of Jesus,
And the land of Mohammed, calling:
Liberate my wounded land,
Sweep out the enemy who occupy our land!
Beladi!

Palestine, my only hope,
I'll restore the pride of my uprooted
Under the banner of struggle!
Beladi!

Palestine, your people will never die,
Nor will they be silenced,
Al Assifa will always have its hand on the gun.
Beladi!

---

* Beladi: "my homeland" in Arabic.
** Al Assifa: Fateh's military wing.

Al Assifa is marching there,
Making traps, securing the land;
Dealing death and destruction
To every thief and traitor to my country!
Beladi!

From *The Call*

Awake, Ye Brave Sons and Daughters of Namibia!

Kaluenya, Namibia

Awake, awake ye brave sons and daughters of
Namibia!
For centuries you have been in chains;
No independence, no democracy, no freedom.
Colonialism and feudalism exploited and oppressed
you all.
Awake, awake, ye brave sons and daughters of
Namibia!

You have known all kinds of misery.
Indignant, you have been resisting and struggling.
You have been trying to hold your fate in your own hands.
And now, the time has come.
Awake, awake, ye brave sons and daughters of
Namibia!

Unite as one man, ye oppressed masses!
Kindle the raging flames of revolutionary struggle
To burn all the colonialists and their puppets,
And none of them shall escape unpunished.
Awake, awake, ye brave sons and daughters of
Namibia!

Look, ye Namibian masses, alone we are not!
We march with millions of the African masses
And the militant peoples of the world.
In unity and solidarity lie our strength and our
victory.
Awake, awake, ye brave sons and daughters of
Namibia !

From the ruins of colonialism and feudalism,
We shall together build our homeland anew,
Enjoying independence, sovereignty and racial equality.
Colonialism, racism and other evils will come to an end.
Awake, awake, ye brave sons and daughters of
Namibia!

Join your hands, ye army of workers and peasants!
Join your hands, those unwilling to be slaves,
Dig deep the graves to bury the colonialists,
And plant flowers to let the masses enjoy a happy life.
Awake, awake, ye brave sons and daughters of
Namibia!

Under colonialism and apartheid,
We have been nothing.
Now in the revolution, our will is like steel, our future is clear.
May our unity and wisdom guide us to a brilliant future.
Awake, awake, ye brave sons and daughters of
Namibia!

In our long and noble struggle,
Let us march, march side by side with African
masses,
Let us strengthen our solidarity with the people of
all countries
To win national independence and liberation.
Awake, awake, ye brave sons and daughters of
Namibia!

From *The Call*

Ode to the Fighting Gaza

S. A. Hussein, Palestine

Gaza, you are
A maiden tempered in fire and blood,
The glowing face of the Arab people,
The symbol of determination to throw the arrogant enemy into the mire,
And the flames that turn the enemy's long nights into hell.

Gaza, you are
A nursery which brings up the seedlings of heroes,
Fearless and undaunted,
From every grain of sand,
From behind every tree,
From every cave,
From every hut that may look shabby but is still full of vigour,
And from every tent that may suffer hunger but still stands erect as an oak.

Gaza, you are
The source of determination and dignity,
The epic of epics,
Where fathers and sons,
Men and women
Compete to join the fight.
With their pure blood,
They wash your soil
And uproot disgrace from our land.

Gaza,
When night falls,
And wind rustles,
Dancing are men's shadows.

From the orchard here,
From the school there,
From houses without door or window,
From the thick jungle,
From the minarets,
Fighters storm enemy positions.

Gaza, where
On every inch of land that the enemy have trampled,
On every road that the enemy pass,
At every place where the enemy camp,
Laid in store
Are fear, death and destruction.

Gaza,
Those aggressive rotten to the core,
Greedily suck your blood.
They live in lust knowing no morals,
Meantime,

Born on your land,
Are thousands of heroes.
For liberation and dignity,
They shed blood
Or lay down their lives.
One warrior falls,
Thousands of others rise up from his bloodshed.
They pledge:

"Oh Gaza,
We Arabs here have
No food, clothes or shelter,
But we are brave
And good at fighting.
We are resolute,
And strike like hurricane.
Every village here is like a mine,
Ever ready to blow up the enemy."

Oh Gaza,
Their words we have heard
Their deeds we have seen.
Oh Gaza, you are
The source of determination and
dignity!

From *The Call*

Decisive Battle

Gochera, Zimbabwe

On the hills yonder in the battle for national liberation,
Many of our sons and daughters fell,
To take revenge upon the white settler for Zimbabwe.
Move on, sons and daughters,
To annihilate the settler in your land!

Oh! Hear our battle-cry!
To ravage the settler's fortress,
To silence their guns of cold blood murder.
Move on, sons and daughters,
To annihilate the settler and save your Nation!

We block the settler's gun with our body,
Our death will not be in vain.
Orders are given. Forward ever
Through the shower of bullets,
Move on, sons and daughters,
To annihilate the settler, your enemy!
The path to victory is to be opened up blood.
Arouse the masses of the people
To form a wall of iron.
Sons and daughters, march to crush the exploiters,
Your freedom is in yourselves alone — Zimbabweans!

Oh! Zimbabweans, your family is murdered.
The oppressor has ravaged your beautiful country.
Awake! Oh, sons and daughters, take action!
Take up arms and save your Nation!

From *The Call*

Struggle

Lee Ying, China

In the masses of spring clouds
The thunder rolls.
Oh, the seventies of the twentieth century,
Your every minute
Ignites in my heart fiery excitement.
Listen, the roaring of the slaves has roused
booming of the battle drums;
The siren of workers' strike is calling up shots
of the gun.

Many a nation has lifted up her head from
the pools of blood;
Many a state has been born in the thick of
the storms;
Even on small islands in the remote part of
the vast oceans
Struggles are going on like steel burning hot . . .
Oh, this is our great era!

Countries want independence,
Nations want liberation,
The people want revolution!
When the dancing flames
Are brightening up the peoples' eyes that glare,
Beat louder your battle drums,
Blow your combat bugles and
Raise your alarms!

Oh, our world,
Today, for the first time I see
How you look.

From *The Call*

Forward, Zimbabwean People
Shadreck, Zimbabwe

Advance!
The war drums are booming.
Listen, fighters in the front and everywhere,
Listen, Zimbabwean people,
The bugle call of victory is sounding.
Do not look back.
Do not hesitate.
Today, the voice of national liberation struggle,
Echoes throughout the country.
A new dawn will soon appear over our land.

Advance!
The war drums are booming.
Roll up your sleeves,
Keep your eyes wide open,
Never let money and promises cheat you,
As the voice of national liberation struggle,
Echoes throughout the country.
We are closing our ranks,
To wipe out the white settlers.

Stand up with ever greater courage,
Victory now attends us.
Today, the country glows red in the dawn of struggle,
Flames against the exploiters are burning
higher and higher.

March, march to the war drums' boom,
Do not hesitate,
Cast your illusions to the winds.
We hold arms with the masses in the struggle,
And become tempered men of strong will.

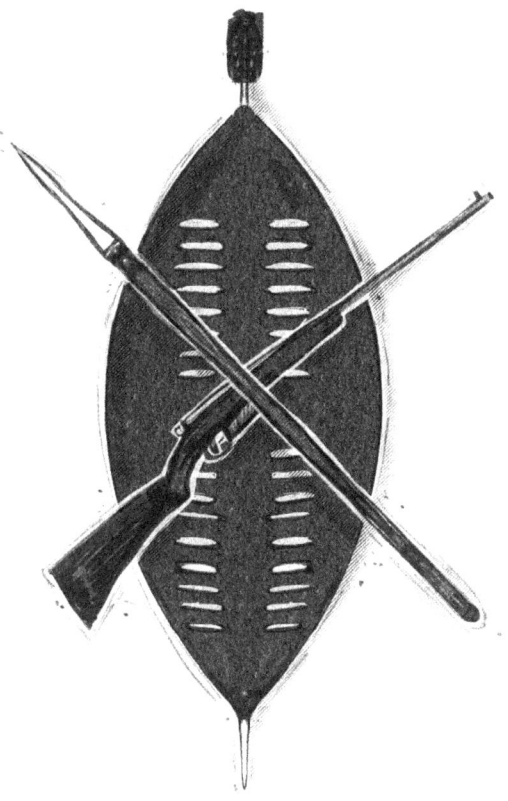

Let us advance with firm strides,
And smash the Smith regime ! ! !

From *The Call*

Kind Mother

Z.N. Chisekesi, Zimbabwe

How rich you are Mother Zimbabwe,
How kind-hearted you are!
You receive those white settlers
And yet they murder your family.

As reward for your kindness
The inhuman settlers give your sons blows and death,
You, who everyday dress them,
Who give them shelter and fertile land,
You see each morning your families detained.
What sad fate is yours, Mother Zimbabwe?

But don't worry, Mother,
Your children are ready to shed blood,
Blood that will surely liberate you.
We, your sons and daughters will free you,
We see your face silhouette in our dreams.

Zimbabwe, how much the enemy persuades,
How much money he may give,
Don't follow him or be deceived!
Let him go alone to where he came from!
Remain here and nurse your own children!

If the enemy hurts you, Mother,
Call freedom fighters to the rescue,
For they are greater than the oppressor
And wholly devoted to you.
They challenge settler supremacy.

Mother Zimbabwe,
Bid your children say little but do much,
Then shall the people rule
In the land, Mother Zimbabwe,
For which your fine sons and daughters
Are ready to shed their blood.

From *The Call*

I Persist in the Fight

Palestine

Persist in the fight! Persist in the fight!
For my fatherland, I persist in the fight!
Should they take all my grains, I persist in the fight!
Should they kill my children, I persist in the fight!
Should they destroy my house, oh, my house!
Beside the shattered walls and on the ruins,
I persist in the fight!
With spirit never to bow, I persist in the fight!
Taking up my baton and shouldering my bag,
I persist in the fight!
Holding high the battle flag, I persist in the fight!
If one of my hands is cut off,
I shall use my other hand to hold the battle
flag; I persist in the fight!
For my homeland, I persist in the fight!
With full confidence and firm determination,
I persist in the fight!
With my bare hands and my teeth, I persist in the fight!
Even if I am wounded all over,
With all the wounds on my body and blood
stains, I shall still persist in the fight!

From *The Call*

The Revolutionaries' Anger

Palestine

March forward!
March forward courageously like a gust of wind!
Oh, azure sky of my motherland,
Have you seen
The revolutionaries' anger?
Oh, vast land of my motherland,
We are bravely marching forward,
Fearing neither blood-shedding nor death,
Needless to say set-backs and difficulties.
We want to hold our heads high and
To live decently on our own land.
In the past years,
Here our forerunners met,
And fought to defend you.
They have written immortal epics
In the history of our motherland.
The dark night will soon pass.
The dawn of truth is no longer far away.

Listen to the cries of the angry masses.
Our blood will not be shed in vain!
Under the lofty banners,
We remain loyal fighters,
Though the day may come
When we have to lay down our lives.
Listen!
The thunder rolls,
The lightning flashes.
Before our sworn enemy,
We are the lightning,
We are the fire,
And our objective will be achieved!

From *The Call*

Kamal, My Son

Wadya Kamal, Palestine

Kamal Nasser was a Palestinian guerrilla leader and a well-known poet. He and two other responsible members of the guerrillas were murdered in cold blood by Israeli Zionists in Beirut, Lebanese capital, in April 1973. Wadya Kamal, Kamal's mother, wrote this poem in memory of her valiant son.

Kamal Nasser once wrote in his poem "The HonoU1· of My Motherland":

As I write the history of my motherland
With my fiery youth and combatant's blood,
I'll put down a glorious page for the people,
    An immortal page in the march of the fighters,
        Shining with splendor of undaunted heroism.
        Fighting stubbornly and heroically falling for his
        motherland, he, indeed, kept his vows. - Ed.

Kamal, my son,
The enemy did not let me see you
When you were taking your last sleep.
They thought I would never see you again,
But I do find you everywhere,
For in every youth I see you.

Your firm voice
Still resounds in my ears:
"I am a revolutionary
And shall not die.
On the march of the fighters,
I'll always advance with my comrades!
I've lit up the torches with my life,
And my body adds more fuel to the flames.
I shall never die,
Together with the people I'll live forever!"

Kamal, my son, you
Whom I brought up are saying:
"Mother, don't be grieved,
A new life cannot be created
Without sacrifice.
Our motherland is calling on me,
To plunge into the great battle,
And dedicate my life to the revolution."

You brought me unbearable grief,
Not merely because I am your mother,
I love you, my own flesh and blood.
You love our motherland
With the purest love in the world.

I am proud,
I am excited,
For I am the mother of such a fighter:
"Mother,
Tears only make one lose confidence.
Let me be firm,
Let me march forward.
It is my duty to fight,
And I know how to win honour for my country."

Kamal, my son,
My future is the same as yours —
To fight in the fiercest combats.
You are the symbol of our young generation,
You've died in glory.
The enemy cannot make me yield,
Nor can they defeat me.

Filled in my body and soul
Is the fighting vigour and zeal.

In our youth you'll live forever,
Your firm voice can be heard everywhere:
"Let us hold high the banners of our struggle,
And charge the enemy.
Forever we shall live!"

From *The Call*

PLACE AND LAND

Chapter of an Old Image

Adonis, Lebanon

As time goes
The horses of dawn are astray,
with loose reins,
Drawing the old image
Of my troubled lovers
On the sad shores of the desert.

Oh my old form
(How does a stranger resume his old form?)
And in what language
Shall I greet the Euphrates
The cradle which lulled me to sleep
And quenched my thirst with its kind waters?

I shall hew my veins into a river
That carries space;
I shall tour with the setting star
Or the rising sun
In their aerial forms
And return to my half that lives
On the sad shores of the desert.
How I wish to sing the song of my troubled lovers.
How I wish to fold my life
In a parchment,
To advance
In the tracts of cinder.
How I wish to reveal myself to these birds,
To this inanimate matter
How I wish to become pebbles or silk.

When it was the season for the lilacs, the swallow,
The season for the seagull in love and the feasts,
I arrived in Baghdad
On a docile yet impetuous carpet.
The fields of grass and plants,
The sands of water, the deserts,
The negro-eyed ships in the Euphrates
A green throat, welcoming the arrivals
With no frontiers
Escorted by rains and clouds,
Coming from the earth, from spring.

I ring the bells of hidden blood
Under the mantle of earth,
I climb in the erect flame,
Under the ice of rejection,
I run with the Euphrates
In a magical time
From the old source of childhood, the old age.

All the blood of the Euphrates
Runs in my body, in my yearning
And here I am girdling the plains,
I am the guardian of huts and fields,
I bold the hand of summer in the hand of winter.
I run dreams on the dust
With no voyage, no absence
I release a flood of duration.

I chase away from my shores,
The sailors of departure.
I descend into my blue depths
In the family tree
Looking for a replacement
Looking for the gate of strangers.
I came to Baghdad
In the branches of palms, the waters of the river,
In the chests of swallows

* * *

The Euphrates told me
What the herbs had told him.
About the saga of rivers and shepherds
The Euphrates told me
All that he had seen.
And in the stones I heard
The song of the seasons,
I heard what the grey clouds said . . .
I saw the miserable hordes
Plaited like a braid.

Together, we read, we wrote, we knew
That we are the orphaned owners.
We shouted, we made our parents' graves, our windows,
Our chained volcanoes
A river that would wash the city . . .

We ran to the herbs listening
It's a magician extending his hands
Emerging through the cracks of dust

From *Lotus*

In Front of the Gate of Allah

Badr Shaker El Sayyab, Iraq

Prostrate in front of your gate
I cry in the darkness:
"Oh, tender of ants in the sand
You who can hear the pebble
Falling to the bottom of the stream."
My cry is like the echo of thunder in the mountains,
Like the heaved sigh in the midday heat.
Do you hear my cry, oh God, do You
And if you hear, do you reply?

Oh, hunter of men,
Crusher of women,
Destroyer of worshippers
With meteors and earthquakes,
You who make houses deserted
Here I am, prostrate in front of your gate
Feeling the refraction of doubts in the conscience.
Shall I rebel? Shall I become angry?

I need no more from life than what I have.
Would a sinner revolt, while under your protection?
I have enough corn to fill the darkness,
The crops are asleep in my fields,
I washed my bands of its soil
So that tomorrow others
Will come to plant,
And others to gather crops.
And time shall sow the graves and ears of corn.

I want to live in peace:
Like a candle melting in the dark
I die with a tear and with a smile.

I'm tired of the midday heat
I wrestle with the seas and my conscience,
And from my nights with the palms
With the lamp and with my thoughts
I follow the verse
In the darkness of the deep
And the depth of the desert,
In the labyrinth of doubts and madness.

I am tired of my great struggle,
I cleave my heart to feed the poor,
I light, my cottage with the candle of my eyes.
I cover it with old flags
That smell of old defeat.
I'm tired of my last spring,
I see it in flowers, roses and semination,
I see It in every spring that crosses the borders.
I am tired of life acting the coy,

I live on yesterday,
And call it my tomorrow.
As if I am an actor from the world of death
Hauled from its darkness by fate
With candles lit on its big stage,
He laughs to the dawn, with a heart
Full of the noon's heat.
I am tired like a child
Tired by its crying.

I want to sleep under your protection
My covers are my sins and misdeeds
My cradle is the quiver of the fallen.
You would refuse to touch me.
I wish I could see You. Who sees You?

I come to your holy place
Amid the procession of the sinners and the tormented,
Our broken voices crying,
Like daggers cutting through the air, with a moan:

"Our faces are ruins
Like children's drawings in dust
They know not beauty and elegance.
Childhood is gone. Youth is dimmed
And melted away like a cloud,
We carry the same faces,
Eyes do not attract looking eyes
And do not reveal ourselves
To You, exploder of beauty. We are lost
Wandering in the gardens of faces Oh . . .
For a world that sees water lilies
On the surface, and misses the oysters
In the bottom, and the rare pearl inside.

Prostrate I cry, biting the stones
"God, I want to die."

From *Lotus*

The Hanging of Zahran

Salah Abdel Sabour, U.A.R

The light was buried deep 'beneath the earth,
Sadness filtered through the thatched roofs . . .
A thousand arm'd dragon,
And each arm a dark and [somber] alley,
From the moon call to prayer till night had set in
But half a day . . . and . . . Oh, my God,
That those misfortunes should have happened in so short a time,
Since Zahran's kindly head drooped from the rope.

* * *

Zahran was a child,
Whose mother was dark ... and whose father was half-caste
In his eyes sweetness shone,
On his temple was a pigeon tattoo,
And his arm bore Abuzeid Al Hilali's image,[1]
Holding his scimitar,
Below this image was some hazy writing
to be found . . .
The name of a village Denshwai.

* * *

Zahran grew up lusty and strong,
And his heart was pure,
On the ground he trod softly
And with comely grace,
He was cheerful and of singing fond
He loved poetry on a winter's night.

* * *

---

1 Legendary hero of Egyptian folklore.

In Zahran's heart
A small flower grew,
Its stem was green with the water of life,
Its crown was scarlet like the flame kindling his heart
When he passed by the market place one day,
One of those days,
And purchased a tiny shawl,
He strutted proudly in it like a turbaned Turk,
Peering with mischievous eyes . . .
Oh, how wonderful is youth,
When searching for love,
When striving to capture a heart.

And then did Zahran wed Djamileh,
And then did Zahran beget a son . . . and yet another,
And the long night followed and drew on
And in Zahran's heart grew a fine young sapling
That would bring forth subtle shrubs one day
Its stem was black from life's heavy loam,
And its boughs red like Earth's molten clay.

* * *

For on this morn did Zahran pass the market place,
And the fire devour a child
Gentle Zahran was a friend of life,
And as he saw fire wipe out that life,
He lifted his arms to Heaven in mute prayer
And asked for Mercy to descend upon the Earth
[Maybe] t'was the vehemence of his wrath
At so much blood split,
Or perchance did he try to quench Earth's fiery flames
With anodyne rain from Heaven.

* * *

The scaffold on the road was built;
The Ghoulish hangmen did appear,
Chief executioner Mesrour made his entrance
With the enemies of life,
Manufacturing death for the lovers of life,
And thus did Zahran's gentle head come to hang,
Since that day does my village feed only on treats;
Since that day does my village live in desolate despair
Since that morn my village freer the treasure of life
Yet Zahran had been a true friend of life;
He had died with his eyes full of life;
Why then does my village fear the brightness of life!

From *Lotus*

A Crown for Africa

Vernard Dadie, Ivory Coast

I will twine for you a crown
Made of laurel and hibiscus
Jewelled with open-winged butterflies
And of the calm of flowering [under bush].

I will twine for your and emerald crown
With the pearls of Atlanta's treasures.
A crown of the surf of my candid tears.
And a garland
Made of the song of rosy springs
And the innocence of waves.

I will twine for you a crown
Of sky blue and sapphire
And of the twittering of the breeze
By the fragrant mornings where the breathing of beings
Takes its shape in the air.
I will twine for you a crown
Of the harmonies of spring songs
Which makes envious the nightingale
In its wedding frills,
And of the fur sandals
Of an angry lioness.

I will twine for you a crown
Of pure flames mixed in a rainbow,
Of ancient hours of fortune
Together with
The ardour of a flaming millennium.

I will twine for you a crown
Of blue dawns
And a necklace of rosy gems
Which time will never dare to tarnish.
I will twine for you a crown
Of the essence of flowers
With a pendant made out of life and of human wisdom.

I will twine for you a crown
Of soft beams of light.
With the glowing Venus of the tropics
And in the orbit of the feverish twinkle
Of the Milky Way.
I will write
In letters of fire
Of fire
Your
Name
O, Africa!

From *Lotus*

Whither Bound, O Africa?

M. F. Dei-Anang, Ghana

I sat beneath
The star-flecked dome of heav'n,
And watched the moon
Sail silently
And patiently
Along her course.

She did not fret
Nor seem to care
What Nature had
In store for her;
Just silently
She smiled
Amidst the clouds on high.

And then,
O Africa,
Land of the great Pharaohs
And the vast pyramids
With strange architectural laws,
My fatherland,
I thought me then
That, like the moon,
Thou, too, hast spread thy sail!
But whither bound,
O Africa,
Oh, whither bound?
Backward?
To days of drums
And festal dances in the shade
Of [sun kissed] palms;

Backward?
To untutored days
When maid was ever chaste
And lad abhorred unhallowed ways
For dread of ancient gods;
Backward?
To dark thatched huts
Where kindness reigned
And solace dwelt,
Backward, to SUPERSTITION?

Or forward?
Forward! To what?
The slums, where man is dumped
upon man;
Where penury
And misery
Have made their hapless homes,
And all in dark and drear?
Forward! To what?
The factory
To grind hard hours
In an inhuman mill,
In one long ceaseless spell?

Forward! To what?
To the reeking round
Of medieval crimes,
Where the greedy hawks
Of Aryan stock
Prey with bombs and guns
On men of lesser breed?

Forward, to CIVILISATION?
Forward, to [dustily] tools
And sordid gains,
Proved harbingers
Of mortal strife?

Or forward,
To the crafty laws
Of Adam Smith
That turn the markets upside down
And steel men's hearts
To hoard or burn
The food supplies of half the world
E'en when the other half must starve?

Or backward?
Backward to the primal source
Of ethic qualities:
Man's love of fellow man
And fear of God
Emanating from a chainless soul
Full and frank and free?

The moon sails patiently
And silently
Across a star-flecked sky,
A down predicted path:

Sail cautiously, O Fatherland,
Along thy course well-tried;
But whither bound, O Africa?
Oh, whither bound?

From *Lotus*

Thinking of You

Thanh Hai, Vietnam

I stop my spinning wheel's turning for a moment   And look out the window;
Two song-birds perch
  On the young green branch
Of an orange-tree:
  The hen in black and white
Close beside her mate
  Whose beak ruffles
His spouse's feathered form.
  The flowers on the branch
Are freshly opened
  A chaptet of flowers
Caresses their brows.
  The newly-wedded pair, I think,
  Look lovingly at the heady flowers.
Seeing them, my thoughts
  Fly far afield,
The distaff falls from my hand unnoticed,
  The blooms send a pang
Through my heart, and despite myself,
  Tears start to my eyes,
Do you remember, my friend
  How we spoke of love
When the orange-blossom
  Was in bloom; how,
Beneath those same orange trees
  I plucked a golden fruit
And gave it you
  Who left to join the columns . . .
Three autumns have come and gone.
  The oranges ripen
And the orange trees bloom again:

  The songsters left
To return with the flowers.
  Pining for you,
Often look out of the door,
  And my distaff
Gets twisted and warped
Mother tells me to
  Do my hair.
This is far from my thoughts.
  Who is there
For me to please?
  Who's eye is
There to catch?
  I peer in the old mirror
And see only myself.
  I read your first letter anew—
  The blue ink fresh still,
But no picture comes
  Of your hand's quick lingers
Or your warm sweet smile . . .
  This morning
I stop my spinning wheel's turning for a moment   I look at the branch
Of the orange tree,
  I hear the songbirds
Sing in unison.
 O, my beloved
I am waiting for you
  As the orange tree
Awaits the spring
  To flowery

From *Lotus*

Hymn of Spring
Thanh Hai, Vietnam

You are already with us, spring!
Yet you should not have returned so soon
For have I not today walked without respite
To hear the rapturous song of spring?

O, the tunes that are sung in village and alley,
By countless beings, gushing from every brook and river,
An impetuous surge, overwhelming the enemy and trampling his—
murderous hand
To win their daily rice!

O, such tunes resounding through the liberated land
Where the light of day already pierces the shadows.
They come running from every red hillside
And from the green fields stirring in the breeze,
Unfurling and vibrating with hope,
Wherever flies the banner of the Revolution!

And the song which our silver-haired comrade is humming,
He who has shed so many tears at our side!

From high on the hillside, his glance takes in
The magnificent spectacle of springtime.
We have grown up in battle, and victory is near!

O this hymn of spring,
How heady it is, and how sweeping!
Is it the voice of a flag flying,
Or the voice of the trumpet that calls,
Or the voice of the surging of humanity,
The rising tide of the Revolution?

O hymn of spring, you are also the song of my heart;
O spring this morning, I still await you,
Yet it seems that already you have been with us a long time,
For have I not today walked without respite
To hear the rapturous song of spring?

From *Lotus*

The Sea in the Night
Vuong Linh, Vietnam

Whose is this lantern disguised as a cluster of cold stars,
Which, twinkling, calls the sea to rush inshore?
It flows, the sea, glimmering on the crest of the waves,
Like a cloud of glow-worms dancing on a slope.
From on high, stars, thinking they see other stars, their friends,
Dart with all haste towards the marine deep.
There is a little fish who, swimming at random,
Thinks he spies a good prey and hastens to seize it.
The stars shatter in an instant into a thousand fragments
On the crest of the foaming, swashing, lapping waters.
Whose is that boat casting its net on a deserted shallow
Its outline drowned in those of a high mountain?
There then remains, sparkling, only an eye of fire
Flaming on the marine expanse in the deep night.
There is a young soldier who, stars in his eyes,
Second by second, follows the sea in its colourful variations.
The mountains and water, he feels them enclosed in his young heart,
And the moment is sweet as when love dawns.
The ground, he feels it firm beneath his firmly-planted feet,
And in the night already moist with dew, he holds his head high . . .

Translated from the Vietnamese.

From *Lotus*

The Lamp and the Mill

Muʿin Bseiso, Palestine

"...and the poet returned, carrying
no cross or slogans . . . nor the mirrors on
which he embroidered his wounds, and
which burdened his shoulders . . . and
in spite of the locked
passages big and small, he stretches his hand
above them to greet the [splendid] new that
goes to the heroic land he loves."

Still you,
And my lamp on that wound of yours
And your dagger-like, flying name
Is before you wherever you go,
Engraved on all the big passages
And the small,
And a hand is being buried, like an axe, into your back.
And on every march...
"The snakes" have "the big gate"
and "the devils young", "and many flocks,"
Change your lamp, night does not conceal it,
Nor will the mirrors' worshippers come to rescue it.
The lamp does not eat its light.
Oh, if only night squeezed
Even one drop of oil, for small lamps
Still you
And my lamp that wound of yours
When they tilled the land, you tilled,
And when they planted it, you planted

"The olive forest" never gave you
The oil that could fill your lamp
"They cursed" forest and land
But you never cursed.
Go then and plant new
forests and trees,
And may night fall not
In the scorching heat of noon
"And the mills" that have lived
For long generations on your corn
Fed all the "Locusts of the Earth",
Denied you the weight of a grain.

You are not "Samson"
Nor is your beloved "Delilah"
Let her grind, and go to cut
Stones to build "new mills"
Not in new lands.
You did not bleed as the disc of the sun
To look for new land
The volcanoes that die out
Are not abandoned by "big fires,".

Translated by Dr. Shafik Megally.

From *Lotus*

The Green Rock
Bouna Boukary Dioura, Mali

To those upon whom the rains weep.
To those whose motto is: to live and toil
To those whom the winds sweep
Clad in their simplicity
To those whom the sun tans deep
Untamed their eyes, their hearts the hearts of lions
I say: "Courage" for in your hands our lives you keep.
Behold! For we were told one day
A barren rock to spray
Until it turned green,
Hard is the barren rock.
But when it's green 'tis seen to live forever.
The slothful stood aside
And on and on "Tis madness", they would say
And yet we started the same day;
For four years and one 'twas endless toil
But when the rock was covered with mossy soil
It was midnight, midnight in September
And we gave it a name to remember: Mali.

At dawn the witch-doctors,
Who once parasites were called,
In ringing choir sang and told
The coming day would be like none before.
And truly it was: Rebirth for evermore.

Witch-doctor, you who once did sing
In raucous tone
Of Koras and of guitar string,

Your song "a warning note"
For in it you did say that we were black
And black we are indeed on this green day
The first of many a wondrous day
That God has e`er made before;
Come my friend, walk with us on our way
For our rock is hard and lives for evermore.

Hymn of my country
Hymn of my green-clad rock
Awaken each dawn of day.
To you my ancestors.
Victims and martyrs
Of the bird of prey
With iron talons,

We bless you for your blessings,
We bless you for your stubborn power
An o'er your graves we'll shed a shower of tears.
As for you, my son, my brother
You'll live to see another day
When I am gone away.
'Tis now I would have spoken
To tell you that the gates of life to me were open
For I'm a witness and did see the year nineteen-sixty

And I've a message to convey,
I your witch-doctor, your messenger
Wish to say: let this my message be your totem.

Speak not of the coming day,
'Tis here ablaze with sunlight
Heed not the ones who sneer.
Work, for death is near
And gives no warning; it is not like the rain
With thunder and lightning
To say it comes again.
Make right and duty your guiding light.

For if you seek your right alone y
You would be baser clay
Or only duty without right
You'd be unworthy of the light of day.
Rise with the sun
Set with the sun
For the sun is steady and ends what is begun.

To you all, to us all on this green rock
To those who have passed away
To those who tread the thorny way
To those who will come one day
I say: "Good fortune, fare thee well
Good fortune too
[To] those who see and tell.

From *Lotus*

It is There That We Were Born
Marcelino Dos Santos, Mozambique

To my brother

- 1 -

The land of our birth
Has been there as far back
As time itself.
Our ancestors
Were born
And lived on this same land;

It is as if the blades of grass filled with life
Were the veins of a body proud and tall
A red and liquid fragrance of the soil
And trees and granite rocks so straight
Their arms embrace the soil

In the course of their daily toil
Shaping the fertile stones
Of a world to be started anew
They trace in every colour
The great design of life.

- 2 -

It is here too
That you
And I were born,

Hot land
Of the rising sun

Green land
Of the fields of plenty
Tender land
Of the welcoming arms

It is to us
That this land has been given
Given, filled with life
And loving anguish.

- 3 -

We grew, lulled to sleep
By the song of the Chirico bird
And budding thus amidst the human vale
Our feelings deep gave life
To fertile waves of crystal.

And when the wind
Whips the skies

And the sword falls back
Tearing into flesh
And horror taints
The cruel mien.

Our love never wavers
This is the land
Where we were born,

Her suffering
Is our wound

And the cloud of bitter poison of today
Is but a moment of pain
Which the rain will wash away
Ours is a land of hope
Open to the frank embrace.

In the furrow of the ancient footsteps
Unfettered circles shine
And like younger brothers
Of a bygone age
We carry in our arms
The heritage of our ancestors.

And with the very fibres of our hearts
We shall continue the human task
The great design of life.

Translated by Nihad A. Salem.

From *Lotus*

Song for Jerusalem, War and Revolution

Fadel El-Azzawi, Iraq

— FIRST SONG —

Jerusalem is a book read in the house of dreams
Jerusalem is the garden of my house in Baghdad
Jerusalem is a poem written in free verse
Jerusalem is peace
Jerusalem is all the wars waged for the sake of the future,
Jerusalem is a path leading to God
Jerusalem is God's path leading to me
Jerusalem is I.

— SECOND SONG —

The hawk slumbering in the valley of the winds
Has a body as fast and fierce as the wind
I wander in the valley of the winds
Looking in the dictionary of war for he who is absent,
He comes, he raises his cup to the wind
I write poems for the mud swept away by the winds
And compose dreams about the continents of the wind
Was the hawk a woman in league with the wind
Talking of the children of the wind?

I recognize your joys as they lift you up O my week
Do you recognize my sorrows as they bring about my fall?
The trees sing. The children of the sea dive towards the moon
Come and ask the strangers of History: wine for the powers that be,
Thoughts for the sirens.

The poet interned in the hospital of the words
A savage going to war and Israel dies at his door.
Israel is a slain horse
Glumly shutting in the night of revolution
The gates leading to a swamp of peace
And the dagger sinking in my heart misses its mark.
Oh my people, my people.
Years that are coming from bottled cities
Masks for death. Fertilizers for love. And trees for joy.
What can the wave sing to the shore if it carries
Sulphurous rocks, if it spreads the sands of the world with groans?
Charming is the jungle in a night dress
Laughing in the face of the wave. In distress I look:
Peace that is not peace — a capital of the waters

And the offspring of blonds. Weeping
Hyphenating the words.
Congested silence in the laughter of my forefathers
Shall I dare hold this suspended sea?
Shall I dare voyage in the past of the waves.
A sun in the night comes to my body,
Serving my members.
Bells and the sea with me, (I hear my voice in the uproar)
Calico sails.
A storm like the eyes of the monster in the forest
I dream of the wave and the jungle.

O beach of my days. O queen twinkling in the wind
Where shall I open my palm for the wind.

The generations on the shore boil with anger
Swaying in the machinery of the winds
Confused allies in front of me, drawing lots upon my head, in the wind.

— THIRD SONG —

The night returns to the haven of the king
whose advent is immanent within himself.
I hear Your voice in the future O woman,
O bird of the past, in my stumble,
in the [Six-Day] war,
in the evening of the hour
when the sea gets swallowed up.
The heaven of the Arabs
who are reverting to the idiom
of the desert with me.
There is no funeral of love in my face.
Joyfully you look at the moment, keen as a blade.
For us: the death returning from Samerra.

In the stream of things I sing. The sparrow adventuring and the girls
Swing against the forest, full of glee
The wind on the grass singing
O my homeland, O freedom of my Jerusalem, O my homeland
As a sinking moon in a room of mourning
Your death glows in the branches of time
Gleams around my neck, shimmers in my book of verse,
And in my first love scintillates
O my homeland.

The night flies to the Capital of the third love. I go to war
With the sun and get drunk in the eyes of Moses. I live by the Sea.
I am Sinai. I am the captive of my voice. How shall I sing to war and
what shall I sing?
The desert lies before me.

I cross the night of the defeated cities and the titles
And the sun on my hat, and the peace reigning on the plateau

I breathe the scent of the past
I speak of my folk, gleeful as a sparrow on the coast
As the pregnant days swinging in the execution chambers.

To war I pray. Are you a Jew?
My Gods get farther and farther away in the dry sea.
I carry my anchor on my shoulder. I have
The haven of the Port of the Winds and the poems of Hend Rustum
My caravan has descended by the river: the commandoes of the world
among the branches Arafat Yasser Arafat
I drown in the revolution and the voices.
I shut my eyes and accept to go to war
As if I had the peace with me.

The night comes to the king of the sun who is lounging outside himself.
I hear your voice in the past, O child of the man in love,
O Ammar Ben El-Haitham.
In the seven day war the sea becomes accustomed to the Arabic Language
And the desert.
And I return to the sun of the coming king in the [Six-Day] war
A sun of freedom
Rising in my skies.

— FOURTH SONG —

When they started to march upon my cities
Their tongue . . . the tongue of war
Pierced my ears.
But I am the sea . . . ever far away
Ever out of reach.
And in the islands of the martyrs my hand bestows upon the murderers
Their love of air. And I cross with them the muddy roads
Loving my people that hates war. This is my blood.
My homeland is a sky open to the sparrows and the war planes
I was killing alone without joy and without hope
My cry of anguish choked
I was alone. To the water and the gallows.
The island swallowed in gloom,
Waiting for the sword to cross the river and the neck of land
To revive even as the wind revives the exhausted cities.

When they started killing my hand, and dying after me
I knew the hand of love as it confesses
Under the throat of the victim
I am the impossible man
Who travels through time towards the gallows
I am Jerusalem and the gallows
I am love and the gallows
I am war and the gallows
I am peace and the gallows
I am an absolute idiom
I am Jerusalem wherever it may be.

Translated by Shafik Magar.

From *Lotus*

Palestine

Hussein Marawan, Palestine

Glory be to you
Though your wound is all salt and fire
Yesterday there was a slogan here
And thoughts turned in the heads
Tomorrow they will be posed anew
Red, digging a trough for themselves in the bones.

And a thousand morrows will pass
And the jars will be filled
With tears and speeches
And poems and literature covered with spices
And maybe the resolve will melt out of too much dialogue.
Until the curtain is raised
And steel clashes, the wall crashes
And the boots of shame step over your face
The roar arises from the gulf to the Ocean:
No! The light shall not die at the top of the lighthouse
So let the wolf from across the seas come out
And follow in your footsteps
It shall reap nothing but the wind
For victory is born among the claws.

A black-lipped year passes
Turning the water in your eyes into steam
Baring the fangs
Shaking the centre of the earth.
So let the enemies in the infuriated west
Send the rats of Europe and the scum of gambling dives

For the end of every soldier
Protected by a borrowed spear
Is flight and retreat
And let History bear witness
That we shall not wage war
Or take to its black path
Except in defence of our homeland
Against the inroads of a barbarian
Who has run amuck.

The world is turned upside down
So let the earthquake take the flowers of the valley
Let the blade cut short the song of the birds
Let gun powder burn out the eyelashes of children
For on the skulls and destruction
On the mutilated remains of great tyrants
Grow the sparks.
Do not fear, for the sword knocks at every door
So drink the new oil with your bitterness
So that belligerency may flare up in your blood
And unveil your face
For your face today is a blazing flower
And your tightly closed lips are the red rose of victory.

Glory be to you
Though your wound is all salt and fire
Make yourself a shawl of death, of bloody wrath and raging fury
And fill your veins with venom,
And old hate, and bitterness
For despair has flown away

From our Arab people, and our patience has boiled over
And every wrist has a vengeance to wreak
Twisting the dark around the light of day.

Everyone has talked too long about the resolution
About the wing of a green dove covered with freshness
For the sake of numerous teeth
And the eagle refuses to be called a canary
The arrow in the bow has become fed up with waiting
While on the forehead of Jerusalem there is a bonfire and shame

So how long are we going to wait?
While the very stones of the venerable pyramid
Shake with impatience
And the bull snorts in the airport?

Do not grieve, for in every home
There is an arm ready to fight for you
And this commando masked with his cloak
Is the man who has retrieved his backbone

So smile despite everything
For your land is lighted
With a thunderbolt.

Translated by Shafik Magar.

From *Lotus*

The Night
Mazisi Kunene, South Africa

The heart of the earth is covered with weeds,
Darkness descends from the path of the skies.
The black tails of cows shake against the wind
Beating the sea with the fence of dusk.
It is as if people crawl in the islands of the light
He who was as tall as the forest
Creeps on his belly dancing in the embrace of a dream
The wilderness of the earth holds its head in its hands.
The little children have fled to their holes
The hole is a great home of the ancestral spirits
Where grief hangs above like ribs
Where the great day sends its forerunners
The white hair, the white hair of the sun.
You will also carry the cripple across the streams.

From *Lotus*

There is a Place
Mazisi Kunene, South Africa

There is a place
Where the dream is dreaming us
We who are the shepherds of the stars.
It stands towering as tall as the mountains
Spreading its fire over the sun
Until when we take one great stride
We speed with the eagle on our journey.

It is the eagle that plays its wings on our paths
Wakening another blind dream.
Together with other generations hereafter
They shall dream them like us.
When they wake on their journeys they will say
Someone somewhere is dreaming in the ruins.

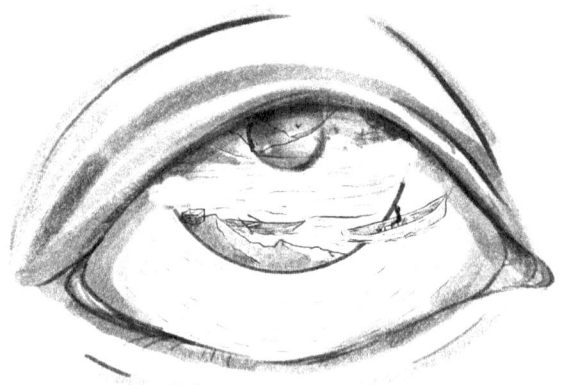

From *Lotus*

Songs to Drive Away the "Gongon"

Oneisimo Silveira, Portuguese Colonies

In the circle of the eve
Papa told of busy cities far
Every eve when there was naught to eat
As many eves as there are days in the year.

In the circle of the eve
Mama promised shirts all new
For the feast of May in Salamantsa
As many promises Mama made
As shirts she ne'er was able to bring.

In the circle of the eve
Bellies thick with crawling worms,
In the circle we did sing
"O moon give us some stew
And some milk we'll give to you."

Dreams of slaves who think they're free
Dreams of children who think the moon to deceive

But the slave ship is here
But the slave ship is here

The Island dies of famine by day
Every day
The Island rises from the depth of its life by night
Every night.

O plaintive voices of guitars
O plaintive voices astray
What can you have to say to the stars?

The mothers' breasts run dry
The human muscles twist and cry
And what of cribs?

O voices black
Voices of masks all streaked with pain
Life beckons you to sing for the earth

For the earth
For the earth
For the earth

Translated by Nihad A. Salem

From *Lotus*

A Palestinian Wedding

Ahmed Dahbour, Palestine

On the day that fled from the heart of summer
A woman gave birth
Children smiled to the new-born babe who came
And said: "We'll give him Kamel for a name."
On the day that fled from the heart of summer
The fruits went ripe, and the hymn of a [hummingbird] was heard

And Kamel came
They bore him on their palms on the green boughs of sorrow
He bathed in glow, and they said: "There is the light."

Who can tell whilst fire—a torrential rain
And the whistling bullets of revenge came forth from his hand
Whether he drew his will in the Sacred Land?
Whether he larked to its stones . . . and how?
Whether he blew the slanting trees erect?
– They did not tell much of the Sacred Land
– They did not tell of talking stones and trees that fell
The wise youth said
"The long-awaited will save us with the sword
But lo! we looked . . .
And he himself was the sword.

"Death? Art thou afraid of death . . . O Son of Haifa"
And went on to tell of orphans
And did say even more:
"The world is a family of famished orphans
And Palestine this very year
Is Paradise beneath whose stones the mines down
As for the coming morrow . . ."
And earth lit up in his dark face like a sun.

On the day that fled from the heart of summer
He did not shed a tear of tenderness nor of fear
But the secret scent of sacred streams of Paradise
Cut like a blade in the blade-green heart.
He bathed in glow . . . and they said: "Here is the light."

On the day that fled from the heart of summer
We bid friend Kamel good-bye
Said I: "We did cry?"
If so I beg forgiveness of our camps engulfed in bitter cold

I beg forgiveness of the patience o'er a score of years
I beg forgiveness of the defeated who on us throw the blame
I beg forgiveness of my mother
As she betimes, my crying brother's children, sings to sleep
In her sweet voice and says:

"The man of Gaza was carried and was gone
To the land of Gaza"
"Hurry with you, young O Safadite
The Son of Haifa long before has gone and was gone"
The children smiled to the new-born babe who came
And said: "We'll give him Kamel for a name"
Glory to the day that fled from the heart of summer.

Translated by Dr. Angele Boutros.

From *Lotus*

5 Poems from the Position

Iicro Ando, Thailand

—Position 1—

This I know—
That at the far end of a vaguely illumined wilderness
Stretching outside my consciousness
There is a skull
Of beautiful silver grey
And that from the eternally dark sockets of its eye
A quiet flame is [rising].

—Position 9 —

The hand holding up a lamp—
                        The valley of darkness
                        Roaring and whirling
                                    Under it.

—Position 21—

All the women he painted are crying—
In the unevenness of thickly-laid paints.
In every corner of his picture there streams
Like a whisper filled in the night sky, a dark, lonely sob.
Glossy pale pink and yellow brown distinct from black and green
And such a noble elegance along the line of breasts!
"What's the use of being alive? Why didn't I kill
Myself when I was in Paris, when I was young . . . ?
The crowd squirming around all these pictures
Never notice this soliloquy of his.
All the women he painted are crying—".
"He may not live much longer," his friends whisper.

— Position 30 —

My heavy heavy body
Exposes its sinews of grief
Like a large chunk of meat on a dresser
In my heavy heavy head
A flower of lead blooms
And it won't shrink, it won't wither
On my heavy heavy anger—
On the sunsetting sea, a black arm of crane falls
Between my heavy heavy sleep
And in the crack of a ruined building a cricket is chirping
O, my heavy heavy half-drunkenness
My heavy heavy fever.

— Position 33 —

A white
Conical flower
Trembling faintly
Alone
In a room at night
—I do not know anything

The black
Eyes of desire
Coining out of the forest
Stand
Outside the door
—You may do just as you
want

A Skull
Sleeping under the wall
Cut off
By the shadow of the world
Together with fallen bottles
—I am left only to dream.

From *Lotus*

A Butterfly
Iicro Ando, Thailand

Then, surely you laughed,
Like one starting on a journey to somewhere,
Already away from me, and yet being much closer for that,
As if to print your image on my eyes.

I never forget—you, in purple,
Tall, perpendicularly,
Making your whole body heave with the soft rays
Like a large butterfly breathing.

Only around the spot you were standing
Trees in buds became transparent and calm
And made the town of dust and crowds far away.

Then, surely, you laughed.
At that instant I stood still and gulped . . .
Trying to remember you with that smile.

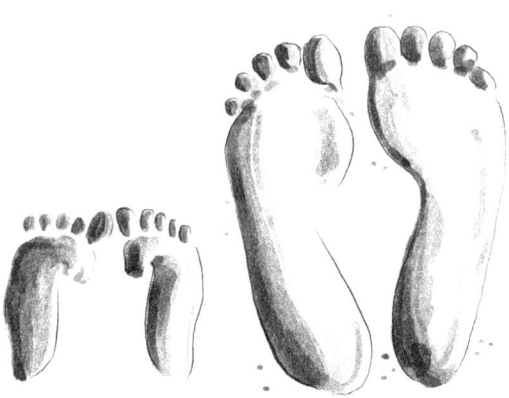

From *Lotus*

Separation
Tran Huu Thung, Vietnam

There are evenings,
Standing in the centre of Hanoi,
As warm as a mother's heart,
When I see half of it tremble
And I thrust out my hands to prop it up!

There are evenings,
Standing in the windy plain,
Amidst recently allotted green [rice fields] stretching as far as the stork can fly
When I see on half of the plain,
[Rice plants] withered and the soil parched.
Why is my heart burning for the fight against drought?

There are evenings,
Under the roof of a snug little thatch-hut
Around a basket of hot sweet potatoes
And in good company
Why do I still long for the southern half?

There are evenings
On a river-dike in the moonlight
When a kiss from my sweetheart warms even the sky,
Why is my heart suddenly half frozen
And yearns for the other half?

There are evenings when
Birds fly against the wind
In pairs very high in the blue sky,
Why are their wings like my feet?
Treading on the only half of the land!

So many evenings,
So many
I feel my heart broken
Half of it is missing:
The South.

From *Lotus*

Africa my Sister
Mirzo Tursun-Zade, USSR

Who has not heard of her? Angry Africa! Let her drumsaga roll:
Heard of the slave-girl [black], with the brave and the beautiful soul?
Who does not know about Africa, continent black and remote,
Off the main sea-ways, burning in fires that few cared to note?
Who can't recall the great ships that sailed to her green-gold strands

After live goods, after treasures so rich in that marvelous land?
Magnanimous land, whose body—much blacker than ebony wood—
Caught in a flood of betrayal and force, ran crimson with blood.
Paleface-Carnivora put her to torment both body and soul,
All their black deeds in black Africa, who dare erase from the scroll?
Passed by years, passed centuries—under the alien scourge
This land was made into a slave, with the ring of her earring a dirge.

Tears, tears rebellious, as brilliant as diamonds
    are spilled in the tomb—
deeps of the diamond mines, spilled in the shade of the jungle gloom...
Sister, my sister, afar off I saw you there under the moon:
Clouds, sobbing dew down, formed a faint halo—ring round the moon.
Waves of the seas and the oceans beat against cliffs with a roar,
Cliffs of Oppression, and down on the reefs—your tormentors
    they bore.
From the Sahara-heart ousted, that desert of fiery mirage,
Burning in bondage, the Arabs dreamt and they hoped to assuage

Thirst, thirst for freedom, with the far, cooling streams of their Nile—
This was a continent closed to the world, shut off behind prison walls;
But living Africans came to us, answering Spring's wild call—
Birds flew from Africa, seeking the vernal fresh warmth of the north,
Building their nests in the orchards that scented our native earth,
Breathed for a time that long-waited freedom they never could share,

Even forgetting at times the merciless hunter, the snare,
When they were starting back, with our feathered envoys we sent
Word to our friends, to all Africans, words of encouragement.
Passed by years, passed centuries—new times brought some changes to all.

Now between Africa and the world, distances have given way,
Freedom now walks through the world and knows no rest both night and day.
This alien land so strange to us is growing closer than before,
Its many fascinating tongues reveal their secrets more and more.

Now from the world one cannot hide the blood that [freedom fighters] shed,
Each drop aglow with freedom's light, like a shower of sparks caught up and spread.
Now, something new is beginning: the world a new era will see—
Africa! Africa rising at last, in a fight to be free.
Desert no longer, nor jungle that Evil put under a spell;
Look, she's no longer a slave-girl, but heroine no one may quell!
Deep was the grave they prepared her, forever cast Sun into Night;
Rid of the last of her grave diggers, she will enter a kingdom of light

Out in the forests and grassy veldt, where pyramids lift hoary peaks,
Goes on the battle for freedom; of freedom alone Africa speaks.
Question them so: who works in the open for fraternity?
Cairo steps forward and answers:
It is me! It is me!

Who decided the land of his fathers to free?
Head raised with pride, then Algeria spoke:
It was me! It was me!
Who was the first to be master in his own house?

From far off latitudes came a voice from Accra:
It was me! It was me!
Which is our joyous isle, sweeter than perfumed fountain?

From the Canaries, a soft breeze sings:
It is me! It is me!
Who cries out in their struggle 'Help me, my tribal brothers!!?'

The colonial people answer in chorus:
It is me! It is me!
Who sews shrouds for the enemy?
Are more shrouds needed?

Then the great ocean roars:
It is me! And they are!
Then come the voices of field and of city and many a sea—
All of the world calls this answer to Africa, it seems to me:
'Africa, sister we love, I can hear you, I can hear you still;
All, we shall all march together that road towards love and goodwill.

When your new life is in flower, won the great battle for liberty.
Then you will answer us, brothers fraternal:
Here I am, friends. It is me!

From *Lotus*

To a Child of my Native Land

Marcelino Dos Santos, Mozambique

- I -

Barefoot child
Child of my native land
Green is the world, and bitter too
in its desperate [loincloth],
and the negro bent upon the sand.
A black child
just like you
was murdered
broken
on the fleshless mire
of racial hatred.
A black child
just like you
whose eyes were green
as the rising sun
whose whistle was purple
as that of the bird of dawn.
A black child
who ran barefoot
just like you
opening his innocent arms
to the sonorous arch of dawn.

- II -

It was there, far away,
O child of my native land
It was there, far away
on lands
way beyond the oceans
There, far away
on lands
quickened to life
by sons of Africa
captured
in slave boats of old.
It was there, far away
on the American land
built with the hand
of black slaves
from Africa.
That Emmett Till
a black child like you
a child of fourteen
whose whistle sounded purple
as that of the bird of dawn
became mud,
with his tortured face,
and his blood
cemented
the blood-tinted lake of the race.

- III -

And yet
there
the sky is blue
yet there,
the star is a prayer
and the holy day
rises with crowns and festivities
in the square.
But the negro
is but a road
without gold, without bread
he is a road of fire
for the hatred of Ku-Klux-Klan.
He is an arch of flowers
flowering in pain
desperate and broken
by night and death.

- IV-

Child of my native land
Emmett Till
ran barefoot
just like you
he was fourteen
just like you
he took the moon in his arms
just like you
and now
he lies ['neath] the earth
that his forefathers quickened to life
broken in the fleshless mire
of racial hatred.
Forget not ever
O child of my native land
You
whose eyes open
Upon the disfigured space
of a world that's green and bitter too,
That Emmett Till
was murdered.
Yet what he felt remains
scattered in your fate.
Emmett Till
died lynched,
But his blood came to cement
The blood-tinted lake of the race.

Translated by Nihad Salem.

From *Lotus*

The Gobi
Yavoukhoulan, Mangolia

Gobi,
It is the Gobi.
The Gobi, sometimes,
Like a boiling pot,
Makes stifling steam,
Grasshoppers and crickets
jump like popcorn.

Gobi,
It is the Gobi,
The Gobi in truth,
Has no rivers.
The Gobi itself
Takes the place of rivers.
My Gobi however
Is a vast, vast land,
Where harvests stand in a row
Beneath the burning sun.
The Gobi harvest, in truth,
Is borne by camels.

Gobi,
It is the Gobi.
The Gobi in truth
Is the sea and sand,
The Gobi dunes
Make waves of sand.
My Gobi however
Is a vast, vast steppe
Where the melody of song
Rings
Beneath the [crescent] moon.
It is the melodious songs,
It is the women of the Gobi.

Gobi,
It is the Gobi,
The Gobi sometimes
Like fresh-dawn milk
Turns cold.
Stretches all in yellow
Like the heart I love.

Gobi,
It is the Gobi.
Gobi in truth
Is the cradle of the earth.
The Gobi land, covered
With sand,
Since the dawn of time.
My Gobi however
Vast as the sky
Is rich
With natural wealth
It is the Gobi.
Whose oil we take.

Gobi
The Gobi, in truth
Is the panel of the earth
The mirage of Gobi
Maker of madness.
That is why my Gobi
Is known throughout the world
Plan of an imaginary town
Sketched in the mirage.
Let us instead
Draw a plan
Of new towns there to build.

Gobi,
It is the Gobi.

Translated by Nihad A. Salem.

From *Lotus*

Jaffa
Rasha Hussein, Palestine

The marijuana pipes in Jaffa scatter sleep
The sterile roads are big with boredom and with flies
And Jaffa's heart is silent, covered with a stone
In the streets of heaven the moon is being mourned
Jaffa is moonless then
Jaffa is blood upon a stone.

Jaffa whose breasts once flowed with orange milk
Now thirsts . . . She whose waves had fed the rain.
Jaffa who broke the days upon these sands
Stands with dead arms which died when her back broke
Jaffa who was a garden a bloom with men
Has now become a marijuana den which sleep now spreads

I was in Jaffa clearing her brows of rats
Lifting the debris off the kneeless dead
Burying the stars 'neath dust and walls
Pulling out bullets from her bones . . . feeding on anger
I choose a murdered lock of hair, I burn it and inhale the smoke
Just like tobacco . . . and I rest when weary moments came . . .

From *Lotus*

Earth Awaits
Paul Charles Atangana, Cameroon

The cloud, soaked with water, slowly writhes
Passing through false azures
Of shades both gold and pure;
Fires burn the songs, and the world mourns.

O rains which linger in the bursting sky,
Break forth, for earth awaits!
The hill, the green mounds, the prairie and the vale
Lend echoes gay
To the rumbling, dying wind,

O trees that bend to the breeze of weather fine,
Stretch forth, for earth awaits!
The fields cover the brow of hill and plain,
Quite soon, new ears of corn
Will stand in rows of nine
Within the laden barns that will be full.

O corn which grows along the winding paths,
Dry up for earth awaits!
Flowers of all shades adorn the valleys
The woods are full of routes,
With fields of birds, with songs
With rowdy towns,

O beauties which revel in the sun and spring
Live on, for earth awaits!
Life fills the days with grandiose feasts
The eves with sweet repasts,
The gay moms with echoes
The madmen laugh at all, at proof and things.

O friends who laugh at hands that stretch forth
Laugh, for earth awaits!
The heart of all great men whom fortune
Hopes will find peace
At the end of thick airs
Already the white birds set upon the moon

O humans who wish to see the devil's throne
Go on, the earth awaits!
Earth is the cradle of all that breathes,
Of all that grows;
Of all that turns to green.
She is the grave of man and his empire
O years whose echoes stretch to dimmest past
Escape, for earth awaits!

(Extracts from "Tremors")
Translated by Nihad A. Salem.

From *Lotus*

I am Athirst
Popular Folklore from Egypt

I am athirst, O young girls!
Guide me to the fountain,

Give me to drink from your water—
It is water of the Nile.

Assyout has become the city
Where the ships come to harbour.

Give me a draught of water
To satisfy the sick heart.

And why are your eyes so fair
And mine are so foul.

The lame girl begs the goldsmith
To make heavy the anklet.

A thirsty man asks for water
The river is far, is far.

Such a man longs for freedom
Such a man longs for songs.

From *Lotus*

The Dove
Popular Folklore from Egypt

I climbed to the roof of the house
To look upon my dove.

I found my dove drinking
From the canal of another.

I cried from the depth of my passion:
"O my dove!"
She said "Your time is past—look for another!"

From *Lotus*

I am Athirst

Popular Folklore from Egypt

I am athirst, O young girls!
Guide me to the fountain,

Give me to drink from your water—
It is water of the Nile.

Assyout has become the city
Where the ships come to harbour.

Give me a draught of water
To satisfy the sick heart.

And why are your eyes so fair
And mine are so foul.

The lame girl begs the goldsmith
To make heavy the anklet.

A thirsty man asks for water
The river is far, is far.

Such a man longs for freedom
Such a man longs for songs.

From *Lotus*

The Dove
Popular Folklore from Egypt

I climbed to the roof of the house
To look upon my dove.

I found my dove drinking
From the canal of another.

I cried from the depth of my passion:
"O my dove!"
She said "Your time is past—look for another!"

From *Lotus*

Letter to the People of My Motherland

Hamid Wafi, Sudan

Cold is the night, but my heart never be cold.
How can it be cold?
In my country, the heartland of Africa,
The dirty lackeys of Johnson and Kosygin
Are swaggering arrogantly.
They grab away the food from the children's mouths.
Like filthy rats,
And vermin,
Nibbling away the wealth of my motherland,
And gnawing at the glory of her history.
Cold is the night, but my heart never be cold.

Oh, my people, though far away you are in the distant land,
My blood is infused with your warm radiance in this cold night.
Lost in thought, I am meditating over your image.
Like you, I am longing for the rising sun.
I sing with all my heart,
How I wish, my people, that you could hear my song,
Sing I shall for your reddened heart and
Sing I shall for your victory.
Somewhat timid I am, and you may laugh over this,
But still I shall sing.
On my desk, my people,
My melodies will never turn cold.

Oh, my people,
Can you hear my voice?
From China, the land of Mao Tse-tung,
To you, the wind is carrying my voice.
Mao Tse-tung, like a giant, embraces the people.
As strong as steel,
And like courageous eagle flying in the sky of revolution,

Against the West wind, he makes the challenge,
He destroys the world of tyranny
And smashed are those who give no thought to the people.
Rebellion will create a world of the people.

Oh, my people, though far away you are in the distant land,
To you, thousands of red songs of my heart,
Thousands of Marches I want to dedicate.
Oh, my people, though on the soil Of China we are,
You should always keep in mind:
We are preparing to make a revolution,
And once this revolution breaks out,
Strong will it be like a gigantic current.
Its basis, oh my people,
Is the thought of Mao Tse-tung,
And its mainstay, oh my people,
The teachings of Mao Tse-tung.
Its path of advance, oh my people,
To us, Mao Tse-tung has pointed out.
Along it we shall always forge ahead.

Oh, my people,
Though on the soil of China we are,
You we shall never forget,
Oh my people, here we have come
Not to forget you for even one day.
Mao Tse-tung teaches us:
The people, and the people alone,
Are the creators of history.
Mao Tse-tung teaches us:
The road the oppressed people should take
Is that of Revolution.

Oh my people, you should understand:
Glory belongs to freedom fighters and to revolutionaries,
Glory belongs to the bright red morning rays of Mao Tse-tung.
Away with the stupid rats in one sweep.
Rejoice, people of the motherland,
Dignity of man will no longer be sold on the slave markets.
Rejoice, people of the motherland,
On the horizon has emerged
The bright red morning rays.

Oh, people of my country,
We shall never forget you,
How can we forget you?
We are living on the soil of fraternal China,
In the land of Mao Tse-tung's China,
From which issued words of profound truth.
They were the words of Mao Tse-tung,
Oh great thinker, source of truth.
And what did our teacher say?

He said,
The stupid reactionaries, imperialists, and their accomplices the despicable revisionists,
And the armies of the western world,
Together with all their new weapons
Are all paper tigers,
Not to be helped by armed force or atomic bombs.
Comrades,
The fighting will of the masses is the most powerful weapon,
The people know clearly
What road they should take.

Oh, people of my country,
Let us keep well in mind, the martyrs, heroes,
Who valiantly died in battle.
Oh, people of my country,
Let us grasp tight our weapons
And advance to wipe out the enemies,
To wipe out Johnson, Wilson, Kosygin
And all those aggressive-natured people.
Oh, people of my country,
Our song of march
Is the fighting will of the masses,
This is the most powerful weapon.

May 1967, Peking

From *The Call*

Letter to My Brother

Sutojo, Indonesia

Pearl of the equator,
How I miss you;
Your Lawu, Wilis, Merapi, Merabu,
Sindoro-Sumbing, [Tangkuban Prahu],
The mountain ranges,
All my comrades
And you too, Periangan,
Kindling spark of the struggle.

The wind wafts over the trees,
The misty mountains are far below.
Since [communist] blood runs in your veins
It is not difficult for you to ascend.

I know not where you are today,
But I am sure that
You and father have taken up arms together.
Should this letter reach you
Please convey it to the whole family.

Whilst class-struggle becomes more acute,
We must never forget
The red banner we defend.
As the enemy has raised his sword,
We must raise ours too
And attack!

Class-hatred is burning on,
And blazes everywhere —
In the huts of the peasants,
And also in the prisons.

Today our country is at war;
I shall surely take up arms
With you, my brother,
And join the battle.

From *The Call*

Songs of Palestinian Guerrillas

'Fedayee'

Fedayee1[1]! Oh my homeland,
The land of my ancestors.
Fedayee! Oh my people,
My immortal people!
With will for victory, with fire, with burning revenge,
With the longing of my blood for my homeland, my country,
I've climbed the mountains and waged the struggle,
I've overcome difficulties and broken the chains!

Fedayee!
By the thunder of the wind,
The fire of the gun,
And the will of the people,
I carry on the struggle!
Palestine, my home,
Palestine, land of heroism.
A Fedayee,
Under our flag I swear
By my people, the fire of my wounds and my land,
I'll live a Fedayee, I'll die a Fedayee,
Till I go back to my homeland,
A Fedayee!

We listen to Chairman Mao's teachings,
And make mountains bow to our will,
Southern slope planted with peaches, apricots, pears,
Northern hill sown with tung oil trees and tea.
In the valleys green pines sing in the breeze,
In our yard leafy bamboos etch a fine pattern,
Clothed in emerald are now all former bare mounds,
Over the hillside, shimmer flowers and fruit like rainbow clouds.

---

1 Fedayee, a Palestinian commando fighter.

From *The Call*

A Hundred Mountain Ranges

Hanh Can, Vietnam

On the vermilion dirt tracks
I've been battling the US foe three full years.
Ranging these mounts far and wide.

The nearer ones, our guns have rolled through,
The farther ones, our cannons, our feet have travelled over.

At midnight our batteries roar the jungle out of sleep,
A hundred mountain ranges awaken.
Yonder US barracks sizzle in a blaze,
Here jungle and mounts cheer and artillery rumbles.

From *The Call*

Uncle's Verses

Ngoc Khuyen, Vietnam

Who is reciting a poem of Uncle by the pass
In the jungle on the border in the evening
glow on the Truong Son?
The marching troops rock mount and hill,
The inspiring lines winging their steps.
The shadow of guns is woven into the blue sky,
The rhymes of verses are in tune with the
"Long March" air.
Uncle's words breathe vigour into us
And speed us up hill and down dale toward
the enemy.

(Ngoc Khuyen)

From *The Call*

Namibia, You Will Be Liberated

H. Kaluenja, Namibia

For nearly a century,
You were in bondage.
Your children, humiliated and starved,
And their history was distorted.

Today they have risen in arms,
In order to redeem you,
Motherland, Namibia,
The land of the inconquerable.

Your mountains, deserts and plains
Know one great truth —
Your sons and daughters,
Persistent and dauntless, keep on fighting.

The peaks of Eros and Brandberg know that
Their caves will always give shelter to us,
Who are the heroic guerrillas,
The heirs of our early liberators.

Our heroes who fell for the motherland
Knew that we shall rise,
And defend you, Namibia,
The land of the valiant fighters!
Namibia, you will be liberated,
Not only because you are beautiful,
But because you deserve
Your right to be a free land.

Your liberation should pave
The way to social equality
And economic prosperity
For all your children.

Namibia, you are beautiful,
And you deserve liberation,
So that the imperialists' humiliation and enslavement
Will come to an end.

From *The Call*

Three Zimbabwean Poems

Zimbabwe

How Long Shall It Be

How long shall it be that we shall suffer?
How long shall it be that we shall be oppressed?
We're tired of drinking tears —
For how long shall we endure this?

Trees rest themselves in winter
When they shed their leaves and have a short respite,
And in spring
They put on their leaves.
With abundant rains,
They will soon be in full blossom.

The children we bear are
The rightful heirs of our motherland Zimbabwe.
But today in dire misery they live
And have nothing they can call their own.
Racism and settlerism, capitalism and imperialism,
Decide, unwilling to accept it they may be,
their fate.

We have no land
On which we can live in peace.
Here and there are hot ashes.
Our hands and feet are full of blisters.

Where shall we go?
From every home and house
We are driven away;
From every piece of land
We are chased away;

In courts,
We are sentenced without cause.
In all places,
We are bullied without reason.

All the wealth of our land has been taken away,
And squandered by the plunderers.
They are eating the fat of our land,
Whilst we have no right to anything.
They are fat like pigs
Whilst we are lean as withered petals.

They lord it over us
And we are strangled with fetters.
In the land of our forefathers,
We possess nothing —
Not even human dignity.

Great Chaminuka, merciful mountain,
Won't you hear our cry?
Great Monomotapa*,
Hear our cry!
How long shall it be
That Zimbabweans must suffer?
How long shall it be
That we Zimbabweans must be oppressed?
How long shall it be?

---

* The old thirteenth century kingdom in Zimbabwe.

Rise Up Angry

Brothers and sisters,
Why should you have hands
If you can't use them
To break the chains
Of oppression and exploitation?

Brothers and sisters,
Why should you have eyes
If you can't see
That the country is being raped and plundered
By forces of oppression and exploitation?

Brothers and sisters,
Why should you have ears
If you can't hear cries
From jails, prisons, detention and concentration camps?

Brothers and sisters,
What crime have our people committed,
To live in such a plight
In the country of their birth?

Brothers and sisters,
Take up the challenge!
Rise up in arms
And fight for the liberation of your people!

Brothers and sisters,
Join the national liberation forces!
Rise up angry   And liberate Zimbabwe!

The Enemy are Paper Tigers

It was only one day
When I realized there'd be a day
Of freedom in our country Zimbabwe;
The day we ambushed our ferocious enemy.

These white racists,
Had seemed to be the most ferocious
enemy,
But today they are paper tigers,
And we are valiant tiger-hunting fighters.

We decided to lay an ambush,
So I hid behind a thick bush.
The enemy came along the highway,
And my heart was beating with desire.

Pa-pa-pa — the commander started to fire,
I was the second with desire to fire.
The enemy tried to fire back,
But their struggle was in vain.

I stopped firing to listen,
And only heard the bullets from our LMG.
Hey man! The LMG was so effective,
The enemy were dying like rats.
I fired again — da-da-da-da . . . da-da-da-da
This time the enemy never returned the fire.
I knew they were dead;
We had won the battle.

We made a fine retreat from the ambush area,
With high morale — singing revolutionary songs.
In the hands of the freedom fighters,
The well-equipped enemy had shown their
true colours of paper tigers.

It was on such a victorious' day,
For every countryman to know this truth:
It's only the armed Zimbabwean people

Who can liberate the country:
WE ARE OUR OWN LIBERATORS!

From *The Call*

HOPE AND ENDURANCE

Martyrs
Conte Saidon Tidiany, Guinea

The burning blood continues to flow
On the black sand of roads.
Blood flows and fertilizes the black earth.
The obscure dead pass, and pass once more,
In the memory of leaves and skies.
The executioners have sung their song and kept quiet,
They had forgotten our dead frothing at the mouth.
The black sand of mourning days,
Will remember implacable evenings,
Faces of flint buried in heaps,
In the deep hole of eternal crimes.
Sadist deathly hands,
In a dispersed and renewed gesture,
Have struck breathlessly,
On the prodigious wings
Of the people of universal front.
The black sand of mourning days
Will remember the songs of the abyss,
The far off tam-tams,
The circular rhythms in the moonlight.
The dead covered with sparks,
Breaking the starless night,
Will appear from the horizons full of disdain.
And on the shore glowing with anger
Immaculate leeches will ring the bell.
Banquets of black entrails 'of the Black,
Armour of parchment of wax,
Fragile and fugitive when facing the burning stone,
Will be shattered like the spider web,
In the fog of the seasons' end.
The night is yesterday.
Tomorrow,   Tomorrow the break of a new day.

From *Lotus*

We Shall Be There
Eustache Prudencio, Dahomey

We lived
Simply
Happily
Since the dawn of time.
We were all brothers
We ate our fruits
and drank our springs,
inhaled the wind of our countryside

We worshipped our Gods,
We sang and danced to them
and bathed in the light of the moon

We lived
Simply
Happily
Since the dawn of time.

And then one day
They landed on our shores
The sharks

And peace was gone
the songs
the dances gone.
They pounced upon our huts
The falcons

As if they did not have enough
of oceans and air

They had to conquer our lands
Why?
But why?
They had
the guns
They had
the alcohol
And most of all
the lies and hate.

Our land was not enough for them
They carried away
Our brothers
Our sisters
Our sons
For other continents

We had to cultivate our fields
To fill their safes;
Our pay
Was humiliation
And violence

It was All Saints Day!
Songs of the sun,
We keep hope
for a better life;
And we danced
and sang
with the rays of the father sun
like we did in Africa
in our forests and clearings

We had a heart of gold
in a chest
that was black
and we taught them
the rhythms and the hot tunes of home.
The negro is so generous
but they sang them
so badly!

And now we sweep
the entire world
with our tam-tams
with the joy of life.
Our laughs are inimitable
because they are dear and frank
because they are pure and beautiful
because our teeth are white and strong.

Our hands are not empty
We shall all go to the rendezvous
of the five continents
with our songs and dances
with our hearts burning
with friendship
with goodness
and with peace
with the genuineness
of our culture.

Not a single finger, no,
Not a finger shall be missing
from the hand of light
which shall hold the torch
of the universal.

From *Lotus*

Solitary Confinement

Faiz Ahmad Faiz, Pakistan

Deprived of my health, my pen and scroll,
I grieve not
For I have dipped my fingers in the blood
of my heart.
The seal on my lips, I. take no account of
For I have. given a tongue
to every link in my chain.

From *Lotus*

Be You Near Me

Faiz Ahmad Faiz, Pakistan

Be you near me,
My murderer, my love
When the night marches;
Stated with the blood of the skies the night marches
Waiting, laughing, singing
Clinking her blue anklets of pain.
Be near me
When hearts sinking deep in bosom
Desperately wait for the sigh of friendly hands veiled in sleeves
And the gurgle of wine is like a distressed child
Refusing to be comforted
When no words avail
When no thoughts march
When the night marches
When the mournful, desolate black night marches
Be near me,
My murderer, my love
Be you near me.

From *Lotus*

Listen my Heart

Faiz Ahmad Faiz, Pakistan

HARK! my heart, [someone] calls again
No, no. There is no one,
It must be a wayfarer bound for some other door.
The night deepens, and the stars are scattering into dust.
In distant apartments, drowsy lamps begin to reel.
Every roadway sleeps, weary of waiting
And unfamiliar dust obliterates all footprints.
Put out the lights, put by the wine and the wine cup,
Lock up your sleepless doors, my heart,
For no one will come here now,
No one!

From *Lotus*

The Shadow

Faiz Ahmad Faiz, Pakistan

O my shadow
I forgot myself in midsummer,
When I met you,
I waited for great friendship
That would have the perennial
Transparency of noons.

It is then that you followed me,
Silent as ever.
And I felt stricken
By the mystery of our destiny.

Today I see myself in you like in a mirror,
In order to know myself
And to find in your frontiers
The very signs of my own beauty.

Have you crawled
From the bottom of the graves?

And what message to me
You never dared tell?

To see my reflection in you,
To ask you about my mystery
I find out
The very lines of my own destiny.

My loneliness is born
Of your presence,
And the one that resembles you
Standing at your feet
Waited, waited
For a great friendship
But nobody came to him.

When shall we begin
To love each other,
Angel of loneliness,
To stretch our hands at each other
And be intimate once more.

From *Lotus*

The Dark Star

Saleh Gawdat, U.A.R.

Whose is this dark star
With its mazes of vague blue
Christ's wounds accusingly point at it
Earthly orders indignantly reject it
He who gives light to His chosen stars
Denies it the gift of Heavenly glow.

O Star of "Zion," surely the strife
Predicts your dark and gloomy days
Hexagonal as the spiders' web
And hollow as the skull
Shame, plunder and treachery
Form the contours of your shape.

You claim that Moses' faith is yours
Do you believe in the Voice that addressed him?
Do you heed his testament
While committing what he forbade?

Where, [O] where is his call for Life
For charity, for mercy and for Truth?

Where, [O] where are his melodious psalms
Were are his inspiring songs?
Where are his Commandments,
When you ignore what virtue and honour are?

Ask, [O] ask justice: who buried it?
Ask the principle of right: who made it an orphan?
You snatched Palestine from her people,
You prolonged her darkened days.

Alas! that the land of prophecy and faith
Becomes the seat of a criminal lot!
Oh that the soil of Bethlehem was given away
To those who never mean to grant it honour!
Oh that Mary's Church was abandoned
While fire is raging all around the sanctuary!

We are a people determined to struggle
A giant in the Arab homeland has stirred up
Springing out of its age-old urn
Awakened at last by a treacherous blow
Deep inside, he burns with justified rage.
Death is in the rift, it dawned on him,
That caused brothers to stand apart,
Moved by the bite of a vengeful snake,
He clearly perceived the image of the snake-master!

United, we make an epic of our days and nights
Should daily bread be hard to get
We'll tighten our belts.
Death shall be welcome
In [defense] of dignity
If in battle our fighters be wounded
Their wounds are their medals.

We have found the long arduous road
To our blow for victory
Up to this peak of hope
Our valiant troops march
Our stars will shine in the skies
While yours lies in darkness.

From *Lotus*

My Voyage

Sardar Jaeffery, India

Time shall inevitably bring that day,
When the candles of eyes shall be put out.
And lotus-like hands shall wither,
And every butterfly of utterance shall fly away
From the petals of tongue;

When all forms and faces shall disappear—
Forms and faces that open up like buds,
That laugh like flowers
At the bottom of a black, black sea,
The circulation of the blood
The beating of the heart
All these are tunes that will slumber
And go into eternal sleep,
And on the velvet of the soft azure
The smiling diamond lips
This paradise, and this land of mine
Its mornings and evenings,
Without perception, without understanding
Shall shed dew-like tears
On a handful of human dust.

All shall pass into oblivion
All shall be taken away,
Every trace of the beautiful temple of memories erased.

Then no one shall ask
Why don't we see Sardar in this feast.
But I will be back again
And talk of children's lips
And sing through the beaks of birds
When seeds laugh inside the earth
And the roots toy with their tender fingers
With the soil.
Then I will open my eye in every leaf
That's green, in every young bud,
In my green hand
I will weigh the drops of dew
I will take the colour of tamarin.

I will turn into the echo of lively tunes
Into a beautiful harmonious melody;
I will emerge and unveil myself to the world,
As a new bride radiant in beauty through a light veil.
And when the wind of winter
Sweeps autumn away
My dry leaves will be heard
Laughter will come out of my dry leaves,
Under the young feet of a passer-by.
All the golden rivers of the earth
And all the blue lakes of heaven
Shall be filled with my existence.

Then the world shall see
That each of its stories is mine
That every lover is called Sardar
And every beloved is Sultana.

I am a fleeting moment gone astray
In the haunted house of time
I am a tremulous drop that knows no rest
Ever on the move
From the vessel of the past,
Into the cups of tomorrow.
I sleep and wake, then again
Fall into deep slumber.

I am a toy as old as Time itself
In the hands of Days,
I become immortal once I die.

From *Lotus*

Rice Pounding Songs

U Win Pe, Burma

After the rice harvest the women of a Burmese village gather to pound out the grains from the husks. As they work, they sing these traditional folk songs which have been collected and translated by U Khin Zaw.

Set down the mortars, line them up neatly,
Girls of Shwe Naung, take up the pestle-stones;
Then sing we and chant it, merrily in time,
As gracefully we pound away.

What means that noise, that bustle we hear?
Oh, a lady of Shwe Naung is giving alms,
With the music of drums and gongs.

There is red-gold radiance over there;
Perhaps the sun has risen.
No, it's the dyed robes of the monks
On their rounds with their begging bowls.
Come, fill them with alms-food!

This [chukrasia] which I planted,
Isn't it lovely? Tiny buds on slender stems.
But if you pluck them before they flower,
My plant will wither away, you know.

Hey there, maiden at the loom,
What cloth are you weaving?
Oh, need you ask, in these thin times?
It's a cotton coverlet for me.

I live in a house of teak,
Bright at night with torches.
It's true, my parents are rich;
Yet if you dare not come yourself,
You can at least send a letter.

My handsome brother, a word with you
Before you leave for lower country;
If you find a wife there do not leave her.
Bring her to us, we've use for her.
She can fetch us water, gather firewood,
And pound our rice—oh, lots of uses!

I've bought a pair of sandals,
Such pretty red sandals.
But I shan't wear them yet.
When you and I are truly wedded,
Then, I shall wear them.

From *Lotus*

The Spring has Come and Asks for You

Zulfia Israilova To Hamid Alimjan, Uzbekistan

The almond trees were wash'd with rain,
At break of day the Spring appeared,
She filled with birds her vast domain,
To make us gay, the Spring appeared.

Oh, how you loved that nightly gloom,
The pungent smell of humid ground,
The apricots, about to bloom,
The bursting burgeons' crackling sound.

And, driving off the winter day,
The Spring her trumpet loudly blew,
And, humming low your favourite lay,
She went abroad to search for you.

To find you she became a breeze,
And rushed through gardens, searching there,
And looked in woods, among the trees,
On [riverbanks], in deserts bare,

But could not find you anywhere,
And, full of wrath against the world,
With stormy cries she rent the air,
And boulders down the hill-side hurled.

She went to search upon the plain,
And asked the youth who watched the herd:
"Where is the bard?" In tongue-tied pain
The [shepherd] answered not a word.

Then as a sunbeam from the sky
She slipped into my darkened home,
And asked my tears: "What is it? Why?"
And kissed my babies in the gloam.

My babies ... yours ... But here, as well,
She could not find you as she willed,
What way to look, she could not tell,
And asked my heart with sorrow filled:

"Where [is] the bard who watched for me
In every nook, on every way;
Who felt my charm in wood and lea,
Whose anxious thoughts I swept away?

Why has he left the verdure fine,
Uryk and tulips flowering gay?
Why, leaving an unfinished line,
He [dropped] his pen, and. went away?

Where are his verses, full of charm
In which I bloomed with radiance rare?
In which I drank of nature's balm,
And saw my beauty still more fair?

Why do you sob, in mourning clad,
And say no word in deep despair,
Your frosted tresses look so sad ...
Where is the bard? Oh, tell me where?

I take her mutely by the hand,
And lead her through the garden gloom,
And near a leafless bush we stand
Before a solitary tomb.

The Spring then hurried out of sight,
With her she bore my grief away,
And there, above the grave, that night,
An almond bloomed, in fair array.

And then the song you used to sing—
A nightingale intoned it too,
And nature, roused by fragrant Spring,
Was live with memories of you.

From *Lotus*

Turning Point

Hajime Kijima, Japan

I
Seventeen
I
Extremely hungry
I
Seek for foods everywhere
I
Wander into the prohibited areas
I
Escaping the pursuit by policemen
I
Find half-rotten potatoes
I
Swallow and swallow
I
Vomit and vomit
I
Become thinner and thinner
I
A deserted dog
I
Eat junks in the shadow
I
Only in my desperate dreams live
I
Unconsciously into vacuum by my inward carnal desire
I
Making love with some unknown glamorous girls in cinema posters
I
Absolutely solitary

I
Zero
I
Just one being among the innumerable poor
I
Just an adolescent in the [ever-crowded] streets
I
Marching with the unfamiliar faces
I
Equally having the right to demand for rice
I
Growing into a citizen armed for ou
revolutionary spontaneous feelings.

From *Lotus*

Al Hallag's Agony

Abdel Wahab El-Bayyati, Iraq

THE NOVICE

You fell in darkness, all was blank
Your soul was stained with dye
From their wells you drank
And felt a faintness
With ink and dust your hands are sullied now.
I behold you bent upon the ashes of this fire
A spiders' web your silence, a cactus on your brow.
O ye who to your neighbours give your all
You rapped at my door, when the singer sang no more
And broken was the guitar string.

How can I help when you are in the Presence seeking light?
Where shall I end, when you are at the beginning of the end?
Doomsday is our date; scatter then not the words of the wind upon the sea.
Nor touch the udder of the scabby goat
The inner heart of things
Is their outer shape—Think what you will
How can I be of help? When in eternal sands their flame so red
Flickered and then went dead
And here I behold you a supplicant in tears
Drowned in the temple of light
Silent, conversing with the night.

A JOURNEY AROUND WORDS

How lonely is night
When the lamp is out
When packs of wolves, and hunters of flies
Have eaten the bread of hungry toilers.
When black clouds, rain, and wind
Have devastated the morning's garden.
And how lonely is autumn, on these hills
As it crawls into the veins of Zaqqum[1] trees in the misty shade.

Oh! Ye who intoxicate me with your love
And bewilder me with your nearness
Ye, who bar all doors
The poor have granted me these rags
And these words;
Stretch your hands to me
Across the years of death and siege,
Of silence and search for the roots and wells.
Tear up these curtains.
And let the executioner come.
I offered my all, the guests have eaten
And departed.
And here I am turning [seashells]
Perhaps they are rose leaves blown by the wind over a dead body.
Perhaps they are phantoms.

---

1 A mythical tree mentioned in the Qur'an

THE CRUCIFIXION

In the years of barrenness and famine
He blessed me
Embraced me
Talked to me.
He stretched His Hands to me
And said
The poor have given you their crown
The waylayers, the lepers, the blind, and the slaves;
He said to me: beware,
And closed the window.
Then the judges rushed, the witnesses and the executioner
They burned my tongue
They plundered my garden
And spat in my well, oh my bewilderer
My intoxicator,
They drove away my guests
How can I cross the banks
When the fire is naught but dead ashes
How can I? O you who bar the doorway
While sterility and waste
Are my table, my last supper in life's feast
Open the door to me
Stretch out your hand to me . . . Ah!

Translated by Dr. Shafeek Megally.

From *Lotus*

Remember

E. Epanya Iondo, Cameron

Remember that night
When shadows hid your face from light
And left it in shadow...
Remember that night
When one-eyed shades
Danced the Baseke , and in their eyes
Nine times the flame of life was thrust
Remember the silence...
When a stifled cry rang deep
In blades of fire, and of blood
The voiceless cry with bared breast
Of the gory monster, satiated, at rest
[Drunkenness] on his drunken breath.
Remember the shouts of the gutted village

Yours and mine
Astride the crushing misery
With the wooden painted face.
Remember that night
The sound of drums reaching a pitched height
Tschak-Grong-Grong-Grong-Theup!
He was killed
But who was killed?...
Do tell us who was killed...
He was only fifteen
Fifteen years of age, of hope, of courage
He was killed I say
For having dared to mutter
That night has left the metal-hued silence
 That shape has come into the face of day
That the river stared in its own liquid mirror

Victorious in its proud array
That in your eyes and mine
Is born the source of hope
That the chains and the rope
Of dead and captive have become
A maze of arms that make us one,
That voices rise in angry fear
Of armed villages far and near
Those voices and the sound of [waterwheels]
Dance in my painful flesh
A nameless fugitive dance:
He was killed

Remember
Remember the old woman worn with care
Thrust by the sudden fire
Her limbs beating the air
Willingly bare, her knotted hands
Covering the movement of her flesh so bare
Real and reeling with despair
Blind and mute, black and terrified;
Man too was petrified
Slave of a stinking fear.
Remember . . .

Remember the prison of New-Bell
In the pitless hell of hopeless waiting
In the sound of rustling whispers
When we no longer dared to voice our fears
Except in choking words soaked in tears
Dry tears and stifled sound
Panting with fear: "Will it be me the next time round?"

Remember
Remember the light
Remember the light
Coming through your eyes and mine
Your silent eyes so eloquent.
[They] cannot wipe away the light of day

Remember Remember
They cannot uproot
This bright black stone from its root
Remember that your executioners and ours
Had become mere slaves to crime
That they no longer then could hear
The song of birds
Heralding the rising morn
That they could never measure
The beating pulse and coursing blood
In the vaulted tree of freedom
Remember

Translated by Nihad A. Salem.

From *Lotus*

Blind Steersmen

Frank Parkes, Ghana

How can I, who cannot control
My own waking and dreaming, ever hope to make my voice heard in the wrangling for mankind's soul?
How can I, dumb in my own [self-defense]
Dream of forging words of salvation for bilions with their cares and well-drugged silence?

Madness is virtue's beholding redemption in pools of blood squashed from dreams
and inexpressible fears of men whose sole bastion is the booth
(Which also is the paschal knife)

Sanity lies in submitting to the [bittersweet] dream created in factories of democracy
by tired, drained-dry brains, doped to senselessness by fact-effacing ether (Which is their sole refuge)

And I, blown by thick puffs of factory smoke
Mad neither for my sorrows nor the world's
Seek faith in the vision I know is false
In sanity I know is mere soul-effacement

And my doubts catch up with me in the flitting cloud
Which cannot provide an anchor
Which is as empty as a dream
And barren as the tomb

I, feeble, spineless speck, dare not hope by warm word
To wreck the sovereign people's dream
The salvation of the world lies in a deserted garden—
In a blind worm's crawl.

From *Lotus*

Poem of the Future Citizen

Jose Craveirinha, Mozambique

I have come from no matter where
From a nation which is not yet there
I have come and I am here.

I was not born alone
Neither I, nor any other
For we all are brothers.

I have much love to give
Love born of my inner core
That I have and nothing more.

I have a heart
And a voice raised high in a common dare
And I come from a country which is not yet there.

Ah! I have much love to give,
Love born of my inner core
I!
A man, any man you see
Citizen of a Nation yet to be.

Translated by Nihad A. Salem.

From *Lotus*

"I am alone, but we are all"

Katsumi Sugawara, Japan

I meet him,
In the morning.
Then I become "we."
We meet them
On the [tramcar],
Then we become a group.
Wind carries our songs,
Flags and [placards].
A group unites with another group

Again I
Change into numberless "we."
Then I become
A drop of the stream,
My thoughts, like sperms,
Flicker about in the crowd.
Why am I
So [openhearted] today?

I think:
The air cleanses up at a stroke
My loneliness.
I am alone,
But we are all.
The herald of time
Pursuing the difference of time
Runs around the globe.

Our voices echo even in Rio
I think it wonderful,
It is autumn there,
While it is spring here.

The main-like sandstorm of Kharakhorum desert,
The white mountains looking down on the Fjords.
It is summer there,
While it is winter over there.

I know:
All the seasons of the world
Meet on this very day.
Various races
All over the world
Make a pattern of peoples.
I am alone,
But we are all.
I am jostled by people.
In the midst of the crowd,
I can only see the narrow sky.

The sky is like the sea with the sun beyond.
Numberless yachts waiting,
With all their sails swelling up.
Moss stirring on the earth
Seems to stand still.
Voices no longer reach us separately,
Except in the one louder tone.

And I feel
My being expand
And fuse into
The harmonious voices of our class.

I am alone,
But we are all.
When the enormous bellows
With tens of thousands of open valves
Resound high
Blowing and blowing up
Through the light-blue space,
All of us step forward
Afresh onto the first day of May.

From *Lotus*

Excavate

Virga Belan, Indonesia

- 1 -

Dig out a wall
in the moon
A well of carbon
dioxide
A well that would accomplish
the message of the world
out of the atmosphere
of ours.

Dig out a well—
A water source
that washes out the dust
from the feet of Colombus,
brushing away
our contemporary tears.

Dig out, behind the night
Dig out, to end at once
our deep sorrows

For the goodness of Man

- 2 -

We could sink
our ego into it
And it must be heralded
To the far ice-plains of Antarctic
We shall shed
all disintegration processes
and its complicated laws

Into its cylinder

And it must be danced
By young maidens of Asia

Melted into the echo of [tam-tams]
By the sons of Africa

- 3 -

Therefore dig out
except of your little finger
From the very bottom
A thousand meanings of life
Dig out
A world
so blue
A world
entirely new
poured with scents
of roses—
A world
of steel and glass
A world
so adolescent
its fate and manifestation

- 4 -

This pattern of freedom is like the dew
The pattern of our creative endeavour
This is a pattern of struggle
which is so divine
A grand pattern of our resurrection
This is the pattern of the dawn
The pattern of trembling sun
This pattern is the drawing of fluttering fish
in the nets
of our desire.

Ah, therefore dig out,
Dig out a well
in the moon
And stake a banner
on earth

Before nature will bear
new fruits in its
bosom
new side-branches at its
branch

Even before the twilight
lift its curtain.

Translated by the author.

From *Lotus*

Thoughts at the Gathering of the Storm

Mazisi Kunene, South Africa

The great smoker smokes wild hemp in the skies,
The smoke clouds move patiently
Giving life to a million images.
The axe-rays of the sun cut and pass.
There is no blood from the skulls.
They wander and assemble on the horizon
Until in their anger they are bound like gigantic knots.
They hurry back wiping out the centre of the sun,
The skies are torn with plural rains
The rains are tears that will remain with the earth.

We do not know when the world will end.
So we stand on an ant hill
Eulogising a thousand years
Saying tomorrow, there will be tomorrow
Suspended with our shadows on the clouds.
It is then that the great smoker of time
Will smoke again in the abyss of the south.

I Sometimes Fear

Sajjad Zaheer, India

I sometimes fear:
The silver threads of friendship
Golden bonds of love
Might break
Like dry twigs;
Eyes opened and closed
But might not speak,
Hands work
Fingers write
All about everything
But, forget, somehow,
To support the tottering steps of
Little children
And in the nights
Cool
When lights are off
Stars fragrant,
Like jasmines
Ways of love, forgotten,
Hearts hardened
Its anxious streams—choked—
This indeed is death
Worse, far worse, than,
When all weep
Funeral pyre is lit,
Wreaths of flowers placed on the grave
And candles lit—
But this:
Eternal prison
In the round mausoleum of silence
Where not even echoes are heard
Of one's own desperate cries ——————— I sometimes fear . . .

From *Lotus*

Our Cause and the Discovery of the Moon

Abdel Kerim El-Naem, Syria

Prepare all spaceships
Aim at a glimpse of the spheres
Prepare your meteors
And plunge into the nebular labyrinths
My Blood
And the brimming cups of fiery love do fill my mouth
And the sinews of our heroes above the golden canal
Bring back
My fathers' youth . . . Set free the eagle with the lowered wings
To greet the Arab Nation.

O you who have returned
You whose echo rings: a laurel on the distant paths
What profits man from the conquest of space?
How does he triumph?
A million men take their own life, there on Reddein Street
A thousand deserts . . .
Your eyes which shed terror in Vietnam
A modest speech [inscribed]
On the pages of that quiet planet:
"Man came to space bearing the banners of peace."
What pregnant idiocy?!
That spreads fire in the mouth
To quench the thirst of parched lips?!

If man were modest, would he consider
The enslavement of space and earth enough?!

What peace is this
Which crowned with bombs spreads o'er our cruel heritage
What peace is this
For which laurel crowns of Napalm an woven!
What peace is this
While my people search the wastes for a glimpse of light
And infinite night bearing the murmer of my flute
Paces imprisoned by the side
What peace is this?

What does man reap when he the moon does tread!
Thinks he to bring back sight
To the blind who live in night?!
Or does he hope from the Huns to get
Humanity as it was in Baghdad?!
Will he give back the Palestinian what he from him did take.
All is the same
And will become in childrens' hands dance
A trip . . . Glittering gold.

Do suffer man the pangs of hunger and of pain
Watch every ship that comes back to you across the waves of sound
Across the ether . . .
You'll get your fill of tales
From the sea of Quiet to the sea of Storms
A charge of melody moves

And wracks your crucified frame, and breaks
Against the gates of a hunger
Which in the cells of poison drifts.
You start . . . Do bow your head
For your eternal morn has reached its night.

You'll get your fill
The spheres of Universe are now your own
A thousand devils on your shoulder dance
For your eternal morn has reached its night.

Broadcasts will crowd
To spread their magic shadows into plagues and cogs
And bring back from its devilish paths a tired vessel
I care not for
My brother there brings forth the morns, victorious
And I am rendered strong by tales of him
For I am but a throb that takes its life from him
Who loves his country, the people, the spheres and the moon!
And sows into our tales
The sparks of songs of hope
And raises the banner of man
That he fall not in any land
What good
If the moon be tamed?

Translated by Dr. Angele Boutros.

From *Lotus*

Tell God: tell Him:

Hastings W. Okoth-Ogendo, Tanzania

Tell God
That lunch time I found my friends eating dirt
Turning over the dustbins each one his own
Mincing potato peels and rot in jam tins.

Tell Him
That in my heart I cried for I loved these destitutes.
In their rot and dirt and garbage,
In their shame and hardship and brutality, I loved them dearly

Tell God that I watched these people enter his holy church,
Tell Him that I heard His priest preach blessedness to them
But the priest did not belong to them any more
These destitutes belonged to a hell he would never enter
They were not his friends any more.
"Blessed are ye poor" he read without conviction,
But these people had lost hope; all hope of glorious heaven

Tell Him
That His priest walked away to the New Stanley;
Beneath the [beckoning] branches of the Thorn Tree
Where peace, comfort and heaven transcend the sin and agony of human love.

Tell Him
That I felt the agony of human suffering and longed for his presence
Tell Him that I looked for Him but found Him not
I shouted for Him but He answered me not
Tell Him that I prayed and bled to Him but He did not come to
Digo Road.

Tell God, tell Him to cast aside his heavenly bliss and come to this hell
For the sick, the suffering, the abandoned cry for his presence
Tell Him that the poor and the destitute long for his dear manifestation
Tell Him that the orphan, the deficient, the lunatic, the maniac hunger after him.

Tell God, oh! Tell Him
That he stays too long in the Cathedrals and fine churches of modern architecture
Tell Him that He stays too long in the holy and sinless altars of our places of worship
There is none there, oh, God but the holy priest

Tell God to come to the slums, oh, tell Him to come
QUICKLY!!

From *Lotus*

Don't Run with your Hands Hanging Down

Hiroshi Osada, Japan

Those men who go running in that distant vacant lot,
Those men who run along that long wall,

Down that too easy slope
They run away for ever with their faces looking down.

Those men in their hats,
Those men who chat like weary pimps,

Like when they drink lukewarm coffee
They mix their words on their stiffened tongues

Who are you? You are the ones
Who run with your hands always hanging down;

Your breath that enshrouds your words
Smells of rotten grease;

Your words are the headlines that drown a clear pain:
You talk picking up the largest type.

Who are you? You are not
A typesetter maddened by a blow of sorrow;

You are not a young wife who sheds silent tears,
Nor know the pain of the dream of a baby who dies without a cry.

Like an awning is stretched over us
A life of warning, perjury, lust and suicide;

But you are the men who run in a distant vacant lot,
The men who run away along that long wall with their hands hanging down.

Translated by Sususmu Sato, from the Japanese.

From *Lotus*

Muse Without Music: The Poet in Search of a Tongue

Ivan G. Van Sertima, Guiana

Last night while the world slept,
I came down to the sea,
lured by the mounting call of an inner music:
Down to the sea,
down to the sea I came,
through the tunelled lanes of my brain's grey city,
through the million streets of the mind's dark maze,
to the sea I came,
searching for a voice, searching for a voice.

Last night while the world dreamt,
I came down to the sea,
I could not sleep though I was in search of a dream.

Time has etched a million wave-marks,
like a mosaic of wrinkles
upon the sand-face of my soul:
And I come down to my sea in the long dark nights,
looking at the waves, looking at the sands
searching for a voice, searching for a voice.

A million waves, unthawed,
gush from the frozen channels of forgotten time,
vomiting the silt of my past,
Flooding my sands with the fossils
of two sepulchred decades of the heart's dark history:
And I come down to the seas of my soul,
taking the living plastic into my hands
warm with the vital essence of a million hours.
trying to mould,
out of the ten thousand faces and places
voices and images,

forms and fancies,
thoughts and impressions,
a voice for the soul's release
and total revelation.

I have gone down like this
to the oceans of men,
sounding their depths,
forging a link to my spirit,
with the echoes that ring out from the deep dark hollows within them:
But their songs have not quenched me
their tongues do not speak me,
their patterns are alien to the webwork I seek.

And I must still go down to my sea in the long dark nights,
searching for a voice, searching for a voice.

Would that the flame of my thought
fanning so faintly now over the far waters,
may from a flicker foment,
flare to a furious force,
full to a fountain of fire,
and from the fevering ferment of forms,
forge me a frame,
fording the fathomless!

From *Lotus*

Would that the voice that I seek
could like the winds of my soul
breathe me a music
milked in the multi-mooded murmurings of the mighty spirit!
A voice, broad and deep,
broad and deep like the river of time itself,
bearing upon the sensitive stream of its subtle symphony
all the vague and vivid etchings
that the waves have made.

From *Lotus*

Poems from USSR

Alexander Pushkin, USSR

Poets from ancient days are used
In sweet alliance to unite;
True votaries of a single muse,
A single flame their souls ignite.

From *Lotus*

Motherland

Begzyn Yavoukhoulan, Mongolia

On the morning when I appeared on earth,
When I slept in my cradle soon after birth,
When my father gave me my name
I knew
And at the same time did not know you.
You are my breath—today I know—
My cradle, my home and my future fame,
You are my happiness and my woe,
You never forget me wherever I go;
Mother—is your true name . . .

From *Lotus*

Memory

Jean-Baptiste Mutabaruka, Rwanda

Remember the sweetness of an eve
by the fountain,
of the dancing grass
that bends to the wind of water rushing
to the depth of the vale.
Remember, remember the carefree race
in the dry plains, burnt with the flames
of the forest gone to dust.
Remember your first days in school,
the rebel letters of the alphabet,
the endless number of multiple divisions
written in the soft and pliant dust.
Remember the maternal tenderness
of your mother's soft hands upon your face,
nerves on edge from the hard rays of the [dogdays] sun
[priceless] treasure, unequaled, mother.

From *Lotus*

Presence

Jean-Baptiste Mutabaruka, Rwanda

Eternally present
way beyond spaces, living form
of a loved old friendship
Slow, majestic procession
of clouds that seem
the shining glow of the sun
reflected in the water stream
Indolent murmuring
of old memories newly-clad
of our common childhood.
You are no longer but a thread,
a thin thread in the foggy desert of days
the empty days, absorbed in vain
And yet, still, hail
to you whom I do not forget
eternal presence of a friendship old.

From *Lotus*

Orb of Earth

Kaisin Kuliev, USSR

Orb of Earth, you are only a melon to some.
They
cut you up into slices and sink their teeth deep.
And to others: a ball to be put into play
with a kick or a pass—just a toy they hold
cheap.
Orb of [Earth], you are neither a melon nor ball.
Orb of Earth, I'm in love with your dear wrinkled face—
Do not cry, let me dry every tear you let fall,
heal your wounds with a song in my tender embrace.

From *Lotus*

By Night I am On Guard

Malek Haddad, Algeria

By night I am on guard, and this vigil
Upon the threshold of my dream, bides the [password];
Or is it a regret by Autumn stored
For the meagre balance the morrow wipes away.

By night I am on guard over my thoughts,
I work them out as I listen to the hours
Ring for the call of a [broken down] record,
Deep within a desert which its fawn does mourn.

By night I am on guard by the powder puffs,
Hypocritical regrets which I thought burned out.
Knowing me alone, the past rises up
And keeps me company till the crack of dawn.

By night I am on guard at the door of fantasy
The garb of blue, too bright, knitted in the sky
The singing tone my mother's words did have
And the wondering bee whose honey is taken.

By night I am on guard, harkening to a dream
Of a boat that floats upon the eyes of a myth
Rut the [seagull] blue as it came on the sand
 Turned out to be a slave-boat, its ashes adrift.

By night I am on guard as the train goes by
That screams but once as it goes into space.
And wet, on the docks, I held in my hand
The kiss that was thrown by a look that raced by.

By night I am on guard, and the dogs of the village
Have left in my eyes those marvelous plains;
It is never too soon, it is never too late
To have in ones eyes the light of the night.

By night I am on guard and I hear the Rhuminel
Repeat sundry times that sundry times were right
The weavers by night of the rainbow new,
Those who pay their bread by reaping the harvest.

By night I am on guard by the [bygone] tongues
Words that I knew when a shepherd I was,
And I lied not when I said that at my door
This is the one who was the first to knock.

Translated by Nihad A. Salem.

From *Lotus*

Look no More

Peter Mwathi, Uganda

Look no more dear heart
For swaying palm fronds
On a strange deserted shore,
The murmuring of a mountain stream
On a high [unheard of] mountain;

The forlorn cry of an unknown bird
In a green valley at sunset:
Yes dear heart,
Look no more.

From *Lotus*

Poem of the Conscripted Warrior

Rui Nogar, Momzambique

He went there
Afraid
Of being afraid.
(Oh Our Lady of Anything
In my village
I left my wife behind).
He went there
With the shame
Of feeling ashamed.
(Perhaps I might even kill children;
I have two children, oh Lord . . .)

He went there
Involuntarily
He went there
And the courage was not his own
And the hate was not his own
Not his own
Not at all
But he went
Infected with blood lust
He killed killed killed
Until one day

Oh! irony
On that day
There was sun
There was hope
There was his wife
There were his children his mother a letter

There was so much
But all crumbled away
All
In the treacherous cackling
Of the grenades
With yellow beaks
And red tails . . .

From *Lotus*

And the Man Returned

Shazel Taquah, Iraq

I asked the eucalyptus tree, and said:
It might know that once upon an eve
We planted a moon upon its boughs
A young moon with eyes of night
For whom we lit incense and candles bright
Protecting it with solemn vows
And the kohl melted in awe
Burning our fingertips, but little did we know.

"A stranger passed, and greeted not!"
Said the eucalyptus tree,
Await his return with grief and longing
For yet another spring . . . "
I wish the tree did know
That of my ribs, my breasts and
Cheeks I made for him a pillow
I wish the tree did know
That I'll ne'er see him again
For, O eucalyptus tree,
T'was but a spring we lived
And off it went, bitter
And sad, and greeted not!

Leaving me with grief and patience
With the sad moon hovering in our night
A moon with eyes and hair of night.
I watered the eucalyptus tree
If the men were to return, and he be among them
Beloved tree, shed flowers on his passage
And kiss his cheeks,
Sprinkle scent upon him
And tell him of my love.

Tell him:
I love him still
And dream
When the young moon comes upon our shores
With kohl upon its eyes
Prone upon the shore
Flirting with the river,
Tell him I love him still
And of my heart, my blood, my tears
He'll have his fill.
With candles, flames and camphor sticks
I vowed to die for him.
I prayed that God guide and protect him
Return him to my arms.
I watered the eucalyptus tree.
Forget not, O tree, and bring him back to me

O fresh—boughed tree . . .
His [comrades] wept in silence,
The guns again did sing . . . bidding him farewell
Over the city circled the bird of death
The eucalyptus tree leaned forth in prayer
And on its boughs a moon bid him farewell
The sky went dim . . . the voices faded away
The last of the stars were lost
And from the edge of the city came a turbulent dawn
Tolling in an angry tone within the streets
Washing the pathway of the sun.

Translated by Nihad A. Salem.

From *Lotus*

The One Who Left before Time

Adonis, Lebanon

Did you ask me? First must you die, or burn like a wound
And in my ashes descend
Then you can ask . . . Is it about my country that you ask?
My body is my country.
And who are you? Did you go forth with the fleeing stars
Did you descend with rushing floods
Did you appear from gaping lips of walls

A flower?
And did you wear the wings of butterflies, and live within a rock
Did you stretch forth your palm, and lie beneath the trees
Did you become the whisper of the woods
And did you hear the mountain bells
tinkle around the necks of clouds?

Who are you? Ah . . . Yes . . . Once upon a time
We walked together once upon a time.
You are the slave of the road
A rag upon the road
You are a [graveyard] and monotony
And I am the beginning and the lead in what is new . . .
Under my lashes myriad horses
Roam, and ghosts and places
Caravans of bread and seeds
Which carry every wood

And every mountain move
And rains returning before their time
And time departing before it should
And flowers closed, and rivers, and the vales

All horses roaming, their neighing
Now a wound, the mountains whispering loud
Planting the face of silence
With red rain, and palms.
And from my paths I wove

For patience: wings
And I embraced the springs, the silver white, and mirrors too:
O trees of days, which sun
Revolves not in my orbit
O trees of dizziness,—
And I said - This is our fire, and this
The solemn wake of brotherhood
And sterile time is but the horn of a dying bull
And prophecy,—

O you poor of the world, prophecy Is poverty,
And every poverty
Begins with—
... "Go with him
Wrap him, wound him
O star of questions, teach him the storm, the fall Up high ..."
I have nothing save my blood and face
I have no longing
Save for the revolution's fire
... "—Wounded, are you?
Who are you?
Ah, yes ... Once upon a time ...
Die first ... "

I was born with the prophet's cape
My face is the flame of a wife
Dreaming: "How fall the swords
How does the soldier e'er return . . . "
My face is like a star
Embracing all is solid, dead, and alive
I rise in the name of the grass
When bread becomes like hell
When dead papers in their ancient books
Become a land of fear
I rise in the name of mud
To wipe away the mire
To engulf time I seek the help
Of the first breath, and I bring back
My first psalm
That I may change the words.

And revolution is colour and the bow of colour
Which from the ashes of the world
Does waken time which sleeps within a lake of ice
Dumb as a nail
And pours it like a grange
Within the fire
And gives it forth to time arisen from the dough of generation

Upon the children's feet,—
To those who sow the seed of virginity
To those who bear the light and flame
And when I fall upon my bed, I do recall
The smell of day, I do recall
My victim night
My first night upon the pillow fresh

I know my death is what remains
I know that revolution now remains ...
I washed my hands of my life
And of this butterfly
I reconciled the century and the fragility
How many days do I abandon, to receive new days
Bake them like bread
And wash them of the rust of history and words
And melt into their texture heat or even a symbol,

For in my veins runs a century of slaves
A century of sins
Pulled by death, and round my face
There is a dying civilization
Here am I like the river
Not knowing how to hold the shores
Not knowing save the source, the end, the way
Where comes the sun
Like the magic black herb
Where rises the sun
Like a red mare
Where becomes the sun
The oracle of misery and joy
An oracle, a lion, or an eagle
Which lies like a crown
Upon the brow of time.

Translated by Nihad A. Salem

From *Lotus*

Man of Africa

Ahmed Sekou Toure, Guinea

Your life is synonymous
With concrete participation
In the People's life
Your usefulness is synonymous
With valorisation for the People
Of what the People gave to you.

Your tomorrow is synonymous
With the People's permanent progress
For, both object and subject of history,
Of this endless process of transformation
More like a race in depth
Than like a blind test of speed,
Man this social and biological product,

Forever in motion and in a state of becoming,
Thanks to his powers of feeling and perception,
To his capacities for interpretation and adaptation,
Thanks to his genius for infinite creation,
Acts upon nature and upon Society
In a manner more or less effective and dynamic
According to the level and quality of his consciousness.

Any true value is social or historical
For the People, their life and eternal hope
Inherent in their struggle for happiness,
As well as in the very nature of man's action,
The significance of this thought and of his being,
Remain fundamentally and forever,
The only and the true life-giving source
Of cultural inspiration and creation;

And the more these do reflect a qualitative
Synthesis of realities present and to come,
The more the man of letters, the architect, the historian,
The musician and the artist, becomes then
An authentic incarnation, more so even, a "container"
Of what contains him, and which alone can valorise him
In space and in Time: Society and History.

Translation by Nihad A. Salem.

From *Lotus*

All That You Gave Me

Anoma Kanie, Ivory Coast

All that you gave me, Africa
Lakes, forests, lagoons lined with
All that you gave me,
Music, dances, tales told by the evening fire
All that you carved upon my skin
Pigment of my ancestors
Indelible in my blood
All that you gave me, Africa
Makes me walk just so
with a step unlike any other,
My hip broken beneath the weight of time,
My feet wide with all the walking,
All that you've left me, Africa
And even this sloth stuck to my heels,
I bear it all with pride upon my brow
My health is no longer mine to lose
And I go along
Singing of my race which is neither good nor bad
Nor worse than another
All that you gave me, Africa
Swamps made golden by your zenith sun
Your beasts—which they pretend preserve,
Your mines, unexplained treasures
Obsession of a contrary world
Your pain at having lost paradise,
I protect it all for you with an unforgiving hand
Down to the light on your horizons
So that it may remain forever intact
This mission entrusted to you by the heavens.

Translated by Nihad A. Salem.

From *Lotus*

The Corpse

Mohamed Taleb, Kenya

I dreamt about a corpse
Who had come back
To fulfil his hopes
And he said
I've come to gather
The harvest of my deeds and seeds
That I did sow and grow
On my last visit

I shook hands with a man
Who died the next day
And he had never dreamt
Of a Nobel prize
Which to everyone's surprise
Was actually bestowed
Four thousand miles away
Ten minutes before.

I kissed a face in tears
That had mourned the years
Fed on hopes
Now hanged dead on ropes;
And she daily postponed her happiness
By crying on purpose
So that she always had
Something to live for.

The corpse fulfils the hopes
The corpse fulfils the hopes.

From *Lotus*

The Top of the Stairs

Nazek El-Maleika, Iraq

The days have passed, bedimmed.
When we met not, even in the shimmer of a mirage
And when I, alone, feed on the sound of footsteps in the dark
Behind the cruel [windowpane], behind the door.
I stand alone . . .

And days have passed,
Cold, creeping and dragging along my dubious boredom.
While I harked, counting their anxious minutes beat
Has time gone by? Or have we lived a timeless time?
Sunk in the tide of dreams
And days have passed,
Laden with my longings. Where am I?

Still staring at the stairs
And stairs do start, but where do they lead?
 They start in my heart where a dark maze reigns,
They stark. Where lies the door to them?
The door to the stairs . . .

Days have now passed.
When we met not. You stand beyond the edge of dreams
An edge lost in unknown
And I now walk, I see, I sleep
And while my days away, dragging my honeyed pain
Which flees into a [bygone] past.

My days are gnawed by sighs. When will you return?
Days have gone by and you remembered not
That somewhere in a corner of your heart, a love forgotten lay
Its soles now torn by thorns
A love that pleads in fear
Give it now light.

Come back. To meet
Does give us wings to cross the night
An empty space does lie
Behind the tangled trees are seas
Raging seas that know no end
Torn by waves made of the foam of dreams
Come back. Or else my voice will die
To your ear behind the hated bend . . .
And I'll remain lost in the heart of forgetfulness . . .

Nothing but stretching silence
Above the grief . . .
Nothing but of forgetfulness the echo
Whispering in my ear that he will ne'er return
Nay, he will ne'er return

Translated by Nihad A. Salem.

From *Lotus*

Blue Horse

Takiguchi Masako, Japan

Sunken murmurs come from the [seabed].
Through the creases of the water I see a horse:
Its eyes are blind.
Once on its back it bore men
—memories long fading out:
a blue horse plods along the [seabed].
Since when does a horse live in the sea?
The blood that once stained its back—
was it the horse's own?
or whose was it?

Without caring how it looks it moves on,
with one leg brushing aside the clinging, seaweeds;
its blind eyes secretly assume
the colour of indigo far and lonely.
The blood oozing from its wounded belly
is washed away by sea-water—
is carried from water to water.

In autumn
cold mist rises over the sea.
Then by the rock at the sea-bottom,
the horse sits alone, with folded legs,
abiding the chill,
abiding the waiting.

From *Lotus*

The Beda Flower

U'thein Hau, Burma

Close friends of the water
The beda hyacinths are floating on the stream.
There is no wind, but they drift with the current
In a movement that is endless and timeless.
On the bank sits a boy with a reed pipe who mimics the [coucal] bird;
The [coucal] leads, and then the piper follows:

"O beda, who come with the flow-tide and go with the ebb,
How I shall miss you when you have gone."
"Upstream and downstream you float;
From where did you come, and where are you going?
And when the sun sets and the current slackens,
By what bank will you come to rest?"

Freely adapted from the Burmese original.

From *Lotus*

The Seaboard Cafe

Aguinaldo Fonseca, Cape Verde

A small far away light
The lighthouse spitting its fire
On the black face of night
All is salt and sadness.

The winds and the surf on its back,
The cafe trembles in the night,
It is but a boat afloat in the bay.

Strong and brutal love
Amid the drawn-out knives
And the abandon of a girl in one's arms.
Despair lingers in the air
through heavy smoke—rings hanging there,
Bottles, glasses, bottles
—Oh what thirst, you sailors . . .

[Tattoos] sting the skin
Screaming with pain and break-neck
of adventures in the ports
Men of all races
Nameless men, men without country
—mere people of the sea
Voices hoarse with salt and wind
Whose wet eyes reflect the sea

Sadness and [boredom] now arrive
Nibbling stems of age-old pipes
they arrive and then they go
dragging off a staggering drunk.

Cards, tables, benches
bottles, glasses, bottles
and the barman's face
wakens old [bygone] revolts

All is rotting with vice
All is rotting with dreams
All is rotting from the sea!

Translated by Nihad A. Salem.

From *Lotus*

Chimera (1972)

Alpha Sow, Guinea

A landscape of valleys in the far horizon,
A landscape which my soul remembers well,
The waiting, the fever, the impatience to see her.
Kale, appearing suddenly with the gait so proud!
Time—old desires which bless, and bless again!
A regal head inundated with black tresses;
Eyes of tenderness in a Nile tinted ebony,
A tree, of a neck underlining a path!
Her fairy ankles pinned on a legend,
Kale walked in my eyes, coy
Loving, blooming, laughing, ripening
She was beautiful in her wild pride,
In times of distress, I sang not of her.
I bore her in my heart, incurable memory
Sheltered from torments! Legendary Treasure,
Of passing experiences, of premature plans and of Chimera!

Translated by Nihad A. Salem.

From *Lotus*

The Last Supper

Amal Donqol, Egypt

An Elegy:

Give me the power to smile
When dangers strike the heart of joy
And death, like a porcupine, stalks near the wall
Bearing fear's censor to children's eyes.
Give me the power ... not to die.
My heart is weary of knocking on every door
Where I seek a shadow of regret in the eyes of the dead
And I see silence ... Like a tender bird
Strike at the eyes and at the heart, and howl
In the smile of every mouth.

- 1 -

The winds have hidden in cellars now to rest ...
From swinging bodies on the gallows hung.
We stood to guard the door, to guard the halls
While Mamlouks' horses beat the earth with violent hooves.
Following the trail
Asking the roads for passage of the winds, of any wind
While we cast down our eyes.
They went ... the wild hooves striking down the earth ablaze
And hid in narrow winding streets.
... And back we went bearing the news to them
And called them by their name
And shook their shoulders, but in vain ...
Their heads hung in our palms ... Quite dead.
While we did guard the door ... and guard the sign
The winds had sought our help ... and we protected not.

- 2 -

The harnessed steeds . . .
Did neigh, yet are the knights the knights that were . . . tomorrow
The spurs strapped on the feet . . . sunk in the hearts.
And swords rendered cold
Nov hired by the slave-driver . . . to protect his caravan,
And swords were content to hang on parade . . . a show.
And burdens
Borne by guillotine blades in dark of night
Whose nobility we buried in the year of tears.

. . . The ghost of knights still lurks upon the city's brow
Silently coming when the water comes
Silently billowing the folds of its robe
Stretching its form . . .
And fear stretches in the night a hand.
And then it goes, carrying shrouds, across the roads
Carrying shrouds, like riding garbs
And spurs strapped to the feet . . . sunk in the hearts.

- 3 -

Greetings, "Death's eve my" heart, and you greet not
—Pray who has died?
— . . . I
— . . . You
— Yes I
— You cannot die at will my friend
— The necks of doves are wrung
And even my tongue is twisted by a foreign tongue
— You know not who you are
— I:
E'er since my father died
Every man loved by my wealthy mother
Every man loved by my mother: is my father in baptism
— Perhaps Ahmos was raised by a woman
— . . . The old sun's gold is molten now
And fallen o'er the dust's debris

I cry over a hill of ash
A Clow now opens wide the eyes
To see . . . But what to see?
(The clock on the wall of Hator's temple ticks no more
And virgin Troy is over... ended on the illusion of a horse)
— I, Osiris, have embraced the moon
And at the banquet I was guest and host
And I was placed at the table's head
The black guards surrounded me
I looked up at my brother's face . . .

His eyes looked down . . . he trembled,
I, Osiris, consoled the moon
Forgave the faces
And foretold what happened and what was to be
I broke the bread when my glass with ancient wine was filled
I said: "My brothers, here is my body to devour
My blood I give thee, drink it deep."
The candle hid his eyes with the lashes of its wings
To bide the crime,
Deflect the light from daggers' tips.

— The sacred tears of "Isis" may one day give back life to you
Though we no longer give birth now to Isis new
We heed no longer to the sound of tears
Our ears are heavy since we drowned in noise,
Now we hear bullet sounds . . . alone.
(Which terror and quiet spread in shades of guns)
— Security in the shadow of death
— Sir . . . we have descended from our mother's womb
With a hand pressing down the wound, The other pressing on the trigger butt.

- 4 -

When the coast swallows up the sunset lights
Darkness and cold cough loud upon its shores,
And hunger bears to shame . . . Its newborn babe,
Words . . .
And then runs from the cold . . . to warmth of cars.
The lamps: just debris . . . of a once-lit moon
Smashed by the peacock's fist upon the road
And handed then to women . . . to be nailed upon their breasts.
Strutting with pride because of it . . . whilst it is naught but dust

Words . . . words
And then runs from the cold . . . to warmth of cars.
And I "Joseph", beloved of "Zuleicha"

When I came to the Sultan's castle
Owned nothing . . . but a moon
(A moon that to my heart was fireside)
How hard I strove to hide it from the eyes of guards,
From all the eyes turned red with rust
. . . It shone bright through the night

They took me with it behind bars . . . that I may dim its light
They left me hungry for more than a night . . .
They left me hungry
The pale moon, in my palm, seemed like a cake.
And until now . . . stuck in my throat remains
A silver of its white-haired grief . . . cutting me like a thorn.

Give me the power to smile
For the [sunrays] fall like a spider's web
And lamps die down
My foot touches upon the first step up
My hand touches the [banister] . . . I'm afraid to fall
How can I remain?

Death's green decay, and smells of embalming
Spread on the house's court, flow in my blood from vein to vein
. . . My heart is weary of the dark, I cannot see
Oh! Had I eaten not the pale moon . . . had I not
It might, e'en for a moment, now have lit the dark
Yet I was starved
And now I've lost the moon.

Hungry art thou my heart on sale in stalls of lies
Hungry . . . to the point of death
What then shall I eat now
In order not to die?

From *Lotus*

Morning

David Gutmann, Zambia

In those few hours a hundred separate dreams
Until the motors kicked like lions and the teacups
Clanked at the doors, night in her coverlet.

On the hillside, pirouetting songbirds
Guided puzzled game through the afforestation,
And the old, old villagers huddled by their fires.

Love, joy, freedom—they are not under the branches;
The spiders in my curtain hide them in the night,
Yea only the night, where these things live.

From *Lotus*

Marriage

Elaine Caulker, Sierra Leone

Two birds, two beautiful birds,
Feathers green and yellow and blue.
Two birds, two beautiful birds,
My Love and I.

A band, a thin gold band,
So fragile, strong as steel
encircled us, to make us one.
My Love and I.

Four wings, four delicate wings
soared high, so eager to fly.
Two flew west, two flew east.
My Love and I.

Feathers battered, wings all torn
Yet foolishly we struggled,
And again and again, we hit the ground.
My Love and I.

Two birds, not beautiful birds,
No more feathers, shiny and new
But now both fly together.
See how well we have learnt!

My Love and I.

From *Lotus*

Home 1968

Femi Fatoba, Nigeria

Tongues Blazing
Sinews flexing
Sinews withering
Lions tearing
Vultures pecking
Mad elephants among vegetation

From *Lotus*

Moon

Femi Fatoba, Nigeria

Moon,
Mother of a [milkyway] of children
Your journey is sweet
I want to go with you
Beyond the clouds
But where,
Where is my face
My face is still in childhood.

From *Lotus*

Olawunmi[2]

Femi Fatoba, Nigeria

That pitcher bearer
at the stream,
Who went home
wet-limbed and [pitcher full]
with a parched throat.

---

[2] Olawunmi is my mother's name.

From *Lotus*

Man and Sea

Masako Takiguchi, Japan

From across the sea I hear the voice:
the voice of the dead.
Even those who are alive
speak from across the sea.

The words of the sea that keeps breaking,
the words of the solitary sea.
The layers of water of different temperatures
that have swallowed a lot of time.

The light from across the sea—
The light of life and death hitting each other.

The fresh mind that springs from light,
the sky that revolves gently round the axis of horizon.

The ever-trembling fear and hope
of the living
who wend their way to the sea:
the call of the dead.

The far end of the sea where fish glitter and jump.
What was it that men wanted to say
when alive?—
Oh the long centuries that are now passed.

From *Lotus*

The Soldiers

Masako Takiguchi, Japan

"Give us back that unknown thing,
That life of ours that fluttered within us".

Their hands extended over the earth as if wanting to speak—
More numerous than telegraph poles,
More pathetic than the rustle of reeds.

Mounted on a [handcart] that creaked jarringly,
Turning the wheels with hands that were numbed in the end,
Abruptly they ceased to be.

That distant border of life
Still gleams with the colour of fresh blood.

From *Lotus*

Poem of Salt

Ovidio Martins, Cape Verde

I was born on the beaches' farthest tip.
And so in me I engulf
All the oceans of the world
My mail is brought by the waves
which bring to me and drag away
messages and secrets too.
And my notes
(my small nostalgic notes)
are composed of salty sighs
Picked by sirens
Riding on the water's crest.
In the [seashells] and the conches
Of the [seashores] of the world
Songs of love
Do locked remain.
I was born on the beaches' farthest tip
And so in me I engulf
All the oceans of the world.

Translated by Nihad A. Salem.

From *Lotus*

Songs in Prison

Salem Goubran, Palestine

- 1 -

Opening an Account

This is the first night . . .
Outside, the sound of rain
And in the dark I see, from my open window
The shadow of the palm tree
The cold is like needles . . .
The blankets: spittle and decay
The silence: ringing curses
And I, alone, am a prisoner behind bars
Alone, alone

How deep the waves of loneliness...
Alone in the night I sink in thought
I whisper, murmur and remember
My street?
What a nuisance you are, o enemies of my street
......
......
This is the first night
Yes, the first and not the last night.

- 2 -

The Shame

"To the police who told me, as I stood in my chains: And now write poetry..."
In iron chains in my hand
And on my brow rests the sun
Before it sets away...
The face is the same face, the eyes two snakes
"... Greetings Salem..."
"Have you come to jail again?"
"Do you still hate the Jews?"
"How long have you been here? "
"Court?... The "Deir Hanna" tale?"
"Nothing like suffering excites poetry
"Come! write for your fellow-prisoners poetry...
O you of the yellow eyes and yellow conscience,
I shall bear my chains
I shall make the prison hear the songs so I sing
For people in the streets and in the vales
The chains in my hands: a shame to burn the conscience
Yes... but not for me
Just for your lowly rule
You small police authority...

- 3 -

To "Victorians Jaffa"

On the day of your victory. I gave the
prisoners
Two packets of cigarettes
I sang poems of the struggle
And laughed out loud at the jailer and the chains
My people behind the prison,
Stand like a sea of towering waves
O Jaffa the red ... I kiss your shining face
You are good news, and harbinger of more to come
This is the yield of but the first harvest
Stretch then your arms my people,
For the field is full of riches ...

From *Lotus*

Accused Thou Innocent

Beland El Haidari, Iraq

In a room on the seventh floor
they met . . .
They talked
They slept together
And down came the curtain
In a room on the seventh floor
But I remained crucified by the wall
And as you wished me
I remained like a nail
Plunged in their eyes
Plunged in their bed
Plunged in the wall
In a room on the seventh floor

. . . .

I heard her master
Ask him about his wonderful love
About a body
—Forgive me master—
She told him that he burned like fire
Burns me like fire
And once they talked of a lost world
Of a seed in a lost world
But I
As you wished me . . . and as you created me
Did not understand the dialogue
For I had risen above their beautiful love
Above a body like fire
And as you'd warned: "All men are criminals"
"All are criminals"
"Even the innocent love in all the eyes"

And as you wished me
I remained like a nail
Plunged in their eyes
Plunged in their bed
Scratching the wall
In a room on the seventh floor
Seeking in the murmur, in the laughter and the dialogue
A date for vengeance
The anger of revolutionaries
For a death to become a rope around their necks
And a nail in their palms

. . . .

Forgive me master
They were obstinately innocent
They were obstinately innocent
And when in my city morning dawned
The news bulletins told
The story of a room on the seventh floor
Of a date for vengeance
Of the anger of revolutionaries
And round their neck there was a rope and in their palms
A nail.

Translated by Nihad A. Salem.

From *Lotus*

Thou Restless Heart

Faiz Ahmed Faiz, Pakistan

There is gathering darkness
Comes rolling in endless waves as if,
From each single vein of the night,
Crimson blood [was] spurting forth
In streams of a gush blackness;
And the pulse of the entire universe
Beats as though the ecstasy
Of both the worlds were weaving off,
leaving exhaustion in the wake,
And a kind of ache,
Felt all over the body!

This warm blood of the night
well, let more and more of it
Run out; for this darkness
Itself is the rough that shall give
A crimson glow to the coming morn,
Soon the day will break,
Thou impatient heart,
Just wait awhile!

Underneath the delicate membrane
of the musical instruments
There still are heard echoes
of the clank of chains;
The serried strength of material mean

Holds the [whip hand] still;
Into the sparkling, blood red wine
There roll down tears too;
While in the stumbling feet
There lingers still
A shade of reverence
For the old forms of conduct,
And the old established laws
But wait awhile
Wait till the [frantics]
Have waxed really frantic
Till thy sedate drinking houses
Turn into real taverns
Where the drinking is deep,
And desperate and wild.

Then will melt into the air
This our whelming awe
of material means;
And the dead weight of old
modes of thought and conduct,
Too, would be lifted—
Though near so unabated still
Might continue the clank of chains!

Translated from Urdu by Sufee A.Q. Niaz

From *Lotus*

The Sailor and the Darwiche

Khalil Hawi, Lebanon

He roamed the unknown with Ulysses, and with Faustus, gave his soul to obtain knowledge, then he despaired of knowledge in this age. Like Huxley he disowned the age and sailed for the shores of the Ganges, cradle of ascetism. There he saw nothing but dead mud, hot mud.

When he had suffered from [seasickness]
From obscure light across the darkness of the road
And the stretched unknown, born of unknown, of certain death
Spread like blue shrouds for the drowned man,
When in horizon's raid spread open jaws of caves
Wrapped in the glows of fire
When winds had dodged him
Winds did toss him to the ancient East.

He landed in a land which story tellers had sung:
A lazy bar, the legends and the prayers,
The palms of tepid shades and flabby crowns,
A humid place to kill sensation
In his fiery nerves, to kill all memories,
The loud and distant echo
The lure of distant ports
O for the abstinence of naked [dervishes],
Dizzy with whirling, they have crossed life

Circles, circles
Round the ancient dervish,
Feet rooted to the earth till he became
Immobile, sucking all that dying earth can give
In the folds of his skin grow parasitic plants
Moss grown old on time's back, creepers boldly wide,
Unaware and in an endless trance

His share of the fertile season raging in the veins,
Bright, elegant patches flowering
On his old and tattered skin

—Come, tell of treasures which transfixed
Your eyes on the deep unknown
I have not moved from here for many a thousand year
—I have not moved from the shore of the ancient gangs
However for the roads of earth may be
All roads at my door come to an end
And in my but the twain do come to rest:
God and fathomless time.

... And I see, what do I see?
Death, ashes and fire ... !
Descent upon the Western shore
Stare and you shall see ... or can't you bear?

... This foaming Ghoul
Which causes feverish mud to foam, and ports to turn to fire
And pregnant earth to writhe and moan ...
And now and then eruption in the mire
Eruption that was Athens, eruption that was Rome
A fever's glow which rattled in the dying breast
Leaving behind some pimples few
And ashes from the residue of time
This suffering Ghoul

Seems to me but the child but seconds born
Whose wrinkled hand now weaves
The shrouds for him, as death draws near
And you see me
Sitting here for many a thousand years
Sitting on the shore of the ancient Ganges
And in my but the twain do come to rest:
God and fathomless time.

—Have you been granted visions true beyond your share?
Let me be! For in my eyes the lights have died
Let me go, to where I do not know
I'll not be lured by distant ports
For some are burning clay
And some are clay of death
How often did I burn in burning clay
How often did I die with death of clay
I'll not be lured by distant ports
Leave me to the sea, to the wind and to death
That stretches shrouds of blue to the drowned man,

A sailor in whose eyes the light did die
You die, the light in his eyes did die
He can no longer saved be by valiant deeds,
nor by prostration of prayer.

Translated by Nihad A. Salem.

From *Lotus*

Song of Ocol

Okot P'bitek, Kenya

Do I hear you whisper
Who is that man?
What is his name?
Do you not know me
And my brothers-in-power?

All the time
I was reading Econ
At Makerere,
And my friend the Resident Magistrate
Was sweating and cramming for the Bar,
You were busy
Performing the get-stuck dance,
Spending weeks at funeral parties,
Or in the bush
Chasing wild animals
Or collecting wild honey,
Thoughtless and carefree
Like children dancing around the hut

After a meal;
We spent years
In detention
Suffering without bitterness
And planning for the revolution;
Tell me
My friend and comrade,
Answer me simply and frankly,

Apart from the two shillings fee
For Party membership,
And the dances you performed
When the Party chiefs
Visited your village,
And the slogans you shouted
That you did not understand,

What was your contribution
In the struggle for Uhuru?

Comrade,
Do you not agree
That without your present leaders
Uhuru could never have come?

And surely,
You are not so mean
As to grudge them
Some token reward,
Are you?

I have a nice house
In the Town,
My spacious garden
Explodes with jacaranda and roses,
I have lilies, bougainvillea, canna . . .

Do you appreciate the beauty
Of my roses?
Or would you rather turn
My flower garden
Into a maize shamba?

What did you reap
When Uhuru ripened
And was harvested?

Is it my fault
That you sleep
In a hut
With a leaking thatch?

Do you blame me
Because your sickly children
Sleep on the earth
Sharing the filthy floor
With sheep and goats?

From *Lotus*

Epistle of the Dead

Tsuguo Ando, Japan

The first atomic bomb, thrown over Hiroshima at 8:15 a.m.,
on August 6, 1945, printed on a granite step the shadow of a man
who was sitting there to rest—printed it to remain there for ever.

The rosy, mineral sunlight creeps around.
Now on the earth
The grey marshes are rampant, eager to cover all this world.
It multiplies millions of times faster than our toiling, drudging lives.
But, alas, it has been long since we began to cherish the earnest wish
to wipe away that sterile shadow.

*

We have ceased, since that day, to walk on two feet.
Nevertheless, we, whose arms and legs have grown in dissimilar lengths,
Can no longer bring ourselves to walk on four.
We put both of our palms
Flat on the earth, as if it were the greatest submission,
And crawl about on our knees gladly.

Since we saw, that day, the huge, dark-purple mushroom cloud
In the rosy, mineral sky,
Our bellies have swollen like those of pregnant women,
And drip oil from the navels drop after drop.
The secreted oil is now much, now little, we comment—how noisy!
How we quarrel, saying, You have stained again where I wiped clean!

And how we laugh at the quarrel [boisterously] and bitterly
Till our ribs become visible!
No longer is it necessary for us to hide our private parts,
Nor have we leisure to bother about it.
What troubles us now is
How to treat these troublesome, swollen, [dark red] navels of ours.

*

Whether, on our navels,
Grow eyes
And noses,
And whether, on top of their bald heads,
Downy hairs, lank like dryland rice plants, sway—
The morning time when we examine and scrutinize it
Is the most solemn time in our daily routine.
So we cannot help
Crawling about on our knees gladly
In the rosy, mineral sunlight.

*

It has been long since we began to wipe away our shadows
that spread over the earth.
It has already been long since we began to forget our dark homeland
where we had started.

Translated by E. Tanaka.

From *Lotus*

The Age of Rubber Stamps

Beland El-Haidari, Iraq

Bring back to us
O age of ours
O age of rubber stamps
O sting of whips
Upon our hides
O chain without a crime

Bring back to us
Our ancient eyes
Our dull black doors
Open to night
Bring back to us
Our shadows shaken by candlelight in the evening dusk

Bring back to us
Our naked children under winter's wrath
Their small hands wishing they could tear the sky
O age of ours
O age of rubber stamps
O chain without a crime
O sting of whips

Bring back to us
Our age-worn eyes
That we may see the victory in defeat
Make of the locusts' legs in our desert
And of the dryness of cacti in our land,
Make of our dead sons' arms
Gallows.

You ask us
Of the wrath that bears us on
In a glorious song.
Well, we are bored
With your conceited face
Stamped in rubber
Stamped in dust
Stained in crime.

Translated by Nihad A. Salem.

From *Lotus*

Canticle of the Obsessed

Boualem Abdoun, Algeria

I testify by the
sterility of my pen
by the plectrum of the four seasons
I testify
by
the
virginity of my writing sheet
by the lyre of the four seasons,
that I loved, that I love, that I shall love an inaccessible vase alas . . .

Will the patience of the school bench bear both our external boredom?
Did I come across you suddenly at the corner of a street
suddenly illuminated by the poignant flash of your number?
Does it matter!
Like a ray of sun suddenly solidified you sprang my soul, undulating
diversity.

You are my desire,
I am the creator of my desire,
I gleaned the beauty of my desire wherever perfection grows,
Desire O painful desire!
My impetus is but a tearing immobility towards you
O double star that I adore
in the monotonous night the rock . . .

O you who are the harmony of my scattered desires!
The gold of your hair and the gold of your perfume, the gold of your
eyes
and the gold of your voice, the gold of your soul and
the supreme gold of your flesh.
Your silken flesh, warm, and golden . . .
Ah I your silken flesh, breathless and golden.

All this, in concentric sheaves, passes by slowly,
very slowly on the livid glass pane of my sleep.
Deep within the alcove the obscene bed offers its stretched belly.
Amphora! ancient amphora of gold full of very ancient wine and
of soft honey appeasing the trembling of my
feverish arms.

I can feel you live and palpitate against me!
And in the hot spirals of the dark,
the dear murmurs flower upon our lips
the murmur of familiar words,
and on our flesh flower the strong vibrations
of familiar pleasures.
Let us be lulled, before the day goes blind, by the tender
buzz of bees kissing the petals of love
by this ebb and flow
by this temporal shudder
and by this rhythm of the sun!
I can feel you live and palpitate within me!
And within the cosmos of dreams we roll together
like a single sheaf
of sobbing atoms.

And you say to me: let us sleep, sleep, . . . sl . . . eee . . . p!
And I answer: let us love, ah I lo . . . ve .
And all my body, brutally torn asunder, howls
echo, cruel echo how your spatterings hurt me!
The gold of my desires hurts my feeble eyelids,
and the dawn of awakening
the dawn of bright red laughter
envelops me like an icy shroud . . .

I am alone.
But would I have been less alone
if you were with me
secretly, profoundly placed?
Answer!
A sob tears the shell-like back of the waves, the roof-tiles and the clouds,
for a moment the permanent murmur exploits it:
Love is solitude.

I am not Narcissus:
The eternal cry of the nymph
the sad internal lover
No! the cold intimacy of the solitary I frightens me.
Here is my body claiming the presence of another body.
Here is the lassitude of a livid body,
will I be solitary . . .
And horizon, the dreamy fog of perfection.
Eternally . . .
The gold of my desire crumbles, and
held aside . . .

Madness, a viper, insinuates itself in my mind.
Of your universal rut?
For already the gold of my desire crumbles, and the ridiculous madness
insinuates itself, corrosive viper, within the reasonfibres of my brain.
But the supreme Place remained fixed in the stupidity of my silence.
Deserved silence
logical silence
cold silence
silence

From the solitary the answer will be born a No, both from me and another.
And I say to myself, with a feeling of joy and despair:
Then will I drink for long yet from the fertile purity of [insatiety]!

From *Lotus*

Requiem for the Saboteurs

Isaac Rammapo, Nigeria

This Night
out here in the night
the keen edge of Winter
cuts, raw; grit stings,
flung from the brooding
brows of tow'ring
sandy-headed gods,
out here in the night.

Chained all through the night,
the saxophone wails,
trumpet whines,
trombone murmurs,
pleading transition into happier mood
night after night
after night
and no kindly hand,
no feather touch to move
the stylus into gayer groove,
end the agony,
stay the blight.

Out here this night
warm bones twirl in fitful delirium
churned in the maelstrom of muted saxophones,
trumpets whining,
trombones murmuring,
this final fling,
out here this night;
for this night
at midnight

the drum's uneasy rumble breaks out in wild unrhythmic tattoo:
flesh fries
pungent with dash of powder
marrow for measure
reeking in Heaven's tardy nostrils.
sharp cry
pinned under brick and mortar
shrapnel-sharpened,
[backbone] broken
dead limbs dragged on purple ribbons
into the night.

This night
the moaning saxophone shall cease
her melancholy piece,
and the bitter cold of winter nights
mellow in the warmth of summer days.

From *Lotus*

The Magi in Europe

Khalil Hawi, Lebanon

"And Magi from the East did come preceded by a star . ..
Seeing the child they kneeled to him in adoration."

O Magi of the East, did you roam
The raging sea to the land of civilization
To see what God
Is newly appeared in the cave?
The path is here, and here the star
And here the travellers' needs!
The adventurous star did lead us here
Across Paris . . . where we saw the cells of thought
And grew surfeited with thought in carnivals,
In Rome the star was hid, the star was wiped away
But lust of priests amid the incense smokes,
We lost it then in London, and were lost
Amid the smog of coal, the riddle of trade!

On Christmas Eve, no star
Nor children's faith in child and cave.
Christmas Eve . . . Midnight . . . Boredom
A branching road ... sad laughter.
We slid down the cursed corridors
Of the city's caves
Eyes shifting from door to door
Eyes that we ask: where is the cave?
We went towards a red red lamp upon a door
Upon which the following words were carved:
"Earth's Paradise! Here no snake does lure.
No devot casts the stones.
Here are the flowers without thorns.
Here nakedness is purity . . . !"
Take off these masks

Made of the hateful skin of lizards!
— We [did] not doff nor did we put on masks.
We are from Beirut, a tragedy, we were born
With false faces and false minds.
The thought is born a whore in the "market",
Then spends her life mending the maiden head . . .
— "Take off these masks"
And in we went like those who did
Within the graveyard night.
Fires were lit, and bodies writhed
The fire dance to music of magician.
The darkness of the ceiling turned
To crystal chandeliers, and turned to blue.
The running not turned
To wine upon the walls . . . the alley mire to gold,
Wine ran into the bodies, made them pure.
No longer were they made of water and clay.

We mingled, nerves and heart and blood.
"You are in earth's paradise ...
Prayer . . . for heaven is on earth."
We kneeled in prayer to chemistry
And to a magician
Who fashioned paradise from graveyard night.
We worshipped him, a God in cave appearing:
O God of the weary
O God of the lost
O God escaped from sunlight stroke
And from the terror of certainty
O God hidden in the cave:
In the caves of the underworld
Of earth's civilization.

From *Lotus*

The Tattoo

Mohammed El-Maghout, Syria

Now
at the third hour of the twentieth century
where nothing
separates the bodies of the dead from the boots of the [passersby]
save the asphalt
I shall sit cross-legged on the street like a Bedouin Sheikh and I shall not rise
until all the prison bars and prison cards of the world are gathered,
put before me that I may chew them like a camel on the street . . .
until all the sticks of all the cops and of all demonstrators flee their owners' hands
to become flowering branches once again
in their native woods.

I [laugh] in the dark
I cry in the dark
I write in the dark
so that I can no longer recognise my pen from my fingertips.

Whenever the door knocks or a curtain moves
I cover my papers with my hands
like a whore at the moment of her arrest.
Who is it who left me this terror as a legacy,
this blood like a mountain cat?
Whenever I see an official paper on a threshold
or a hat from a door ajar
my bones clatter against my tears
and my blood from fear runs in every way
as if in eternal flight from the breeds of cops
pursuing it from vein to vein.

O my beloved!
In vain do I recover my courage and my name.
The tragedy is not here
in the whip or the desk or the warning sirens.
The tragedy is there
in the cradle . . . in the womb.
For I certainly
was not tied to the womb by an umbilical cord
but by a hangman's rope.

Translated by Nihad A. Salem.

From *Lotus*

Bypass the Day: Penetrate the Night

Rival Apin, Indonesia

Before young girls bloom,
before leaves green and flowers colour freshly,
squeezed by the extremities, where the limits can only be groped at
—and he cannot slip away, but must be honest in his self fulfilment—
tears shall notch the cheek,
thoughts burn the heart,
making one dry ash after the burning.

The dry season has arisen
and blows and scatters
the dry breath of death,
truth [happiness] in the first explosion.
From behind brick walls along lanes
death peers out never teasingly.
Man is only the child of a few hours.

The son of man now knows only broken hopes,
birds at the end of their songs.
And his heart, in the dry plain, is cracked rocks bereft of hope.
Now his mouth tastes bitterness,
his chest heaves, and he drags himself heavily into the grave.
Truth happiness in the first explosion,
truth acknowledged in the heart
but broken by thought, for
he asks guarantee to live as an ordinary man.

The first bitterness spreading in the mouth
and poisoning the breast,
the understanding that:
he has darkened the limits
between the ordinary man and the extraordinary man.

Both are the son of man
bound round by a few hours:
"in the beginning was the deed."
Truth acknowledged by the heart but broken by thought,
the extraordinary man asking a guarantee for his life;
for the man who runs like a hunted animal : the ordinary man
comes whipping at his wounds
he who has fled to the final hiding place
because he will not become a hireling.

Through love and faithfulness
let us be honest about
this life which nears in front of us
so beautiful, attractive and full of temptation,
whose road heads towards fear
the devils at the edge of the road
shouting their suggestions.

The flow followed
giving forgetfulness and honours
proves the presence of fear . . .
Is the earth an honour,
is that honour a firm foundation,
honour haunted by fear and regret,
but what must we fulfil?
Search for the final dream—
search for the last song—
but how? Neither shall ever end.

Both go on and on.
They can be brought about,
can, but how . . .
Where the end of distance is to be found,
the final region, at the foot of the sky,
never ending loneliness, never ending rejection,
never ending defense and the [strength] to stand on the foundation
not on the earth, not on the sea.

In the moment intermediate to earth and sea
and the two blues of the sky
the earth has a form and a name
belching tortuous clouds and . . .
The [phase] continues . . .
An awareness of place and time,
victory and defeat
make the fulfilment then return to the road,
the direction which first flowed from the heart.

In the seventh region at the foot of the opening sky,
in the region washed each day by rain
whether by day or night
search for the right moment,
search for the right place, and remember
There is no place nor time for he who born of the light
and who rejects the light.

He who is born in the overturned night
in the suddenly all at once smashed jungle
which at another time was a desert
he will live heading for the beaches a becoming the master
for he believes:
This is the earth, water and air
on which, in which and under which
the Son of Man must live.

He reckons all lives.
He is strong to count all deaths.
He holds his values.
The sea is eternal and has no limits
on which ships, lives sail.
He who has immersed himself in
the blue, the honesty of the sea, its storms and glassiness,
the source of all that lives,
the crater sending forth [strength]
And girls in all beauty after the hurricane,
will rise from the crystal blue sea.

Translated by Harry Aveling.

Creators of the Sun Tame Nature

Z. Afif, Indonesia

- I -

The sun was blotted out by the driving rain,
Frozen, the rocky mountains trembled,
We grew up sheltered in the warm embrace —
The warm embrace of the parents
Who are the peasants

creators of the sun

They are the peasants
— heart of the revolution.
O, no words can describe the scene before our eyes:
The great cause is being realised through the struggle —
The destruction and construction of nature:

waste rocky mountains are conquered

and turn green with flourishing crops.
— From the most arid centre of the earth
water is forced out
to irrigate the fields;
The fable of "the foolish old man who removed the mountains"
Has at last become a reality.

- II -

From different countries of fighting Asia and Africa
We come to a village of new China.
In the past it was unknown,
Today it is called Sha Shi Yu[1]
It's hard to locate it on the map.
Before liberation damnable landlords
Like rapacious, ravenous wolves
Stretched out their greedy claws to this place;
Even sand and rock became tools of exploitation.
Peasants starved, their corpses scattered everywhere.
Yet, who would have thought

    — the cruelty of the landlords
      — ferocious nature
        — and the hard stone

Like a scorching furnace
Steeled and tempered the peasants' bone.
The time came when they stood up, never again to yield;
They smashed the three great knives[2] pointing at their throats
And overthrew the three mountains[3] on their backs.
This is the great epic created
By the invincible labouring people!

---

1 Sha Shi Yu is Chinese for a sandy and rocky valley.
2 The three knives are: 1) forced labour, 2) rent, 3) interest.
  —various forms of exploitation of the peasants by the landlords.
3 The three mountains are: 1) imperialism, 2) feudalism, 3) bureaucrat capitalism.

- III -

From our different countries of fighting Asia and Africa
We have come to a village of new China,
Today they call it Sha Shi Yu,
Revolutionary base to crush Japanese fascism —
Revolutionary base of the Liberation war.
We meet the peasants and dine together
Around us crashing thunder and downpour
But our shouts of solidarity drown their din.
Sons and daughters of the two countries
— China and Indonesia
Discuss frankly.
Together they affirm:

> — The Communist Party and Mao Tse-tung's thought
> are the guarantee
> that the dark old China
> and unendurable sufferings of the past
> never will return.
> We are left with only the memory
> a lesson never to forget.
> It is we who have become the masters of the land
> and permit no monster or demon to ride roughshod;
> At their first appearance we will deal them
> ruthless blows —
> Blood hatred cannot be appeased!

We were impressed,
Lost in thought, wondering
And drawing lessons.

- IV -

The train swiftly speeds along from Tangshan
Racing against the twilight to Peking.
As the wheels carry it further and further away
The sound of drums, gongs and songs disappears on the air . . .
Voice of solidarity!
— Yafei renmin wansui![1]
And the accompanying thunderous applause and laughter,
Hearty and sincere.
As the train moves further and further along
I have a feeling of warmth and intimacy
We were soaked to the skin alike under the rain with muddy feet.
My heart is throbbing:

    — There is one thought
        — there is one feeling
            — there is one aim

Mao Tse-tung's thought has linked us together,
Mao Tse-tung is the commander at the front.
The more I think, the more I long
For my motherland locked in the liberation struggle —
I think of the Party that has guided me here today
And the peasants of Sha Shi Yu—
My wish is not only to partake a meal with you,
Above all it is to take part in your most significant labour —
To be tempered by you into a staunch revolutionary.

---

[1] "Yafei renmin wansui!" is Chinese for "Long live the Afro-Asian people!"

- V -

The train swiftly speeds from Tangshan
Racing against the twilight to Peking.
Vast expanses of green fields slip silently by
Brilliant in the moon and lamp light
The countryside is shimmering
I wonder to myself:

    — If they had not wholeheartedly applied
    the great teachings of Mao Tse-tung
    and unreservedly worked for revolution,
    could the peasants have become so prosperous
    and flourishing?

        This question is answered
        When we look around us
        Every face is radiant —
        Their greatest joy
    Is to live and die for the victory of revolution!

- VI -

From Tangshan to Peking
The train speeds along;
My thoughts outstrip it, flying beyond
To the motherland.
I recall Gunung Kidul
Barren and grey —
It is imprinted deeply on my mind.

Wonosari, O, Wonosari,
Sunbaked and bare the stony soil,
Dead the men, not having rice to eat since birth.
But, Oh, Gunung Kidul
If, even with these poor natural conditions,
More cruel still are the evil landlords
Who fatten themselves by sucking the blood of the peasants,
Is it right to lay blame on the land alone?

Albeit, you, Gunung Kidul
Must likewise be transformed
Just as the Sha Shi Yu production team;
For peasants have revolted, have risen up,
Have taken the road of Mao Tse-tung,
The gun gripped strongly in their hands,

Firmly believing:
"Political power grows out of the barrel of a gun."
In the spirit of
"The foolish old man who removed the mountains"
We will overthrow the feudal landlords —
Crush the Suharto-Nasution fascist military regime
Establish the people's democratic power;

And after that:
— exert all efforts,
using all the tools we can lay our hands on,
afforest the barren land
making sure that no one starves again.

- VII -

Tangshan
Sha Shi Yu
Model production team
The people's commune — Yao Ko Chuang
Pace-setter here,
An incarnation of Tachai.
Thanks to the wisdom and talent well-proved
Of the Communist Party and Mao Tse-tung,
"The foolish old man who removed the mountains"
Is now no longer mere fable
But has become reality.

It is man who decides everything.

From *The Call*

Lead We Follow O Great Helmsman!

Challezh Khaphezh Mouarxqui-Mahidah, *Kenya*

In the world the red sun of immortal thoughts
Of Marxism-Leninism shines bright!
O helmsman of the destiny of the world lead we follow,
Lead us O great teacher Chairman Mao,
Lead us to victory over collapsing imperialism,
Armed with your thoughts we fight all monsters,
And we are sure victory will be ours!

We fight reaction, modern revisionism and [McCarthyism],
Armed with your thoughts we fight on and on!
We'll never go back O Chairman Mao we promise!
Glorified be your name O great father of the world's oppressed,
Your day will be remembered for a red sun,
That vitalised Marx, Lenin and Stalin,
That gave the world a true understanding,
Of Progress and Liberty!

The modern revisionists
Fear You!
The aggressive Yankees and their paper tiger puppets,
Are going to their doom.
The world oppressed in love exclaim,
Chairman Mao lead we follow,
In this era of total victory of socialism,
Steer the course to prove history's victory,
Lead we follow O great helmsman!

From *The Call*

The Flaming Red Book: Eulogy to "Quotations from Chairman Mao Tse-tung"

Lambert Olayi, Congo

Happy as I, will be he who shall peruse the Scarlet Book of Mao Tse-tung,
The book of Knowledge
The book of Truth
The book of Light.
Happy will be the man of this century who receives these best seeds
of the abundant harvesting of Mao Tse-tung,
Even more happy will be those who shall sow them.

Proletariat from all horizons
Oppressed of all the distant climes
Gather round and take from the Scarlet Book of Mao Tse-tung
the wholesome
nourishment, the vitality necessary to all oppressed,
To all those struggling for Liberty.

Scarlet Book!
Lamp offered to all those who march in darkness searching for the light.
Shine on us!
Light up the peoples of the world,
Make wise the oppressed,
Make healthy and clear the sick minds!

Proletariat of all lands
Behold your guide for combat,
The Scarlet Book of Mao Tse-tung!
Study it!
Examine it carefully

Every day!
Its content is the work of an Intellect—a Thinker dedicated to the service of
Humanity for its salvation.
Read it!
Study the Scarlet Book of Mao Tse-tung!

Mao Tse-tung has given us this lamp.
Let the name of Mao Tse-tung be blessed throughout eternity!

Precious guide
        Inspired summary for all the militant
                Marxist-Leninists of the twentieth century!

From *The Call*

We Will Never Yield

Ahmed Khansa

I swear by the Fire
I swear by the Gun
I swear by the People and by our Flag
by those who push fearlessly into Death,
I swear that we will never bow
that we will never kneel.

Thousands and thousands come forth in wrath
waiting and working for the day of battle
for glory that is bought with Life
with boiling blood and wounds;
I swear
we will never kneel
to that scum
to those jungle beasts
who feed on children's blood.

Oh, knight in the battle field
tall, dark and sinewy
like a roaring lion in anger,
Ya Arabi!
Arise and all the world shall know
that we will never bow,
that we will never kneel.

My people! Oh, my people,
break the hacks of your enemies
without a grain of mercy!
Paint your horizons in crimson,
set it ablaze, a people's war
to drown in flames
the raving, hungry wolves!

Lo, tis a battle for the final say!
My people . . . go!
Heroes . . . be!
Be volcanoes
to bring back your stolen land!

We swore,
to remove the mark of shame
to drive out the aggressor
to engrave the name of Freedom
across an everlasting sun
to crush the raving wolves;
Until then,
we swear
that we will never yield.

From *The Call*

With the Father of a Martyr

Fata El Thawra

Without a tear in his eye,
without a moan or sigh
the old man said:
Don't grieve
Don't grieve
though my son is dead
he wrote his name with blood
I am happy because he paid his share
and for such a day
brought him up with care;
Don't grieve
Don't grieve.

Tread on your road of fire
tread on your road of thorns
but beware of pits and falls
the snake is nestling in our home
and darkness nibbling our morn
our flowers are watered with our blood
and we plant,
in our vine yard and field
our mines and traps instead;

Don't grieve
Don't grieve,
The night, the snake and the herds of wolves
their howling carrying the shriek of doom
all will be drowned and swept
in our surging ocean
in our mighty storm.
The storm of those
who are bred by suffering and toil.

From the points of our spears
dawn is already shining
from tops of hills and mountains
shining from our flaming wounds
front our salient eyes;
Hail our dawn
Hail our dawn.

From *The Call*

Pick in One Hand and Rifle in the Other

P. Sekuj

The construction work and song to life
Is resounding in the fields, factories and work-sites
The fatherland is flourishing ever more beautifully
Like a spring daisy
Whereas our enemies look into us with hatred
And even brandish their weapons
But no one dares touch this land of eagles
For it has the Party — mountain eagle at the head

Refrain:
Pick in one hand
We are building up the country
Rifle in the other
We defend the victories of this land
We are marching forward
And thus we will do at all times
Onward, ever onward
With our glorious Party at the head

In kindergartens you see children
Singing like nightingales to their happy life
They are brought up full of care
Their happy life is made by the sweat of their parents
If the enemy will go mad
And dare touch their joy
They'll surely fall under the steel shells
Of the hearts of the [party] and the people that are one

From The Call

Reply to Comrade Kuo Mo-jo: to the Melody of Man Chiang Hung

On this tiny globe
A few flies dash themselves against the wall,
Humming without cease,
Sometimes shrilling,
Sometimes moaning.
Ants on the locust tree assume a great nation swagger
And mayflies lightly plot to topple the giant tree.
The west wind scatters leaves over Changan,
And the arrows are flying, twanging.
So many deeds cry out to be done,
And always urgently;
The world rolls on,
Time presses.

Ten thousand years are too long,
Seize the day, seize the hour!
The Four Seas are rising, clouds and waters raging,
The Five Continents are rocking, wind and thunder roaring.
Away with all pests!
Our force is irresistible.

January 9, 1963

Kuo Mo-jo, famous Chinese writer and Vice-Chairman of the Standing Committee of the National People's Congress.
Line 6: In the short story Prefect of the Southern Branch by Li Kung-tso, a writer of the Tang dynasty, a man dozing under a locust tree dreamed that he married the princess of the Great Locust Kingdom and was made prefect of the Southern
Branch. When he awoke, he found that the kingdom was an ants' hole under the tree.
Line 7: In one of his poems Han Yu (824-768), a distinguished writer of the Tang dynasty, sarcastically compared people over reaching themselves to "mayflies which attempt to shake the giant tree".
Line 8: Changan was the capital of the Tang dynasty and is now called Sian.

From *The Call*

Kuo Mo-jo's Poem

Kuo M0jo

When the seas are in turmoil,
Heroes are on their mettle.
Six hundred million people,
Strong in unity,
Firm in principle,
Can keep the falling heavens suspended,
And create order out of the reign of chaos.
The world hears the cock crowing,
And day breaks in the east.

The sun rises,
The icebergs melt away.
Gold is not pinchbeck
And can stand the proof of flames.
Four great volumes
show us the way.
How absurd for Chich's dog to bark at Yao;
The clay oxen plunge into the sea and vanish.
The red flag of revolution is unfurling in the east wind,
The universe is glowing red.

Line 14: Four great volumes refers to the Selected Works of Mao Tsetung in four volumes.
Line 16: King Chieh was a wicked despot and Emperor Yao a benevolent ruler. Chieh's dog etc. refers to an old Chinese saying: *"At his master's voice, Chieh's dog barks at Yao."*

From *The Call*

Road To Liberation

By a Fighter, Palestine

From now on, my eyes shall shed no tears,
Nor will I complain, bewail and fear,
For tears cannot recover our beloved land,
Nor complaints resist oppression and torment;
The Security Council will never liberate our soil,
And our protests are of no avail.

Pain and hatred deep in my heart I'll bury,
With guns and rifles the situation I'll explain,
Every day, we are annihilating the enemy,
On every inch of land, destroying tyranny.
Area of tranquility must be turned into land of horror,
And those who made others homeless be held in terror.
From where the sun rises to where it sets,
The people of the whole world support Palestine.

From *The Call*

We'll Paint the Spring of Our People's Commune

Ma Cheng-chung (Chinese Commune Member), China

We listen to Chairman Mao's teachings,
And make water bow to our will.
Before the village a pond is dug,
Behind the village a dam is built,
Channels and ditches criss-cross in a web,
As water runs freely to irrigate the land.
A reservoir built with a power station,
Electricity lights up every member's home.

We listen to Chairman Mao's teachings,
And make soil bow to our will.
Silver hoes build up high-yield farms,
Iron ploughs conquer low-lying swamps.
Setting up model plots for scientific farming,
Keeping tight grasp on the Eight-Point Charter,[1]
In our fields red flowers of Tachai[2] also bloom,

---

[1] The Eight-Point Charter put forward by the great leader Chairman Mao Tsetung in 1958 is a systematic formulation of eight basic factors for increasing farm production. These factors are deep ploughing and soi improvement, fertilizer, water conservancy, seed selection, close planting, plant protection, field management and improvement of tools.

[2] Tachai refers to the Tachai Brigade of the Tachai People's Commune in Hsiyang County, Shansi Province, a red banner planted by Chairman Mao Tsetung on China's agricultural front. "In agriculture, learn from Tachai" is Chairman Mao Tsetung's great call to the whole nation.

> Boldly we'll advance to overfultil the Programme.³
> We listen to Chairman Mao's teachings,
> Hearts loyal, vision clear, spirits high.
> A thousand jin⁴ load but a feather,
> Crossing hills of swords, seas of fire but one step.
> We path-breakers in the Cultural Revolution,
> Monsters and demons will trample underfoot.
> With the great earth as paper, our hoes as brush,
> We'll paint the spring of our people's commune!

---

3 The Programme refers to the National Programme for Agricultural Development personally proposed by Chairman Mao Tsetung in January 1956. It was promulgated in April 1960. Here the author means the overfulfilment of the prodution targets set in the Programme.
4 One jin is equal to half a kilogramme.

From *The Call*

Azanian People Shall Triumph!

Azanian Poems

For centuries three
Azania has languished
In a kingdom of slavery
Deep in a swamp of exploitation
Oppression and dispossession
In the hell of white supremacy

For centuries three
Guns have we faced
Bullets have we chewed
Battles have we fought

But for centuries three
Azanian people have fought to be free!
Azanian people shall triumph!

The lone guerrilla fighter in the mountains,
Nor the unarmed student,
Forty-seven millions
Want to save the motherland
From the brutal lackeys
Who sold her out
To Yankee imperialism.

The great road will lead my country to greatness.
Victory and prosperity to those countries

That follow this road,
The road is pointed out
By the universal thought
That being universal
Is applicable to all the peoples.

Mao Tsetung's words,
Treasure of our time,
Have marked out for the world
The road to progress.

From *The Call*

No More! No More!

Azanian Poems

Our villages are groaning
Under the tyrannical yoke
Of feudal savagery

Our cities are the heavens
Of capitalist beasts and
A workingmen's hell

Our countries are run over
By imperialist dogs!
Our virgin lands raped and
Plundered
By white racist brutes

Over all this crime, my people now shout:
No more of apartheid! No more!
Death to the plunderers!

From *The Call*

Song Against Portuguese Aggression

Massa Makan Diabate, Mali

Coryphaeus
To a man, death is slow a-coming,
Though theirs was sudden;
I had to say these words,
As hard as stone . . .

Chorus
To those who died
For freedom,
We shall build no monument.
No stele can say enough of their greatness.
We shall not mourn for those
Who died for freedom,
Their cause is more just than life.
Those who died for freedom
Died a worthy death.

Narrator
One of them told me,
Bullets having pierced his body
And the winter cold paralysing his tongue:
"Life is still there,
It is coming back to live,
Nothing is more lasting."
Another man — still very young:
"Look, we are the men
Who live forever."

Coryphaeus
The eyes fixed on our future,
Always ready to fight,
We often hear them:
"Life is still there,
It is coming back to live,
Nothing is more lasting."

Chorus
We shall not mourn for those
Who died for freedom.
They left us
Their radiant faces
And the red of their blood.

Narrator
On that day,
I saw, high,
Above the tumult,
A man standing erect,
His gun, he had loaded it
With hatred, to the muzzle.

Coryphaeus
Ahmed Sekou Toure! . . .
Your pride is a road that stands the wind,
Your pride brings our paths together.
On that day, your voice, in Africa
Was the sovereign voice,
On that day, in your voice
Africa saw what separates us,
What in vain plots against us.

Chorus
To those who died
For freedom,
We shall build no monument.
No stele can say enough of their greatness.
We shall not mourn for those
Who died for freedom,
Their cause is more just than life.
Those who died for freedom
Died a worthy death.

From *The Call*

Cry Not, Child!

B. A. Mudadi, Zimbabwe

Cry not, child!
Your father has answered the call of the revolution.
He's taken up the gun,
So that you can live like a man.
He is gunning down the blood suckers.

Weep not, child!
Because father has refused to be crushed.
Wipe your tears and
Be prepared to take up his gun
As he falls and
To continue the glorious struggle
Until victory!
Island

From *The Call*

Marching Troops

Hong Thao, Vietnam

Nicest is the glow of youth,
Merriest is a send-off for front-bound lads,
Most boisterous is the rush of a post
Through a dense net of fire,
Most exciting is a combined attack,
Most precious is our people's love.

Flowers blooming good-bye when we start on
a march,
Flowers smiling welcome when we return
with victory.

From *The Call*

Buru Island

Mahyudin, Indonesia

Facing tortures and prison,
Karim, be firm for the people and the revolution,
Defend them
To your last day.

Wives having been killed,
Children roaming without food,
Against the enemy up we rose;
Revolutionary fighters filled with hatred,
Now stand erect in front of them.

Everyone who loves the people and revolution,
Like you, Karim,
Will in full hatred fight back
In revenge for the inhuman tortures.
Never forget that the fascist regime
One day will be crushed into smithereens.

Our eyes see through the iron bars,
Our hearts fly over the barbed wires.
Oh Buru Island,
The storm is gathering.
Karim,
Sing one of our revolutionary songs,
It will be heard all over the world.
Eyes and hearts behind the iron bars
Are steeled and filled with fury.
Fight on, Karim!
Never forget that the fascist regime
One day will be crushed into smithereens.

From *The Call*

SOLIDARITY

Fingers

Ousmane Sembène, Senegal

fingers, skillful at sculpture
At modeling figures on marble
At translation of thoughts
Fingers that would impress,
Fingers of artists.

fingers, thick and heavy
That dig and plough the soil
And open it up for sowing,
And move us,
fingers of land tillers.

A finger holding a trigger
An eye intent on a target-finder

Men at the very brink
Of their lives, at the mercy of this finger
The finger that destroys life.
The finger of a soldier.

Across the rivers and languages
Of Europe and Asia,
Of China and Africa,
Of India and the Oceans,
Let us join our fingers to take away
All power of this finger
Which keeps humanity in mourning

From *The Call*

From the Philippines to Vietnam

Jose Ma. Sison, The Philippines

Curse the birds of prey
That drop their iron eggs
Wantonly
That crush the fields
Viciously
Sowing hunger
Hatching death
Ripping the breast
Of our dear [brother land].

Vietnam! Vietnam!
Every bomb on your breast
Is a blow on our hearts.

The crags of your terror
Are in Mactan, Clark Field
Sangley point and [many-wheres];
The nests of evil here
Comfort the black birds
That torture you.

How many nests of evil
Have been built
On your soil?
How much fire and poison
Have the black birds breathed out?
How many claws
Have ruined and robbed you
Of your children and substance?

Answer us with mortars and rockets,
Land mines and night raids,
Answer us with your fight for freedom,
Answer us with cautious whispers
In your endless tunnels
And shout to us in triumph
After every battle against our common foe.

Let the wasps of your anger
Sting his ugly face.
Let the mountains break
The neck of the black birds.
Their dirty payload of fragmentation
And white phosphorous bombs
Can neither burn or break your spirit.

Nature is the friend of the fighting masses,
Command every inch of it with genius.
Let every bush, tree and rock be a shield,
Ensnare the enemy into the eye of rifle
Or into a pit of bamboo stakes
Hidden by rivers and carpets of leaves.

Let every coconut tree
Be the taut bow of an arrow.
Let the eastern wind
Strike at the western terror in flight.

From *The Call*

Red River Bridge
Rewi Alley, New Zealand

Out of Hanoi city runs
the Red River bridge;
Vietnamese courage,
Vietnamese hands built it
and now an arrogant, purse proud
U.S.A. rips at it with bombs;
"Submit, or else we shall tear
your land to shreds" the madman
yell, withal waveringly.

Dearly so Vietnamese love that bridge;
for them the Red River is part of
their lives, their tradition; a bridge
that realized early hopes; but deep
in their hearts they know the main stay
is the human spirit; what man has
built, man can build again, and build it
better; the thing to do now
is to toughen the will to fight back
so that no bomb can break it.

You escalate into our Hanoi
and on to the Red River bridge; we
carry the war with our American Negro
brothers right into the core of your
national life; no single great base
you have planted in our land and have
squandered your billions on, will be
safe from us; at our rear lies China;

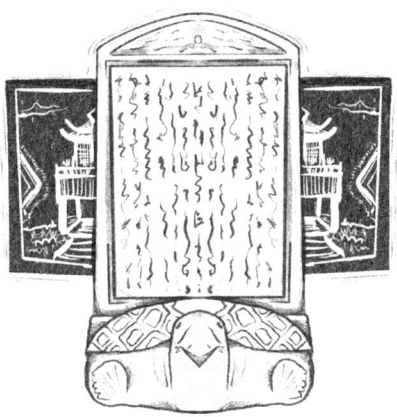

at your rear a pack of [jackals]; with us
increasingly are the peoples of
the world, while you ever become
as helpless as a policeman on
a Detroit street; when it comes
to building again, we shall build
all right; not one bridge but a hundred;
with you and your smelly gang clear
of Vietnam, all can be done.

Peitaibo
August 13, 1967

From *The Call*

3,000 Million and One Thought*

Roberto Crespo y Payno, Mexico

March forward thundering steps
On the long, long road
Coloured like fire
By the sun.
Take this road we must
From the five continents
To the horizon of aurora
That illuminates the whole world.

From Rio Bravo
To Rio de Plata
Men searching the horizons for answers
No longer listen to promises
That on the morrow
Bring them only sorrow.

The October Revolution
Led by Lenin
Gave power to the workers,
And the great Soviet nation
Built herself up into a bulwark
For the struggle for liberation
Arising throughout the world.
There stood on the expansive steppes
A powerful giant,
Resolutely following the course
Pointed by Stalin of Georgia.

---

* Extracts of the· dtiginal poem. — Ed.

Today, what contrast!
To Georgia went a forest worker
Who with emotion remembered
The great days that were defamed
By the renegades.

He was sent to the barren frontier
Truth repressed, traitors rampant.
With clarity Enver Hoxha declared:
Albania may be very small,
But follows a definite course.
If dare to come here the forces
That occupied Czechoslovakia,
They will have to face
A life-and-death struggle,
For a people's war
Never fails to win.

The outcry of the people
Trodden underfoot by the Kremlin,
Merges with the voices
That shout: "Yankees, go home!"

To capitalism and to revisionism
Will soon come the fatal hour
When they will be destroyed
By the fists and swords of world revolution.

The Indian people feed their hunger
With hatred of the present regime.
The Indonesians are shaking off
The pro-Yankee government.

The Japanese people go on the streets to fight
Against the crimes of the selling-out government.
In over thirty prefectures of Thailand
The patriotic forces spread armed struggle.

And in this Southeast Asia,
In Vietnam where ride rough-shod the U.S. imperialists,
The heroic people refuse their rule and shackle,
And united, they wage a valiant struggle.
Heroes of all Indo-China
Have fought for forty years for freedom.

And on the land where Lincohn
Freed the slaves,
There millions of Negroes
Are debased and enslaved.
There they saw fall dead before violence
Martin Luther King
Who had predicted victory
By the voice of reason.

Now the Black Power avows:
Violence for violence.
And what reason can there be
Where men's value
Is determined by race?
The Black people call
On their white brothers:
Unite and for liberation fight!

Six thousand million eyes
That were searching the horizon,
Have found the road
That through revolutionary war leads to triumphant peace

A tremendous struggle there will be,
But favourable will be the outcome.
This has been witnessed by mankind
As being proved by its one-fourth.
Bygone is the feudal yoke
And arise the Big Leap Forward
And the magnificent
Cultural Revolution.

To confront those who still wanted
That she live on "aid"
And continue to be enslaved,
China built her own factories,
Created new techniques of her own,
And was heard throughout the world
Her great nuclear explosion.

In smile are the old
Leading a life
That was undreamed of.
The young who sing
At work and in schools,
See the fruit
Of their labour and their study,
And seeing this coming from their own hands
Feel work a joy.

The golden wheat and corn,
The silver white rice,
The shining mirrors of metal pieces
Of which are made Diesel engines

Under the blue sky triumphantly speeding away.
The majestic black fluid
Bursting forth from the Taching Oil Field
Gives life to millions of motors,
On the land that foreign experts
Once declared as "oil poor."

The radiant red orchestras
Put an end
To the bourgeois domination of the stage.
Gongs, drums and other popular instruments,
Resound with a tonality of heroism,
Where the ivory key-board
Sings to the people of their own Odyssey,
Transforming the piano
That yesterday was only
A window dressing of western bourgeoisie.

Art was given the message:
Make the past serve the present,
And foreign things serve China.
Let a hundred flowers blossom,
Weed through the old
To bring forth the new.

It's the voice to creators of red art,
It's the voice to builders of red forges,
It's the voice to producers of red fruit.
It's the voice to researchers of red science,
It's the voice to makers of red heroes.

It's the voice of Comrade Mao,
To whom I wish to open my heart:
I wish to come to you
With simple words
To express my deep love
For the people you liberated,
Who, guided by a great thought,
Removed mountains with tremendous strength.

You are the light of a new sun
That guides our life
And leads us to go on
Along the correct road.

Mao Tsetung's words,
Quotations, essays and articles,
Are messages to all struggles,
Instructions, support and encouragement.

Mao Tsetung's words,
Treasure Of our time.
To all I must speak out
Of what I feel
Deep in my heart.

I can see that throughout the world
All people will say the same,
It's for this that all Chinese people,
When they glorify your name
And sing of their victory,
Make known to all
That it is your thought that guided their way.
Mankind will say
What I have said:
"Mao Tsetung's words,
Treasure of our time."

Treasure that reaches
Each people in their language,
Journals, pamphlets, books,
Carry your thought
As the guide to the whole world.

There are just wars,
And unjust wars,
As you have taught us.
And now, to win a real peace,
The only just war is the people's war.

Out of the flames comes light,
Political power grows out of the barrel of a gun.
With arms tightly held in our hands
We beat to their knees those
Who refuse to let us live.
People of the whole world,
Arms may be important,
But the decisive factor is man!

Mexico of thousand wounds!
Our love can surely heal you.
By sacrifices we have awakened our great Mexico!
Now you are no longer

From *The Call*

Mao Tsetung and Revolution

Surono, Indonesia

In the east dawn gleams
Red radiates the sky
On peaks and dales
Red flags welcome the tempest

Column after column advances
Raising fists high
The world's in the grip of the people
How powerful
Victorious jubilation of the revolutionary army's millions
Resounding throughout the world
Raising powerful waves
World's revolution leaps

For us
Mao Tsetung and revolution
Mao Tsetung means revolution

Every inch of the earth
Glows crimson red
Thunder roaring in five continents
We tightly hold the guns
Raising aloft the victorious banner
Filled with confidence
We shout
"Political power grows out of the barrel of a gun"
Success and failure taught us
This is the only road
One and indivisible
Gun
Power

For us
Mao Tsetung and revolution
Mao Tsetung means revolution
In the east dawn gleams
Red radiates the sky
"The earth shall rise on new foundations
We have been naught
We shall be all"

From *The Call*

In Memory of G. Jackson

M. Tolliver, U.S.A.

Ah, young George Jackson*, the man
Who had a lot to say
Against oppression and for liberation
But he's not alive today.

And yet such men, while alive
Though in the struggle they stand at the head,
When they die, to the enemy,
(This is true!) Are still more dangerous dead!

Behold ferocious Jackson with a bullet
wound in his head.
He stands before us speaking.
The enemy trembles, squeaking.
He's pointing out and shooting at
The monsters in the night.

All right, you monsters who growl and spit,
We've had quite enough of it!
Close on the heels of Jackson march women and men
Who will make America a people's democracy that's genuine.
Attica has fought well, so did Ashkalon.**
Right on! Arise, you heroes tall!
Your lighting spirit radiates light
Although your bodies fall.

---

* George Jackson, a young American progressive, was imprisoned in 1960 and killed at the age of 29 by the American reactionaries in summer of 1971.
** Prison in occupied Palestine, where prisoners revolted after Attica and other U.S. prison uprisings.

From *The Call*

How Long, Comrade?

H. Kaluenja, Namibia

Each day you ask me how long?
How long shall we continue the march?
How long shall the fighting last?
And how long shall we remain in bondage?

But I have always said to you:
Please, let us go on, Comrades,
To fulfil the Mission the people entrusted to us,
And report back when all is done!

I have also told you that the road is long.
It is hard, and it needs patience.
We need perseverance and courage
And the will both to be free and resist hardships.
I told you that it was victory for Algeria the other day,
And heroic Vietnam yesterday.
Today it is for Guinea-Bissau,
And tomorrow, the day will be ours.

There is no easy way to victory, Comrades,
And that is why we must persist in fighting.
That is why we must remember what the
people expect of us,
To be optimistic and firm in resistance.

If you ask me how long again,
Then I will tell you that
All depends on our efforts,
And we must also win world solidarity.

From *The Call*

BIOGRAPHIES

Salah Abdel Sabour *(1931-1981)* was an influential Egyptian poet who was one of the pioneering figures in the development of free verse. He was also a critic, playwright, essayist, and editor. During his life, he worked as a teacher and journalist, and held positions in Egypt's Ministry of Culture as well as being head of the General Egyptian Book Organisation. His most notable works include *Dreams of the Old Knight* (1964) and a poetic drama entitled *The Tragedy of Hallaj* (1965). He died of a heart attack at the age of 50.[1]

Fadhil al-Azzawi *(1940-)* is a prominent Iraqi poet, novelist, and writer. He earned a BA in English Literature from Baghdad University before earning a PhD from Leipzig University. He founded the poetry magazine *Shi'ir 69* (Poetry 69), which was eventually banned. Some of his most notable works include the poetry collection *Miracle Maker* (2003) and novels *The Last of the Angels* (2007) and *The Traveler and the Innkeeper* (2011). Al-Azzawi's writings have been translated into several languages including English, French, German, Turkish, and Persian. He was imprisoned for three years by the Baʿth regime in Iraq before leaving his country in 1977. He has been living in Berlin since 1983 working as a freelance writer.[2]

Abd Al-Wahhab al-Bayati *(1926-1999)* was an influential Iraqi poet. He worked as a teacher in Iraq before being expelled due to his leftist political ideologies. He opposed both the monarchy in Iraq as well as the rule of the Baʿth party that followed and spent most of his life in exile. Al-Bayati was well-known for his contributions to the modern form of Arabic poetry that defied classical poetic systems regarding meter, themes, and structure. His best-known works include *Mala'ika wa Shayateen* (1950; Angels and Demons) and *Abariq Muhashama* (1954; The Broken Jugs) which was a pillar of Arab poetry's modernist movement. He died in Damascus due to heart failure at the age of 72.[3]

Nazik Al-Malaika *(1923-2007)* was an influential Iraqi poet who was most notable for introducing elements of free verse into her poetry, making her one of the first Arab poets to do so. She was one

---

1   "Salah Abdel Sabour (1981-1931)," Egyptian Figures, January 2025, 31, https://bit.ly/3T2x9fr.
    "Salah 'Abd al-Sabur (1981-1931)," Jehat, January 2025, 1, https://bit.ly/4k2pZD6
2   "Fadhil Al-Azzawi," International Literature Festival (Berlin), January 2025, 31, https://bit.ly/44s6IpV
3   Linda Sue Grimes, 2024, Life Sketch of "Abdul Wahab al-Bayati," Owlcation, https://bit.ly/4eahDI6

of the pioneering writers involved in the Arabic literary movement known as Tajdeed, which brought forth several innovations in Arabic poetry and literature in general. Some of her most notable works include "Cholera" (1947), a poem many consider to be the first modern Arabic poem, and the poetry book *Sparks and Ashes* (1949). She died due to illness at the age of 83.[4]

Yusuf al-Sibai *(1917-1978)* was a prominent Egyptian novelist, writer of short stories, and critic. He was best known for his novels that were described as romantic and dealt with political and social issues in Egypt and the Middle East. Some of his most well-known publications include *The Land of Hypocrisy* (1962) and *Life is a Moment* (1973). In 1973, al-Sibai was appointed Minister of Culture by Egypt's president Anwar al-Sadat and was known for supporting al-Sadat's initiative to make peace with Israel. Al-Sibai was also elected General Secretary of the Afro-Asian Writers' Association, which began publishing *Lotus* magazine. He was assassinated in Cyprus while attending an Afro-Asian conference at the age of 60.[5]

Badr Shakir al-Sayyab *(1926-1964)* was an influential Iraqi poet. Al-Sayyab was one of the most prominent poets in the Arab movement of Tajdeed, whose work introduced several pioneering innovations in Arabic poetry, including developments in meter and the use of metaphors. His most notable poem is "Rain Song" (1960). At one point, he was politically affiliated with the Communist Party and promoted principles of Arab nationalism while being a fervent supporter of the Palestinian cause. He died due to illness at the age of 38.[6]

Mulk Raj Anand *(1905-2004)* was a prominent Indian novelist. He wrote in English and was highly influential for his vivid portrayal of the Indian people and the socio-economic conditions of the country. He was also one of the first writers to incorporate Hindustani and Punjabi phrases into English. His most notable works include *The Village and The Sword and the Sickle* (1942). He criticised the caste system

---

4   Simone Stevens, "Nazik al-Malaika (2007-1923) Iraqi Woman's Journey Changes Map of Arabic Poetry," Al Jadid, 2008-2007, https://bit.ly/44halhn
5   "Rossen Djagalov. The Afro-Asian Writers Association and Its Literary Field," Syg.ma, July 2021, 15, https://bit.ly/4lg0zCN
    Mustafa Marie, "Egypt Today commemorates birth anniversary of Yusuf Sebai," Egypt Today, June 2019, 17, https://bit.ly/45ywk5F
6   "Sayyab Badr Shakir Al-Sayyab - (1964-1926)," Universalis, accessed February 2025, 5, https://bit.ly/4ndkbcs

prevalent in India through his work and played an active role in the Indian independence movement. He also admired the principles of communism. He died due to illness at the age of 98.[7]

Mário Pinto de Andrade *(1928-1990)* was a prominent Angolan writer, poet, politician, and critic. After studying philosophy in Portugal and sociology in France, he became most recognised for fervently opposing Portuguese colonial rule in his home country and actively expressing his resistance through writing anti-colonial poetry. He later played a significant role in the founding of the Angolan Communist Party and then founded and became the first president of the MPLA (Popular Movement for the Liberation of Angola). His publications included anthologies of African poetry written in Portuguese. He died due to illness at the age of 62.[8]

Ali Ahmad Said Esber, also known as **Adonis** *(1930-)* is an influential Syrian poet, essayist, critic, and translator who is considered the most important Arab literary figure in the late twentieth and early twenty-first centuries. His most notable works include *The Songs of Mihyar the Damascene* (1961), his *Anthology of Arabic Poetry* (1964), a collection of Arabic poems over the past two thousand years, and his translation of Ovid's *Metamorphosis* (2002). During his early life, he was associated with the Syrian Social Nationalist Party and remains an avid supporter of secularism.[9]

Nobuo Ayukawa *(1920-1986)* was an influential Japanese poet and literary critic considered one of the most important figures of post-war Japanese literature and modern Japanese poetry. Ayukawa deviated from traditional Japanese themes of the time and focused on the abstract and stylistic elements of poetry. His work is collected in *America and Other Poems* (2007) which includes his early poems about his experience as a frontliner during World War II. His later works are known for representing peace through anti-war sentiments in Japan. Moreover, he was heavily influenced by Western literature and translated works by T. S. Eliot and William S. Burroughs.[10]

---

7   "Mulk Raj Anand," Britannica, accessed February January 2025, 31, https://bit.ly/3HOUDlT
8   "Mário Pinto de Andrade," Britannica, accessed February 2025, 1, https://bit.ly/465EOkI
9   "Adonis (Ali Ahmed Said Esber)," Barjeel Art Foundation, accessed January 2025, 21, https://bit.ly/4eh0Tz9 Jonathan Randal and Scott MacLeod, 2014 "Age of Darkness," The Cairo Review, https://bit.ly/3Tz0tKJ
10 "Nobuo Ayukawa," Kaya, January 2025, 31, https://bit.ly/43SHReL

Mahim Bora *(1924-2016)* was a writer and poet from the Indian state of Assam. He wrote in Assamese and is known for having served as president of the literary organisation Assam Sahitya Sabha and the Assam Literary Society after being elected in 1989. He pursued a teaching career and wrote short stories for periodicals in addition to poetry collections. His most prominent work is the poetry anthology *Rangajivya* (1978; The Red Dragonfly). Bora's writings aimed to reflect the culture and traditions of Assam. He was also known for his translations from Assamese into English.[11]

Bernard Binlin Dadié *(1916-2019)* was a prominent Ivorian novelist, poet, dramatist, critic, and former minister. He moved to Senegal at an early age, working for the French government there. He then returned to the Ivory Coast and became a staunch advocate for independence, fervently supporting the struggle against colonialism. At one point, he was imprisoned by the French for openly opposing their government. Most of his writings dealt with colonialism as well as African traditions and culture. Some of these are *La Ville où nul ne meurt* (1968; The City Where No One Dies) and *Monsieur Thôgô-gnini* (1970; Mr. Thôgô-gnini). Later, he published the novel *Commandant Taurcault et ses nègres* (1980; Commander Taurcault and His Negroes). After the Ivory Coast gained independence, he was appointed Minister of Culture in the Ivorian government from 1977 to 1986. He died in 2019 at the age of 103.[12]

Mahmoud Darwish *(1942-2008)* was a prominent Palestinian poet and is considered one of the most important literary figures in the Arab world. His poetry reflected feelings of exile, loss, and struggle for freedom. The Lebanese composer Marcel Khalife set many of his poems to music, which led to their increased popularity, most notably "I Yearn for My Mother's Bread" and "Rita and the Rifle." Darwish was associated with the Israeli Communist Party, and later joined the Palestine Liberation Organisation. He also believed that peace between Palestine and Israel was attainable. Following complications due to heart surgery, he passed away in 2008.[13]

---

11   Mahim Bora, Kathanibarighat : Mahim Bora, Indian Review, accessed February 2025, 1, https://bit.ly/4ejRmay
12   "Bernard Binlin Dadié," Britannica, accessed February 2025, 1, https://bit.ly/3T35awk
13   Issa J. Ballouta, "Mahmoud Darwish and the Loss of Palestine," Al Jadid, accessed February 2025, 1, https://bit.ly/3HTkkll

Dazai Osamu *(1909-1948)* was an influential Japanese author who is considered one of the most important Japanese writers of the twentieth century. He battled depression and was known for attempting suicide several times during his life. At one point, he held communist beliefs for which the Japanese government arrested him. In 1945, to escape American raids, he lived in an annex next to his parents' house in Tsugaru with his wife and children, where he wrote twenty-two literary works. He is best known for his work in fiction, most notably his novels *Shayō* (1947; The Setting Sun) and *No Longer Human* (1948). His works are characterised by an expressive style, dealing with several personal issues through his writings. He ultimately took his own life by drowning at the age of 38 before finishing his novel entitled *Goodbye*.[14]

Mohammed Dib *(1920-2003)* was an Algerian novelist, writer of short stories, and poet. His French-written works are best known for dealing with the Algerian struggle for independence from French colonialism. He started writing poetry at a very young age before studying literature at the University of Algiers and then working as a teacher in Morocco. He married a French woman and joined the Algerian Communist Party in the 1950s. The French authorities later expelled him from Algeria due to his political beliefs. He died in Paris at the age of 82.[15]

Gevorg Emin *(1918-1998)* was an Armenian poet, essayist, and translator. He graduated from a polytechnic institute as an engineer, before fighting in World War II for the Soviet Union. He wrote that his higher education in engineering helped him become an adroit writer, giving him the proper "discipline and sense of form and construction." He received the Stalin Prize in 1951 and the USSR State Prize in 1976. Some of his most notable works include *Seven Songs About Armenia* (1983), as well as his translations of Polish poetry.[16]

Sengiin Erdene *(1929-2000)* was a prominent Mongolian novelist and writer. He worked as a psychiatrist for a few years before fully dedicating his time to writing. His literary

---

14 "Dazai Osamu," Britannica, accessed February 1, 2025, https://bit.ly/43Vskei
15 "Mohammed Dib," Britannica, accessed February 1, 2025, https://www.britannica.com/biography/Mohammed-Dib
16 "Gevorg Emin," Find a Grave, accessed February 1, 2025, https://bit.ly/4nrRKb8

works incorporate elements of modernism in addition to exhibiting a traditional Mongolian ambiance. He is thus considered one of the foremost writers of modern Mongolian literature. Two of his most well-known novels are *Sun Cranes* (1972) and *Zanabazar* (1989). Erdene was also awarded several Mongolian state awards and was named People's Writer of Mongolia. He died due to natural causes at the age of 71.[17]

Faiz Ahmad Faiz *(1911-1984)* was a revolutionary Pakistani poet. He is one of the most prominent poets in the Urdu language and also wrote in Punjabi. His work is considered essential to the development of Pakistani literature and art in general. His most notable poem is "We Shall See" (1979). He received the Lenin Peace Prize in 1962 and was known for his affiliation and ardent support of the Communist Party. He died due to illness shortly after receiving news of his Nobel Peace Prize nomination.[18]

Rasul Gamzatov *(1923-2003)* was a prominent poet of the former Soviet Union. Known as the People's Poet of Daghestan, he is generally regarded as the most famous poet to write in the Avar language. He was born in Tsada, an Avar village, and started writing poetry at an early age, as his father was a famous bard. Several of Gamzatov's poems became well-known songs, including "Gone Sunny Days" (1939) and the famous "Zhuravli" (1976) which dealt with World War II. He was awarded the State Stalin Prize and the Lenin Prize. He died at the age of 80.[19]

Daniil Granin *(1919-2017)* was a Russian prose writer and chairman of the Union of Writers. He studied engineering and served his country during World War II. He did not begin consistently publishing his work until he graduated from college, after which he began working as an engineer. His works are best known for their reflections on the tough choices one may face in making the righteous or "moral" decisions, as well as their accurate portrayal of war experiences. A few of his most notable works include the short story "The Second Variant" (1949) and his novel *Those Who Seek* (1955). He died in 2012 at the age of 98.[20]

---

17 "Life and work of the Mongolian writer Sengijn Erdene," Mongolian Art, accessed February 2025,1, https://bit.ly/3ZHt30
18 "Faiz Ahmad Faiz, 1984-1911," Library of Congress New Delhi Office, accessed February 2025,1, https://bit.ly/3HMmkfj
19 "Rasul Gamzatov (2003-1923)," Rasul Gamzatov, accessed February 2025,1, https://bit.ly/44gDIjO
20 Efim Schumann, "A survivor speaks," Deutsche Welle, January 2014,27, https://bit.ly/44rnvt9

Colette Anna Gregoire, better known as **Anna Greki** *(1931-1966)*, was a French poet who identified herself as Algerian. She was born and raised in Algeria and later attended college in Paris. She left her studies behind and returned to Algeria to teach, work for the Algerian Communist Party, and support the nation in its struggle against the French. As a result, she was imprisoned, tortured, and eventually banished to France by the French government. Her most recognised poetry collection is *Algeria, Capital Algiers* (1963). She died while giving birth at the age of 34.[21]

Malek Haddad *(1927-1978)* was an Algerian novelist and poet who wrote in the French language. He was an innovative writer who incorporated modernist developments into the novel and poetry writing of his day. He served as Algeria's Director of Culture at the Ministry of Culture and Information after the country's independence from France. Some of his most notable works include the novels *Je t'offrirai une gazelle* (I Will Offer You a Gazelle, 1959*)* and *Le Quai aux fleurs ne répond plus* (The Flower Quay No Longer Answers*,* 1961). He died due to complications from cancer at the age of 50.[22]

Buland al-Haidari *(1926-1996)* was an influential Iraqi poet. Born to a Kurdish family, he was known for his leftist ideological affinities and frequent opposition to the Iraqi government, which led to him living much of his life in exile. He is best known for his role in the free verse literary movement in the Arab world, where he introduced pioneering structures, themes, rhymes, and meters into his poetry. His first poetry collection *Khafqat Teen* (1946, *Beating of Clay*) is generally considered revolutionary in both style and content. He died at the age of 70.[23]

Suheil Idris *(1925-2008)* was a Lebanese journalist, novelist, and writer of short stories. He founded Al-Adab, which was one of the most influential Arabic literary journals of the twentieth century. He also founded Dar-Al-Adab, a prominent publishing house in the Arab World based in Lebanon. Idris was well known for translating the works of writers such as Albert Camus and Jean-Paul Sartre from French into Arabic. Moreover,

---

21 René Gallissot, "GREKI Anna, literary pseudonym of GREGOIRE Colette [Algeria Dictionary]," Le Maitron, December 24, 2023, https://bit.ly/4k3otQW
22 "Malek Haddad," Britannica, accessed February 1, 2025, https://bit.ly/4kkQ2FP
23 "Buland al-Haidari," All Poetry, accessed February 3, 2025, https://bit.ly/4eh9xxB

his own literary works are characterised by their blending of autobiographical components with Arab nationalist ideologies and French existentialist literary elements. His three novels are *The Latin Quarter* (1953), *Al-Khadaq Al-Ghamiq* (1958), and *Our Fingers That Are Burning* (1962). He died due to illness at the age of 83.[24]

Yusuf Idris *(1927-1991)* was a famous Egyptian short story writer, novelist, and playwright. He first studied to become a doctor before shifting his focus exclusively to literature. He opposed King Farouk's regime and was persecuted and imprisoned for his views. Idris then supported the rise of Gamal Abdel Nasser and was an adherent of his political ideologies. His plays and writings were best known for incorporating elements of traditional Egyptian culture into his work, including the Egyptian Arabic dialect. His best-known play is *The Farafeer* (1964). He died due to illness at the age of 64.[25]

Fazil Iskander *(1929-2016)* is an Abkhazian writer, poet, novelist and writer of short stories who wrote in Russian and is best known for his satirical and anecdotal writing style, as well as his extensive use of humor. He was born to an Iranian father and an Abkhazian mother. He politically disassociated from Abkhazia's attempts to separate from Georgia, speaking out against political and ethnic conflicts and stating that both Georgian and Abkhazian sides are at fault. Some of his most notable works include *Sandro of Chegem* (1973), *The Goatibex Constellation* (1974), and *Chik and His Friends* (1985).[26]

Zulfiya Isroilova *(1915-1996)* was an Uzbek writer and poet. Her poems are known for their emphasis on work-related themes, as well as their vibrant imagery and prevailing sense of optimism. She worked as editor-in-chief for *Saodat* magazine and was a part of the Communist Party in the mid-1950s. She attended the Asian-African Solidarity Conference held in Cairo in 1957. Her first poetry collection was *Hayot varaqlari* (1932; Pages of Life) followed by several other publications including "Yuragimga yaqin kishilar" (1958; People Who

---

24   Mahmoud Saeed, "In Memoriam: Suheil Idriss (2008-1925): Founder of Al Adab 'moved the waters' of Arab Literature," 2009, https://bit.ly/4kM76W0
25   "Yūsuf Idrīs," Britannica, accessed February 2025, 1, https://bit.ly/4kM73JO
26   "Fazil Iskander," Britannica, accessed February 2025, 1, https://bit.ly/44bLzz8

Are Close to My Heart). She is a well-respected literary figure in Uzbekistan, as she was selected National Poet in 1965. The Uzbek national award for women was named after her. She died in 1996 at the age of 81.²⁷

Ali Sardar Jafri *(1913-2000)* was an influential Indian poet, lyricist, and scholar, best known for his writings in Urdu. He was a member of the Communist Party in India and was known for his anti-war sentiments, which led to his arrest in the early 1940s. He was also one of the founding members of the Progressive Writers' Association. His writings were patriotic and revolutionary, attempting to give a voice to the oppressed. Some of his most notable poetry collections include *Salute to a New World* (1948) and *Asia Awakes* (1951). He was the winner of the Jnanpith Award in 1997. He died in Mumbai at the age of 86.²⁸

Edward al-Kharrat *(1926-2015)* was an Egyptian novelist, writer of short stories, and critic. He was a Coptic Christian and was best known for his experimental writings as an avant-garde writer. He worked as a translator in the Romanian embassy and was jailed at one point for his Marxist ideologies. Al-Kharrat was actively involved with the Afro-Asian Peoples' Solidarity Organisation and the Afro-Asian Writers' Association and edited *Lotus* issues. Some of his most notable works include his collection of short stories *Hitan Aliya* (1958; High Walls) and his novel *Ramah wal Tinneen* (2002; Ramah and the Dragon).²⁹

Hajime Kijima *(1928-2004)* was a Japanese poet, author, lyricist, and essayist. He is well known for his translations of American literature, most notably the works of Langston Hughes and Nat Hentoff, as well as Ezra Jack Keats. He also wrote children's books. Some of his most notable works include the anthology *The Poetry of Post-War Japan* (1975), the poetry collection *One Planet*, as well as his collaboration with sculptor Churyo Sato for *The Tree*, which placed his poetry alongside Sato's sketches.³⁰

Mazisi Kunene *(1930-2006)* was a South African poet best remembered for his staunch opposition to apartheid in South Africa, known for its segregation

---

27 "Zulfia (1996-1915)," Ziyouz, 2013, https://www.ziyouz.uz/en/uzbek-literature/-41literature-of80-30-s-of-xx-century/-120zulfia1996-1915-.
28 "Profile of Ali Sardar Jafri," Rekhta, accessed February 2025, 3, https://bit.ly/4ld2Iix.
29 Amal Amireh, "Edward al-Kharrat and the Modernist Revolution in the Egyptian Novel," Al Jadid, 1996, https://bit.ly/44gEXQ0.
30 "Japanese Writers and Iowa: 1976-1967," Iowa University, accessed February 2025, 6, https://bit.ly/4l06bBG.

laws. Kunene was exiled but continued to support movements opposing the regime, founding the Anti-Apartheid Movement in Britain. He eventually became the chief representative for the African National Congress in Europe and Africa, as well as a Cultural Adviser at UNESCO before teaching at UCLA. He is best known for his poem "Emperor Shaka the Great" (1979). He died of cancer at the age of 76.[31]

Alex La Guma *(1925-1985)* was a South African writer and activist. He is considered one of the most important South African writers of the twentieth century as his work reflects his staunch opposition to the apartheid system in South Africa. He was the leader of the South African Coloured People's Organisation and a defendant in the 1956 Treason Trial. He was exiled from South Africa in 1966 for his political views and spent the rest of his life in exile. Some of his publications include *A Walk in the Night* (1962), *And a Threefold Cord* (1964), and *The Fog of Season's End* (1972). He won the Lotus Prize for Literature in 1969.[32]

Abdul Hayee, better known by his pen name **Sahir Ludhianvi** *(1921-1980)*, was a prominent Indian lyricist and poet. He worked as an editor and was a part of the Progressive Writers' Association. He was associated with Communism and was persecuted for his political beliefs. The Pakistani government issued a warrant for his arrest, prompting him to flee to Delhi. He wrote in Urdu and Hindi and had a profound influence on Indian cinema, as some of his works include lyrics to songs in Indian films, most notably the film *Baazi* (1951; *Gamble*). He died of a heart attack at the age of 59.[33]

Zaki Naguib Mahmoud *(1905-1993)* was a prominent Egyptian philosopher and critic considered a modernist by many. He promoted logical positivism, a school of thought that sought to reconcile philosophical and intellectual discourse with empirical sciences. He also aimed to portray Arab traditions and conventions in a way that demonstrated they did not contradict scientific thought. Moreover, Mahmoud was notable for his journalistic work, as he was editor-in-chief of the magazine *Contemporary Thought* to which he also contributed by

---

31 "Mazisi Raymond Kunene," South African History Online, accessed February 2025, 3, https://bit.ly/4l3mtta
32 "Alex la Guma," South African History Online, accessed February 2025, 4, https://bit.ly/4lmt81I
33 "Sahir Ludhianvi," Sahir Ludhianvi, accessed February 2025, 4, https://bit.ly/4latrMS

writing a monthly column titled "Philosophical Trends." He died in Cairo at the age of 88.[34]

Mouloud Mammeri *(1917-1989)* was a prominent Algerian linguist, novelist, poet, and writer of short stories. He is of Berber origin and many of his writings dealt with the study and analysis of the Tamazight language. He fled to France during the Algerian War and returned after independence. While in Algeria, Mammeri taught Berber courses and the Tamazight language despite the government's active opposition. Some of his most notable works include *The Forgotten Hill* (1952), *The Sleep of the Just* (1955), and *Opium and the Stick* (1965). He was killed in a car accident at the age of 71.[35]

Yuri Nagibin *(1920-1994)* was a prominent Soviet writer, novelist, screenwriter, and literary critic. His father was executed before he was born. He served his country during World War II, but was wounded and hospitalised after which he returned to the front as a war correspondent for the daily newspaper *Trud*. Some of his most notable works include "Great Heart" (1944) and "Grain of Life" (1948), both of which reflect on his experience during the war.[36]

Sergey Narovchatov *(1919-1981)* was a Russian writer, poet, and critic. He was a member of the Soviet Communist Party and served in the Soviet Army during World War II. Themes across his poetry reflect his experience with revolution and war, and his writing style is characterised as clear and articulate. Some of his most notable works include the collections *The Campfire* (1948) and *The Soldiers of Freedom* (1952). He was best known for being editor-in-chief of the Russian literary magazine *Novy Mir*, meaning New World.[37]

Dashdorjiin Natsagdorj *(1906-1937)* was an influential Mongolian poet and playwright known as one of the pioneering figures of modern Mongolian literature. He studied at the Political Academy of Leningrad and at Leipzig University of Berlin before returning to Mongolia, where he founded the Mongolian Writers' Union. He was skeptical of leftist ideologies and was imprisoned for his political views in 1932. His most notable works include the poem "My Native

---

34   "Zaki Naguib Mahmoud," Philosophy of the Arabs, February 2025, 5, https://bit.ly/3ZHmRVX
35   "Mouloud Mammeri," Britannica, accessed February 2025, 5, https://bit.ly/44cq6G2
36   Jeanne Vronskaya, "Obituary: Yuri Nagibin," Independent, 1994, https://bit.ly/4lnXfpv
37   "Sergey Narovchatov," People, accessed February 2025, 13, https://bit.ly/4l07Nve

Land" (1933), which describes the beauty of Mongolia, and the story "The Three Sad Hills" (1934) which was made into an opera. He died of a stroke on a street in Ulaanbaatar at the age of 30.[38]

Hiroshi Noma *(1915-1991)* was a Japanese writer and novelist. He was born to a highly spiritual Buddhist family and was raised to succeed his father as head priest of his sect. Noma grew up to be interested in literature, was highly influenced by European forms of fiction writing, and was specifically drawn to French Symbolist poetry. At one point, he was a member of the Communist Party. He is best known for his war novel *Zone of Emptiness* (1952) and for winning the Lotus Prize for Literature in 1972. He died in 1991 at the age of 76.[39]

Gabriel Jibaba Okara *(1921-2019)* was a Nigerian novelist and poet renowned for depicting the folklore of his African heritage through his literary works, in addition to exploring the changes that African culture faced because of its eventual interaction with Western culture. He studied journalism in the United States and later worked as an Information Officer for the Eastern Nigerian Government Service before the beginning of the civil war. He then worked in civil service during the 1960s. His most famous works include the poems "Piano and Drums," "You Laughed and Laughed and Laughed," and "Once Upon a Time," written in the 1970s. He died in 2019 at the age of 97.[40]

Amrita Pritam *(1919-2005)* was an influential Punjabi poet, novelist, and essayist. Born in what is now Pakistan, she is considered one of the leading figures in Punjabi literature and one of the most prominent female writers of her time. She wrote expressively in both Punjabi and Hindi reflecting on personal experiences and highlighting various social issues. Among her notable literary work s is the poem "Ode to Waris Shah" (1992), which aimed to depict the destruction and trauma due to the partition of India. She died due to illness at the age of 86.[41]

Jean-Joseph Rabéarivelo *(1901-1937)* was a prominent and influential poet of Madagascar

---

38 John Gombojab Hangin, "Dashdorjiin Natsagdorj (1937-1906)," The Mongolia Society Bulletin 6, no. :(1967) (11) 1 22–15. https://bit.ly/4kOVXnj
39 "Noma Hiroshi," Britannica, accessed February 2025, 5, https://bit.ly/4kPe1O5
40 "Gabriel Okara," Britannica, accessed February 2025, 5, https://bit.ly/44nOGFj
41 "Amrita Pritam," Poetry Foundation, accessed February 2025, 5, https://bit.ly/45EOW41

who mostly wrote in French. He was one of the founders of the literary movement in Madagascar and is considered one of the most important modern African literary figures. He was notable for being a modernist poet who, while adhering to the convention of rhyme and meter remained inventive and incorporated surrealist elements in his later works. He published several anthologies including *Nearly Dreams* (1934) and translation of *The Night* (1935). Rabéarivelo aimed to blend his native Malagasy culture with that of France. He committed suicide at the age of 36.[42]

Richard Rive *(1931-1989)* was a South African short story writer and critic. He was known for opposing the prevailing apartheid system in his homeland and his literary endeavors vividly depicted its cruelty and brutality. He graduated from the University of Cape Town and then earned an MA degree from Columbia and a doctorate from Oxford. He travelled between Europe and Africa and taught at several colleges, including Harvard, as a visiting professor, in addition to working as an athletic coach in South Africa. His best-known publications are *Emergency* (1964) and *Buckingham Palace District Six* (1986). He was murdered in Cape Town at the age of 58.[43]

Anar Rasul oghlu Rzayef *(1938-)* better known simply as **Anar**, is a writer known for his novels and short stories. He is also a film director, dramatist, and screenplay writer. He comes from a family that is immensely interested in art and literature. His mother, Nigar Rafibeyli, and father, Rasul Rza, were both well-known Azerbaijani poets. He is also the president of the Writers' Union of Azerbaijan and was a member of the Supreme Soviet and National Assembly several times. Some of Anar's works include the short stories "Morning of That Night" (1999) and "Me, You, Him and the Telephone" (1967).[44]

Rady Saddouk *(1938-2010)* was a Palestinian poet and journalist. He worked as a teacher before becoming editor-in-chief of the magazine *Risalat al-Ordon*, as well as the *al-Ayyam* newspaper, which became the first Arabic-language newspaper to be published in Rome. He worked as a consultant in Jordanian, Qatari, and Saudi

---

42 "Jean-Joseph Rabéarivelo," Britannica, accessed February 2025, 5, https://bit.ly/448yiqW
43 "Richard Rive," Britannica, accessed February 2025, 5, https://bit.ly/44hmOSd
44 "Azerbaijani writer Anar in photos," 2014, anews,https://bit.ly/3GaYsBh
   "Anar: Me, You, Him and the Telephone (1967)," Azer, 2004, https://bit.ly/43UEWSU

media outlets and was a member of the Federation of Arab Journalists. Some of his most notable works include the poetry collections *I Had a Heart* (1963) and *Rebel Without an Identity* (1966).[45]

Ousmane Sembène *(1923- 2007)* was a famous Senegalese film director and producer, as well as a prominent novelist and poet. He is considered "The Father of African Film." He served with the Free French Forces during World War II and later joined the Communist Party from 1950 to 1960. He first began writing novels and then turned his focus to filmmaking because he was concerned with Western film and false media representations of African culture. Some of his films include *Black Girl* (1966) and *The Money Order* (1968). He died at the age of 84 due to illness.[46]

Léopold Sédar Senghor *(1906-2001)* was the first president of Senegal after the country gained independence from France. He was also widely recognised as an influential poet and one of the most important African literary figures of the twentieth century. He founded the Senegalese Democratic Bloc and played a major role in establishing the ideology of "Negritude" which aimed to undermine French colonialism and unite the African people. His most famous publication is *Négritude et humanisme* (1964). He was the first African to be elected to the Académie Française, the principal French organisation that presides over the French language. He died of natural causes at the age of 95.[47]

Pham Ba Ngoan, better known by his pen name **Thanh Hai** *(1930-1980),* was a notable Vietnamese poet and writer. He is mostly remembered for his revolt against corruption in Vietnam and his disapproval of the American presence in the country. He was involved in many revolutionary movements in the 1950s and 1960s and was best known for his book *The Faithful Comrades* (1962), through which he expressed his opposition to the US-backed Southern Vietnamese government. He was also famous for heading the *Flag of Liberation* newspaper in Vietnam. He died due to illness at the age of 50.[48]

Fadwa Tuqan *(1917-2003)* was an influential Palestinian poet. She was born in Nablus, where

---

45 راضي صدّوق,"رابطة الأدب الإسلامي العالمية". 47. accessed on February 18, 2025, https://bit.ly/4k1uGwG
46 Immanuel Ness, The Palgrave Encyclopedia of Imperialism and Anti-Imperialism (Springer, 2015).
47 "Léopold Senghor," Britannica, accessed February 5, 2025, https://bit.ly/4lfBo3h
48 Thanh Hai Pham Ba Ngoan. Institute of Poetry. accessed February 13, 2025, https://bit.ly/4k02oCI

her brother Ibrahim, a poet and playwright, tutored her in poetry and literature. Tuqan was also the sister of former Jordanian Prime Minister Ahmed Tuqan. She began by writing conventional poetry but moved on to more experimental free-verse endeavors later in her career. Resistance to Israeli occupation characterised most of her works, which include the collections *My Brother Ibrahim* (1946) and *Before the Closed Door* (1967). Her autobiography *Mountainous Journey* (1990) also criticised how women are treated within Arab societies. She won several awards and her work was translated into English, bringing her work to the Arab diaspora. She died of natural causes at the age of 86.[49]

Sonomyn Udval *(1921-1991)* was a prominent Mongolian writer, politician, and activist. She was known for being the first secretary of the Mongolian Writers' Union as well as chairwoman of the Mongolian Women's Committee. She was also a member of the Mongolian People's Revolutionary Party's Central Committee until 1990. Her literary works were very influential in developing Mongolian literature in the twentieth century. Some of her most prominent novels include *Great Destiny* (1973) and *The First Thirteen* (1974). She won the Lotus Prize for Literature in 1971.[50]

U Gtun Kyi, better known by his pen name **Minn Latt Yekhaun** *(1925-1985),* was a Burmese linguist, theorist, and research writer. He was best known for extensively studying the Burmese language and analyzing Old Burmese poetry. He was also a poet and writer of short stories. He lived most of his life in Czechoslovakia and was an ardent supporter of communism. He eventually returned to Burma to become an active member of the Burmese Communist Party. He was shot and killed under mysterious circumstances at the age of 60.[51]

Ramses Younan *(1913-1966)* was a Coptic Egyptian painter, art critic, and writer. He is one of the most widely admired Arab painters of his time and is the agreed-upon first Egyptian surrealist painter. He was a member of the Trotskyist Egyptian group "Art and Liberty" as well as the chief editor of the Egyptian art magazine *The New Magazine*. In addition to being an influential painter, he also wrote

---

49   "Fadwa Tuqan," Interactive Encyclopedia of the Palestine Question, accessed February 2025, 5, https://bit.ly/44qFxM9
50   "Sonomyn Udval," Prabook, accessed on February 2025, 13, https://bit.ly/44qFC2p
51   Aung Zaw, "Tell the World the Truth," 2019, https://bit.ly/45Ak2tw

essays and translated literary works by authors such as Franz Kafka and Arthur Rimbaud. He died in Cairo at the age of 53.[52]

Tawfiq Zayyad *(1929-1994)* was a Palestinian poet, politician, and scholar. He was elected mayor of Nazareth and was a member of the Israeli Knesset. He pressured the Israeli government to change its policies towards Palestinians and Arabs. He co-authored a report that described Israeli prison conditions and how they used torture techniques on Palestinian prisoners, which were eventually published in the Israeli *al-Hamishmar* newspaper. He published several poems portraying resistance and the struggle against Zionism. He also translated Russian works of literature. He die at the age of 65 in a car crash while returning from a meeting with PLO chairman Yasser Arafat.[53]

WE WERE UNABLE TO TRACE

Z. Afif, Indonesia
Kaluenya, Namibia. This person may be the same as H Kaluenja who also has another poem in this anthology.
Nazih Kheir, Palestine
Ma Cheng-chung, (Chinese Commune Member), China
Mahyudin, Indonesia
B. A. Mudadi, Zimbabwe
Ngoc Khuyen, Vietnam
Hong Thao, Vietnam
Fata El Thawra (Translation: Youth of the Revolution)
A Lu Shih
Shadreck, Zimbabwe
Surono, Indonesia
J. F. William, Somalia

---

52   Please provide link for Ramses Younan.
53   "Tawfiq Zayyad," Interactive Encyclopedia of the Palestine Question, accessed February 5, 2025 https://bit.ly/4jYpDgz

LISTS OF POEMS AND IMAGES

LIST OF POEMS

A Lu Shih, Poems of Chairman Mao Tse-Tung Capture of Nanking, 158
Abdel Kerim El-Naem, Our Cause and the Discovery of the Moon, 303
Abdel Rahman El Sharkawi, Laila in Acca My Homeland, 107
Abdel Wahab El Bayyati, The Descent of Orpheus to the Underground, 100
Abdel Wahab El-Bayyati, Al Hallag's Agony, 286
Adonis, Chapter of an Old Image, 185
Adonis, The One Who Left before Time, 325
Agostinho Neto, Fire and Rhythm, 113
Aguinaldo Fonseca, The Seaboard Café, 337
Ahmed Dahbour, A Palestinian Wedding, 225
Ahmed Khansa, We Will Never Yield, 396
Ahmed Sekou Toure, Man of Africa, 329
Akbar S. Ahmed, Diaspora, 103
Alexander Pushkin, Poets from ancient days are used, 313
Alpha Sow,Chimera (1972), 339
Amal Donqol, The Last Supper, 340
Anoma Kanie, All That You Gave Me, 331
Anon, Militant Songs of Palestine, 163
Anon: A popular Arab revolutionary song, Oath of the Revolutionaries, 157
Antonio Jacinto, Monangamba, 150
Arthur Nortje, Apartheid, 142
Azanian Poems, Azanian People Shall Triumph!, 406
Azanian Poems, No More! No More!, 407
Azanian Poems, United in Blood, 162
B. A. Mudadi," Cry Not, Child", 410
Badr Shaker El Sayyab, In Front of the Gate of Allah, 188
Begzyn Yavoukhoulan, Motherland, 314
Beland El Haidari, Accused Thou Innocent, 357
Beland El-Haidari, The Age of Rubber Stamps, 369
Boualem Abdoun, Canticle of the Obsessed, 371
Bouna Boukary Dioura, The Green Rock, 206
"By a Fighter, Palestine", Road To Liberation, 403
"C. J. Driver, South Africa ", To the Dark Singing, 144
Challezh Khaphezh Mourax-qui Mahidah, Lead We Follow O Great Helmsman!, 393
Conte Saidon Tidiany, Martyrs, 265
Cosmo Pieterse, Freely, 145
Cosmo Pieterse, Love Exile Land, 105
Cosmo Pieterse, Old Form: New Life, 106
David Gutmann, Morning, 346

David Rubadiri, A Negro Labourer in Liverpool, 121
Dennis Brutus, A Wrong Headed Bunch, 143
E. Epanya Iondo, Remember, 289
Elaine Caulker, Marriage, 347
Eustache Prudencio, We Shall Be There, 266
F. Laro, Albanian Revolutionary Songs: Revolutionary is Marching Forward, 156
Fadel El-Azzawi," Song for Jerusalem, War and Revolution", 212
Fadwa Toukan, The People's Liberty, 123
Faiz Ahmad Faiz, Be You Near Me, 270
Faiz Ahmad Faiz, Listen my Heart, 271
Faiz Ahmad Faiz, Solitary Confinement, 269
Faiz Ahmad Faiz, The Shadow, 272
Faiz Ahmed Faiz, Thou Restless Heart, 359
Fata El Thawra, With the Father of a Martyr, 398
Fedayee, Songs of Palestinian Guerrillas, 253
Femi Fatoba, Home 1968, 348
Femi Fatoba, Moon, 349
Femi Fatoba, Olawunmi, 350
Fernando Costa Andrade, The Fourth Poem of a Song of Accusation, 152
Frank Parkes, Blind Steersmen, 292
Geraldo Bessa Victor, The Little Boy Enters Not in the Circle, 153
Giang Nam, The Hum of the Spinning Wheel, 125
Gochera, Decisive Battle, 172
Gracade, Fire! Fire!, 159
H. Kaluenja, How Long, Comrade?, 431
H. Kaluenja, Namibia, You Will Be Liberated, 256
Hajime Kijima, Turning Point, 284
Hamid Wafi, Letter to the People of My Motherland, 248
Hanh Can, A Hundred Mountain Ranges, 254
Hastings W. Okoth-Ogendo, Tell God: Tell Him, 306
Hiroshi Osada, Don't Run with your Hands Hanging Down, 308
Hochi Minh, A Milestone, 127
Hochi Minh, Permitted to Take a Walk in the Prison Yard, 130
Hochi Minh, The Flute of the Fellow-Prisoner, 131
Hong Thao, Marching Troops, 411
Hussein Marawan, Palestine, 218
Iicro Ando, 5 Poems from the Position, 227
Iicro Ando, A Butterfly, 229
Isaac Rammapo, Requiem for the Saboteurs, 375
Ivan G. Van Sertima, Muse Without Music: The Poet in Search of a Tongue, 310
J. F. William, The Angel with Broken Wings, 67
J.J. Rabearivelo, Exile, 65

Jean-Baptiste Mutabaruka, Memory, 315
Jean-Baptiste Mutabaruka, Presence, 316
Jitra Pumisakdi (a martyr of Thailand), Ode to The Revolutionary Heroes:
    A Revolutionary Song of Thailand, 154
Joke Moeljono, In Alien Land, 66
Jose Craveirinha, Poem of the Future Citizen, 293
Jose Ma. Sison, From the Philippines to Vietnam, 416
Kaisin Kuliev, Orb of Earth, 317
Kaluenya," Awake, Ye Brave Sons and Daughters of Namibia!", 167
Katsumi Sugawara," "I am alone, but we are all"", 294
Keorapetse Kgositsile, My People no Longer Sing, 146
Khaled Aly Mustapha, The Voice of the Wounded, 79
Khalil Hawi, The Magi in Europe, 377
Khalil Hawi, The Sailor and the Darwiche, 361
Kuo Mo-jo, Kuo Mo-jo's Poem, 402
Lambert Olayi, The Flaming Red Book:
    Eulogy to Quotations from Chairman Mao Tse-tung, 394
Lee Ying, Struggle, 173
Lenrie Peters, We Have Come Home, 83
M. F. Dei-Anang," Whither Bound, O Africa?", 196
M. Tolliver, In Memory of G. Jackson, 430
Ma Cheng-chung (Chinese Commune Member),
    We Paint the Spring of Our People's Commune, 404
Mahmoud Darwish, A Lover from Palestine, 69
Mahmoud Darwish, My Father, 139
Mahmoud Darwish, The Martyr of a Song, 114
Mahmoud Darwish, The Song and the Sultan, 119
Mahmud Hassan Ismail, Self and Sin, 78
Mahyudin, Buru Island, 412
Malek Haddad, By Night I am On Guard, 318
Marcelino Dos Santos, It is There That We Were Born, 209
Marcelino Dos Santos, The Earth Trembles, 134
Marcelino Dos Santos, To a Child of My Native Land, 234
Marcelino Dos Santos, Man and Sea, 351
Marcelino Dos Santos, The Soldiers, 352
Massa Makan Diabate, Song Against Portuguese Aggression, 408
May El-Sayeg, Fateh on the Day of Karameh, 85
Mazisi Kunene, As Long as I Live, 148
Mazisi Kunene, Poisoned Mind, 115
Mazisi Kunene, The Echoes, 149
Mazisi Kunene, The Night, 221
Mazisi Kunene, There is a Place, 222

Mazisi Kunene, Thoughts at the Gathering of the Storm, 301
Mirzo Tursun-Zade, Africa My Sister, 231
Mohamed Taleb, The Corpse, 332
Mohammed El-Maghout, The Tattoo, 379
Muʿin Bseiso, The Island of Ancient Mottoes, 77
Muʿin Bseiso, The Lamp and the Mill, 204
Nazek El-Maleika, The Top of the Stairs, 333
Nazih Kheir, Illusion, 141
Ngoc Khuyen, Uncle's Verses, 255
Okot p'Bitek, Song of Ocol, 364
Oneisimo Silveira, Songs to Drive Away the "Gongon", 223
Ousmane Sembene, Fingers, 415
Ovidio Martins, Poem of Salt, 353
P. Sekuj, Pick in One Hand and Rifle in the Other, 400
Palestine, I Persist in the Fight, 178
Palestine, The Revolutionaries' Anger, 179
Paul Charles Atangana, Earth Awaits, 242
Peter Mwathi, Look No More, 320
Popular Folklore from Egypt, I am Athirst, 244
Popular Folklore from Egypt, The Dove, 245
Popular folklore in Egypt, For a Childless Woman, 147
Rady Saddouk, Song of a Revolutionary Without Identity, 116
Rasha Hussein, Jaffa, 241
Rewi Alley, Red River Bridge, 418
Rival Apin, Bypass the Day: Penetrate the Night, 381
Roberto Crespo y Payno, "3,000 Million and One Thought", 420
Rui Nogar, Poem of the Conscripted Warrior, 321
S. A. Hussain, Ode to the Fighting Gaza, 169
Sajjad Zaheer, I Sometimes Fear, 302
Salah Abdel Sabour, The Hanging of Zahran, 191
Saleh Gawdat, The Dark Star, 274
Salem Goubran, Songs in Prison, 354
Sardar Jaeffery, My Voyage, 276
Shadreck," Forward, Zimbabwean People", 174
Shazel Taquah, And the Man Returned, 323
Sulafa El-Hegawy, The Song of Songs, 89
Surono, Mao Tse-Tung and Revolution, 428
Sutojo, Letter to My Brother, 252
Takiguchi Masako, Blue Horse, 335
Takiguchi Masako, Bury Your Dead and Rise, 99
Takiguchi Masako, At the Peak of a Passion, 94
Thanh Hai, Crossing the Demarcation Line, 128

Thanh Hai, Hymn of Spring, 201
Thanh Hai, Thinking of You, 199
Thanh Hai, To the Soldier in the South, 132
Tran Huu Thung, Separation, 230
Tsegaye Gabre Medbin, Self-Exile, 90
Tsuguo Ando, Epistle of the Dead, 367
U Win Pe, Evening, 76
U Win Pe, Rice Pounding Songs, 279
U'thein Hau, The Beda Flower, 336
Unknown, Reply to Comrade Kuo Mo-jo: to the Melody of Man Chiang Hung, 401
Vernard Dadie, A Crown for Africa, 194
Virga Belan, Excavate, 297
Vuong Linh, The Sea in the Night, 203
Wadya Kamal," Kamal, My Son", 180
Yavoukhoulan, The Gobi, 238
Z. Afif, Creators of the Sun Tame Nature, 385
Z.N. Chisekesi, Kind Mother, 176
Zimbabwe, Three Zimbabwean Poems, 258
Zulfia Israilova To Hamid Alimjan, The Spring has Come and Asks for You, 281

LIST OF IMAGES

Figure 1: Scan from Lotus Magazine 1 no. 1. "Resolution on Palestine." 1968): 140.

Figure 2: W. E. B. Du Bois delivering an address at the Afro-Asian Writers Conference in Tashkent in October 1958.

Figure 3: Scan from The Call. Special Supplement of The Call on the Occasion of Palestine Day. "Political Power Grows out of the Barrel of a Gun." (1968): i.

Figure 4: Scan from The Call no. 3. Tolliver, M. "In Memory of G Jackson." (1972): 19.

BIBLIOGRAPHY

Preface

Abu-Sittah, Ghassan. "Israel Bombs Lebanon After Blowing Up Pagers in "Act of Mass Mutilation." Is Ground Invasion Next?" Interview by Sintia Issa. September 23, 2024. Video, 35:43. https://www.democracynow.org/2024/9/23/israel_lebanon.

Alareer, Refaat. "If I Must Die." In These Times, translated by Sinan Antoon. December 27, 2023. https://inthesetimes.com/article/refaat-alareer-israeli-occupation-palestine

oweda, Farouk. ".أحد ع_____مسـت ولا ..ب_ضـغا" Al-Ahram, translated by Tariq Mehmood Ali, December 14, 2003. http://www.ahram.org.eg/Archive/2003/12/14/ARTS2.HTM

Introduction

Abdel Sabour, Salah. "The Hanging of Zahran." Lotus 1, no. 1 (1968): 44-45.

Adonis. "Chapter of an Old Image." Lotus 1, no. 1 (1968): 70-72.

Afro-Asian Writers' Bureau. "8th Conference of Arab Writers General Declaration." Lotus 4, no. 13 (1972): 10.

Afro-Asian Writers' Bureau. "General Declaration." Lotus 1, no. 1 (1967): 149-152.

Afro-Asian Writers' Bureau. "Oath of the Revolutionaries: A popular Arab revolutionary song." The Call 9, no. 3 (1969): 16.

Afro-Asian Writers' Bureau. "Strongly Condemn Soviet Revisionist Fascist Invasion of Czechoslovakia." The Call 8, no. 2 (1968): 2.

Afro-Asian Writers' Bureau. The Struggle Between the Two Lines in the Afro-Asian Writers Movement. Afro-Asian Writers' Bureau: Colombo, 1968.

Ahmad Faiz, Faiz. "Sacred Space: Hum Dekhengey." Translated by Maniza Naqvi. Times of India. August 20, 2008. https://timesofindia.indiatimes.com/edit-page/SACRED-SPACE-Hum-Dekhenge/ articleshow/3382158.cms.

Alareer, Refaat (@itranslate123). "If I must die, let it be a tale." X, November 1, 2023. https://x.com/itranslate123/status/1719701312990830934?s=20.

Alley, Rewi. "Red River Bridge." The Call 8, no. 1 (1968): 12.

Aydelott, Sabiha T. "Memories of Faiz." Alif, no. 18 (1998): 308-309. https://doi.org/10.2307/521891.

Banya, Kingsley. "Illiteracy, Colonial Legacy and Education: The Case of Modern Sierra Leone." Comparative Education 29, no. 2 (1993): 159-170. https://doi.org/10.1080/0305006930290204.

Besesio, Mu'in. "The Island of Ancient Mottoes." Translated by Shafik Megally. Lotus 2, no. 4 (1971): 37.

Bissay Gracade, Guinne. "Fire Fire!" The Call 9, no. 4 (1969): 16-17.

British Pathé. "Uzbekistan: The Tashkent Conference." British Pathé, January 1, 1958. Video, 1:23. https://www.britishpathe.com/asset/255965/.

Bureau of Education. "Minute by the Hon'ble T. B. Macaulay." In Selections from Educational Records, Part I (1781-1839). Edited by H. Sharp, 107-117. Delhi: National Archives of India, 1920.

bush, jewel. "Related Somehow to Africa." Transition, no. 115 (2014): 68–86. https://doi.org/10.2979/transition.115.68.

Central Intelligence Agency. Biweekly Propaganda Guidance. 1999. https://www.cia.gov/readingroom/docs/CIA-RDP78-03061A000400070008-4.pdf.

Central Intelligence Agency. Peaceful Coexistence. 1959. https://www.cia.gov/readingroom/docs/CIA-RDP80-01446R000100060009-2.pdf.

Central Intelligence Agency. Sino Soviet Struggle for Writers' Allegiance: Who Smashes Whom? 1967. https://www.cia.gov/readingroom/docs/CIA-RDP78-03061A000400070008-4.pdf.

Central Intelligence Agency. The Afro-Asian Peoples Solidarity Organization. 1961. https://www.cia.gov/readingroom/docs/CIA-RDP78-00915R001300050001-1.pdf.

Corera, Gordon. "MI6 and the death of Patrice Lumumba." BBC, April 2, 2013. https://www.bbc.com/news/world-africa-22006446.

Crespo Payno, Roberto. "3,000 Million and One Thought." The Call 10, no. 3 (1970): 16-18.

Darwish, Mahmoud. "A Lover from Palestine." Lotus 1, no. 2-3 (1970): 81.

Dei-Anang, M. F. "Witherbound, O Africa?" Lotus 1, no. 2-3 (1968): 96-97.

Dos Santos, Marcelino. "The Earth Trembles." Lotus 3, no. 8 (1971): 167-169.

Dos Santos, Marcelino. "To a Child of my Native Land." Translated by Nihad Salem. Lotus 3, no. 8 (1971): 170-171.

Du Bois, Shirley Graham. Address by W. E. B. Du Bois given standing ovation by Asian-African Writers' Conference I am an American – I am an African, 14 October 1958. W. E. B. Du Bois Papers, 1803-1999 (bulk 1877-1963). Special Collections and University Archives, University of Massachusetts Amherst Libraries. https://credo.library.umass.edu/view/pageturn/mums312-b239-i012/#page/1/mode/1up.

El-Azzawi, Fadel. "Songs for Jerusalem, War and Revolution." Translated by Shafik Magar. Lotus 2, no. 6 (1970): 82-85.

El-Haidari, Buland. "The Age of Rubber Stamps." Translated by Nihad A. Salem. Lotus 4, no. 13 (1972): 108.

El-Sebai, Youssef. "The Role of Afro-Asian Literature and the National Liberation Movements." Lotus 1, no. 1 (1970): 5-12.

Ernst, M.J., and Rossen Djagalov. "The Road to Lotus: Faiz Ahmad Faiz's Magazine Proposal to the Soviet Writers Union." Interventions 25, no. 6 (2022): 699-718. https://doi.org/10.1080/1369801X.2021.2015701.

Fatoba, Femi. "Home 1968." The Call 4, no. 11 (1972): 24.

Haddad, Malek. "Listen and I am Calling You." Lotus 1, no. 2-3 (1968): 34-35.

Hanh, Can. "A Hundred Mountain Ranges." The Call no. 3 (1972): 10.

Haqqani, Husain. Pakistan: Between Mosque and Military. Washington, D. C.: Carnegie Endowment for International Peace, 2005.

Harlow, Barbara. Resistance Literature. London: Routledge, 1987.

Hussain, S. A. "Ode to the Fighting Gaza." The Call no. 3 (1972): 5.

Jacinto, Antonio. "Monangamba." Lotus 4, no. 13 (1972): 173.

Jawdieh, Farouq. "Be Angry and Don't Listen to Anyone." 2007.

Kanafani, Ghassan. "Resistance Literature in Occupied Palestine." Lotus 1, no. 2-3 (1968): 65-79.

Kanie, Anoma. "All That You Gave Me." Translated by Nihad A. Salem. Lotus 3, no. 10 (1971): 35.

Kgositsile, Keorapetse. "My People No Longer Sing." Lotus 4, no. 12 (1970): 177.

Kunene, Mazisi. "Poisoned mind." Lotus 1, no. 2-3 (1968): 87.

Ludhianvi, Sahir. "Martyr's Blood." Translated by K. A. Abbas. Lotus 1, no. 2-3 (1968): 132.

Makhoul, Marwan. Untitled.

Minh, Ho Chi. "A Milestone." Lotus 3, no. 7 (1971): 192.

Mohan, Jitendra. "African Liberation Struggle: In Continental and International Perspective." Economic and Political Weekly 11, no. 4 (1976): 105–16. http://www.jstor.org/stable/4364352.

Mourax-qui-Mahidah, Challezh Khaphezh. "Lead We Follow O Great Helmsman." The Call, 1968.

Mustapha, Khaled Aly. "The Voice of the Wounded." Translated by Nihad A. Salem. Lotus 2, no. 5 (1970): 149-150.

Neto, Agostinho. "Fire and Rhythm." Lotus 1, no. 2-3 (1968): 25.

Neto, Agostinho. "The Voice of Blood." Lotus 1, no. 2-3 (1968): 24.

Northern Atlantic Council. Committee on Information and Cultural Relations. Afro-Asian Writers' Conference, Tashkent, October 1959. Note by the United Kingdom Delegation, 18 November 1958. https://archives.nato.int/uploads/r/null/1/4/14871/AC_52-D_58_59_ENG.pdf.

Parkes, Frank. "Blind Stersmen." Translated by Heba Enayat. Lotus 2, no. 5 (1970): 73.

Prasbad, Vijay. The Darker Nations. New York: The New Press, 1995.

Pushkin, Alexander. "Preface." Lotus 3, no. 8 (1971): 60.

Saunders, Frances Stonor. Who Paid the Piper? The CIA and the Cultural Cold War. London: Granta Books, 1999.

Sembene, Ousmane. "Fingers." Lotus 1, no. 1 (1968): 100.

Siddiqui, Mohammad Asim. "How to Read Faiz for Those Who Never Read Poetry." NewsClick, January 5, 2020. https://www.newsclick.in/how-read-faiz-those-who-never-read-poetry.

Sison, Jose Ma. "From the Philippines to Vietnam." The Call 8, no. 1 (1968): 13.

Stpansky, Joseph, and Farah Najjar. "Israel-Hamas war updates: Gaza faces heavy Israeli bombardment." Aljazeera, December 7, 2023. https://www.aljazeera.com/news/liveblog/2023/12/7/israel-hamas-war-live-palestinians-face-another-night-under-israeli-bombs?update=2541721.

Sutojo. "Letter to My Brother." The Call 8, no. 2 (1968): 21.

Tolliver, M. "In Memory of G Jackson." The Call no. 3 (1972):19.

Toukan, Fadwa. "The People's Liberty." Translated by Shafik Megally. Lotus 3, no. 7 (1971): 62-63.

Tse-Tung, Mao. Talks at the Yanan Forum on Literature and Art, May 2, 1942. In Vol. 3 of Selected Works of Mao Tse-Tung. 2nd ed. Paris: Foreign Languages Press, 2021. https://foreignlanguages.press/wp-content/uploads/2021/11/B09-Mao-Tse-Tung-Volume-3-1st-Printing.pdf.

Tsoungui-Ngono, Vincent. "Afrasia." Translated by Nihad A. Salem. Lotus 2, no. 5 (1970): 164-165.

Tursun-Zade, Mirzo. "Africa my Sister." Lotus Magazine 3, no. 8 (1971): 66.

Vyas, Chiman L. "The Dove." Lotus 4, no. 12 (1972): 137.

Zedong, Mao. Speech at a Meeting of the Representatives of Sixty-four Communist and Workers' Parties, November 18, 1957. Digital Archive, Wilson Center. https://digitalarchive.wilsoncenter.org/document/mao-zedong-speech-meeting-representatives-sixty-four-communist-and-workers-parties-edited.

Ziyad, Tawfik. "Bury Your Dead and Rise." Lotus 3, no. 10 (1971): 178.

Poems

Abdel Sabour, Salah. "The Hanging of Zahran." Lotus 1, no. 1 (1968): 44-45.

Abdoun, Boualem. "Canticle of the Obsessed." Lotus 4, no. 13 (1972): 94-97.

Adonis. "Chapter of an Old Image." Lotus 1, no.1 (1968): 70-71.

-----. "The One Who Left Before Time." Lotus 3, no. 10 (1971): 109-111.

Ahmad, Akbar S. "Diaspora." Lotus 4, no. 11 (1972) : 110-111.

Ahmad Faiz, Faiz. "Be You Near Me." Lotus 1, no. 1 (1968): 27.

-----.. "Listen my Heart." Lotus 1, no. 1 (1968): 26.

-----. "Solitary Confinement." Lotus 1, no. 1 (1968): 26.

-----. "Thou Restless Heart." Lotus 4, no. 12 (1972): 50-51.

Al-Haidari, Buland. "Accused Thou Innocent." Lotus 4, no. 12 (1972): 102-103.

-----. "The Age of Rubber Stamps." Lotus 4, no. 13 (1972): 108-109.

Al Maleika, Nazek. "The Visitor Who Did Not Come." Lotus 1, no. 1-2 (1968): 123.

Aly Mustapha, Khaled. "The Voice of the Wounded." Lotus 2, no. 5 (1970): 149-150.

Ando, Icro. "5 Poems from the Position." Lotus 3, no. 7 (1971): 55-57.

-----. "A Butterfly." Lotus 3, no. 7 (1971): 58.

Ando, Tsuguo. "Epistle of the Dead." Lotus 4, no. 12 (1972): 64-65.

Apin, Rival. "Bypass the Day: Penetrate the Night." Lotus 4, no. 13 (1972): 86-89.

Belan, Virga. "Excavate." Lotus 2, no. 5 (1970): 133.

Bessa Victor, Geraldo. "The Little Boy Enters Not in the Circle." Lotus 4, no. 13 (1972): 176-177.

Boukary Dioura, Bouna. "The Green Rock," Lotus 2, no. 5 (1970): 18-19.

Brutus, Dennis. "A Wrong Headed Bunch." Lotus 4, no. 12 (1972): 158.

Mu'in Bseiso. "The Island of Ancient Mottoes." Lotus 2, no. 4 (1970): 37.

-----. "The Lamp and the Mill." Lotus 2, no. 4 (1960): 36-37.

Caulker, Elaine. "Marriage." Lotus 4, no. 11 (1972): 66-67.

Charles Atangana, Paul. "Earth Awaits." Lotus 4, no 12 (1972): 28-29.

Chisekesi, Z.N. "Kind Mother." The Call 3-4 (1973): 22

Costa Andrade, Fernando. "The Fourth Poem of a Song of Accusation." Lotus 4. no. 13 (1972): 16168.

Craveirinha, Jose. "Poem of the Future Citizen." Lotus 2, no. 5 (1970): 198.

Dadié, Vernard. "A Crown for Africa." Lotus 1, no. 1 (1968): 81.

Dahbour, Ahmed. "A Palestinian Wedding." Lotus 3, no. 7 (1971): 64-65.

Darwish, Mahmoud. "A Lover from Palestine." Lotus 1, no. 1-2 (1968): 81.

-----. "My Father." Lotus 3, no. 10 (1971): 176-177.

-----. "The Martyr of a Song." Lotus 1, no. 2-3 (1968): 80.

-----. "The Song and the Sultan." Lotus 2, no. 6 (1970): 76-77.

Dei-Anang, M. F. "Wither Bound, O Africa." Lotus 1, no. 1-2 (1968): 96-97.

Diabate, Massa Makan. "Song Against Portuguese Aggression." The Call 11, no. 1 (1971): 11.

Donqol, Amal. "The Last Supper." Lotus 4, no. 11 (1972): 131-135.

Dos Santos, Marcelino. "It is There That We Were Born." Lotus 2, no. 5 (1970): 187-188.

-----. "The Earth Trembles." Lotus 3, no. 8 (1971): 167-169.

-----. "To a Child of my Native Land." Lotus 3, no. 8 (1971): 170-171.

Driver, C.J. "To the Dark Singing." Lotus 4, no. 12 (1972): 172.

El-Azzawi, Fadel. "Song for Jerusalem, War and Revolution." Lotus 2, no. 6 (1970): 82-85.

El-Bayyati, Abdel Wahab. "Al Hallag's Agony." Lotus 2, no. 5 (1970): 100-101.

-----. "The Descent of Orpheus to the Underground." Lotus 4, no. 11 (1972): 142-143.

El-Hegawy, Sulafa. "The Song of Songs." Lotus 2, no. 5 (1970): 151.

El-Maghout, Mohammed. "The Tattoo." Lotus 4, no. 13 (1972): 98-99.

El-Maleika, Nazek. "The Top of the Stairs." Lotus 3, no. 10 (1971): 88-89.

El-Naem, Abdel Kerim. "Our Cause and the Discovery of the Moon." Lotus 3, no. 7 (1971): 66-67.

El-Sayegh, May. "Fateh on the Day of Karameh." Lotus 2, no. 5 (1970): 152-153.

El-Sharkawi, Abdel Rahman. "Laila in Acca My Homeland." Lotus 4, no. 12 (1972): 91-93.

Epanya Iondo, E. "Remember." Lotus 2, no. 5 (1970): 168-169.

Fatoba, Femi. "Home 1968." Lotus 4, no. 11 (1972): 24.

—. "Moon." Lotus 4, no. 11 (1972): 25.

—. "Olawunmi." Lotus 4, no. 11 (1972): 25.

Fonseca, Aguinaldo. "The Seaboard Cafe." Lotus 4, no. 11 (1972): 44-45.

Gabre Medbin, Tsegaye. "Self-Exile." Lotus 2, no. 5 (1970): 116-117.

Gawdat, Saleh. "The Dark Star." Lotus 1, no. 1-2 (1968): 126-127.

Gochera. "Decisive Battle." The Call 3-4 (1973): 22-23.

Goubran, Salem. "Songs in Prison." Lotus 4, no. 11 (1972): 140-141.

Gutmann, David. "Morning." Lotus 4, no. 11 (1972): 63.

Haddad, Malek. "By Night I am on Guard." Lotus 3, no. 8 (1971): 108-109.

—. "Listen and I am calling you." Lotus 1, no. 1-2 (1968): 34-35.

Hassan Ismail, Mahmud. "Self and Sin." Lotus 2, no. 4 (1970): 160-161.

Hawi, Khalil. "The Magi in Europe." Lotus 4, no. 13 (1972): 106-107.

—. "The Sailor and the Darwiche." Lotus 4, no. 12 (1972): 109-111.

Ho Chi Minh. "A Milestone." Lotus 3, no. 7 (1971): 192.

—. "Permitted to Take a Walk in the Prison Yard." Lotus 3, no. 7 (1971): 190-191.

—. "The Flute of the Fellow-Prisoner." Lotus 3, no. 7 (1971): 193.

Hussein, Rasha. "Jaffa." Lotus 4, no. 11 (1972): 139.

Israilova, Zulfia. "The Spring has Come and Asks for You." Lotus 1, no. 1-2 (1968): 109.

Jacinto, Antonio. "Monangamba." Lotus 4, no. 12 (1972): 172-173.

Jaeffery, Sardar, "My Voyage." Lotus ,1 no. 1-2 (1968): 118-118.

Kanie, Anoma. "All that You Gave Me." Lotus 3, no. 10 (1971): 35.

Kgositsile, Keorapetse. "My People no Longer Sing." Lotus 4, no. 12 (1972): 177.

Khansa, Ahmed. "We Will Never Yield." The Call, Special Supplement of The Call on the Occasion of Palestine Day (May 15, 1968): 25. Kheir, Nazih. "Illusion." Lotus 3, no. 10 (1971): 177.

Kijima, Hajime. "Turning Point." Lotus 2, no. 4 (1970): 47.

Kuliev, Kaisin. "Orb of Earth." Lotus 3, no. 8 (1971): 66.

Kunene, Mazisi. "As Long as I Live." Lotus 4, no. 12 (1972): 148.

—. "Poisoned Mind." Lotus 1, no. 1-2 (1968): 187.

—. "The Echoes." Lotus 4, no. 12 (1972): 148.

—. "The Night." Lotus 2, no. 6 (1970): 67.

—. "There is a Place." Lotus 2, no. 6 (1970): 65.

—. "Thoughts at the Gathering of the Storm." Lotus 2, no. 6 (1970): 66.

Laro, F. "Revolutionary is Marching Forward." The Call 9, no. 3 (1969): 12.

Linh, Vuong. "The Sea in the Night." Lotus 1, no. 2-3 (1968): 53.

Martins, Ovidio. "Poem of Salt." Lotus 4, no. 11 (1972): 43.

Marwan, Hussein. "Palestine." Lotus 2, no. 6 (1970): 80-81.

Masako, Takiguchi. "Blue Horse." Lotus 3, no. 10 (1971): 60.

Moeliono, Joke. "In Alien Land." Lotus 1, no. 1 (1968): 112.

Mutabaruka, Jean-Baptiste. "Memory." Lotus 3, no. 8 (1971): 53.

-----. "Presence." Lotus 3, no. 8 (1971): 59.

Mwathi, Peter. "Look no More." Lotus 3, no. 8 (1971): 44.

Neto, Agostinho. "Fire and Rhythm." Lotus 1, no. 2-3 (1968): 25.

Giang, Nam. "The Hum of the Spinning Wheel." Lotus 3, no. 7 (1971): 168.

Nogar, Rui. "Poem of the Conscripted Warrior." Lotus 3, no. 8 (1971): 172-173.

Nortje, Arthur. "Apartheid." Lotus 4, no. 12 (1972): 178.

Okoth-Ogendo, Hastings W. "Tell God: Tell Him:" Lotus 3, no. 7 (1971): 50-51.

Olayi, Lambert. "The Flaming Red Book: Eulogy to 'Quotations from Chairman Mao Tse-tung.'" The Call 2, no. 8 (1968): 6.

Osada, Hiroshi. "Don't Run with your Hands Hanging Down." Lotus 3, no. 7 (1971): 59.

P'bitek, Okot. "Song of Ocol." Lotus 4, no. 12 (1972): 22-23.

Parkes, Frank. "Blind Steermen." Lotus 2, no. 5 (1970): 73.

Peters, Lenrie. "We Have Come Home." Lotus 2, no. 5 (1970): 114-115.

Pieterse, Cosmo. "Freely." Lotus 4, no. 12 (1972): 149.

-----. "Love Exile Land." Lotus 4, no. 11 (1972): 18.

-----. "Old Form: New Life." Lotus 4, no. 11 (1972): 19.

Popular folklore from Egypt. "For a Childless Woman." Lotus 4, no. 12 (1972): 139.

Popular folklore from Egypt. "I am Athirst." Lotus 4, no. 12 (1972): 138.

-----. "The Dove." Lotus 4, no. 12 (1972): 137.

Prudencio, Eustache. "We Shall Be There." Lotus 1, no. 1 (1968): 42.

Pumisakdi, Jitra. "Ode to the Revolutionary Heroes: A Revolutionary Song of Thailand." The Call 2, no. 8 (1968): 20-21.

Pushkin, Alexander. "Poems from USSR." Lotus 3, no. 8 (1971): 60.

Rabearivelo, R.R. "Exile." Lotus 1, no. 1 (1968): 99.

Rammapo, Isaac. "Requiem for the Saboteurs." Lotus 4, no. 13 (1972): 40-41.

Rubadiri, David. "A negro Labourer in Liverpool." Lotus 3, no. 7 (1971): 48-49.

Saddouk, Rady. "Song of a Revolutionary Without Identity." Lotus 2, no. 4 (1970): 39.

Saidon Tidiany, Conte. "Martyrs." Lotus 1, no. 1 (1968): 13.

Sekou Toure, Ahmed. "Man of Africa." Lotus 3, no. 10 (1971): 16-17.

Sekuj, P. "Pick in One Hand and Rifle in the Other." The Call 9, no. 3 (1969): 13.

Shaker el-Sayyab, Badr. "In Front of the Gate of Allah." Lotus 1, no. 1 (1968): 68-69.

Silveira, Oneisimo. "Songs to Drive Away the Gongon." Lotus 2, no. 6 (1970): 68-69.

Sow, Alpha. "Chimera." Lotus 4, no. 11 (1972): 53.

Sugawara, Katsumi. "I am alone but we are all. Lotus 2, no. 5 (1970): 87.

Takiguchi, Masako. "Man and Sea." Lotus 4, no. 11 (1972): 94.

-----. "Soldiers." Lotus 4, no. 11 (1972): 93.

Taleb, Mohamed. "The Corpse." Lotus 3, no. 10 (1971): 34.

Taquah, Shazel. "And the Man Returned." Lotus 3, no. 8 (1971): 111.

Thanh Hai. "Crossing the Demarcation Line." Lotus 3, no. 7 (1971): 172-173.

-----. "Hymn of Spring" Lotus 1, no. 1-2 (1968): 52.

-----. "Thinking of You." Lotus 1, no. 1-2 (1968): 50-51.

-----. "To the Soldier in the South." Lotus 3, no. 7 (1971): 174-175.

To Huu. "Ever Since." Lotus 2, no. 4 (1970): 162.

Toukan, Fadwa. "The People's Liberty." Lotus 3, no. 3 (1971): 62-63.

Tran Huu Thung. "Separation." Lotus 3, no. 7 (1971): 176-77.

Tse-Tung, Mao. "Capture of Nanking by the People's Liberation Army." The Call 9, no. 4(1969): 4.

-----. "Kuo Mo-jo's Poem." The Call 9, no. 4 (1969): 6.

-----. "Reply to Comrade Kuo Mo-jo." The Call 9, no. 4 (1969): 5-6.

Tursun-Zade, Mirzo. "Africa my Sister." Lotus 3, no. 8 (1971): 61-64.

U'Tam'si, Tchicaya. "At the Peak of a Passion." Lotus 3, no. 10 (1971): 21-23.

U'thein Hau. "The Beda Flower." Lotus 3, no 10 (1971): 61.

U Win Pe. "Evening." Lotus 1, no. 1-2 (1968): 48.

-----. "Rice Pounding Songs." Lotus 1, no 1-2 (1968): 49.

Unknown. "A Martyr's Last Word." The Call 11, no. 1 (1971): 14.

-----. "Azanian People Shall Triumph." The Call 10, no. 3 (1970): 19.

-----. "Beladi...." The Call 11, no. 1 (1971): 15.

-----. "Debt in Blood." The Call 11, no. 1 (1971): 15.

-----. "Fedayee." The Call 10, no. 3 (1970): 8.

-----. "How Long Shall It Be?" The Call 2 (1974): 16.

-----. "I Persist in the Fight." The Call 3-4 (1973): 11.

-----. "No More! No More!" The Call 10, no. 3 (1970): 19.

—. "Rise Up Angry." The Call 2 (1974): 17.

—. "The Enemy are Paper Tigers." The Call 2 (1974): 17. —. "The Revolutionaries' Anger." The Call 3-4 (1973): 10.

Van Sertima, Ivan G. "Muse Without Music: The Poet in Search of a Tongue." Lotus 3, no. 7 (1971): 52-53.

Wafi, Hamid. "Letter to the People of My Motherland." The Call 1, no. 8 (1968): 26-28.

Van Sertima, Ivan G. "Muse without Music: The Poet in Search of a Tongue." Lotus 3, no. 7 (1971): 52-53.

Willam, J.F. "The Angel with Broken Wings." Lotus 1, no. 1-2 (1968): 99.

Xavier Andrianrahinjaka, Lucien. "The Shadow." Lotus 1, no. 1 (1968): 82.

Yavoukhoulan, Begzyn. "Motherland." Lotus 3, no. 8 (1972): 168.

—. "The Gobi." Lotus 3, no. 8 (1971): 88-87.

Ying, Lee. "Struggle." The Call 3-4 (1973): 27.

Zaheer, Sajjad. "I Sometimes Fear." Lotus 2, no. 6 (1970): 73.

Ziyad, Tawfik. "Bury your Dead and Rise." Lotus 3, no. 10 (1978): 178.

EU Safety Information

Publisher: Daraja Press, PO BOX 99900 BM 735 664 Wakefield, QC J0X 0C2, Canada

info@darajapress.com | https://darajapress.com

EU Authorized GPSR Representative: Easy Access System Europe – Mustamäe tee 50, 10621 Tallinn, Estonia, gpsr.requests@easproject.com

For EU product safety concerns, please contact us at info@darajapress.com

www.ingramcontent.com/pod-product-compliance
Lightning Source LLC
Chambersburg PA
CBHW072103050526
44107CB00099B/395